P9-DDW-523

stepping across

"Julia Eklund Koza offers both a powerful corrective to popular culture distortions and a fresh critical lens through which to make sense of the music, art, and drama that surround and confound us. This is an informed citizens' guide to living in the postmodern."

Gloria Ladson-Billings,
Professor of Curriculum and Instruction, University of Wisconsin, Madison

"*Stepping Across* documents why we need work that trespasses disciplinary boundaries. It is insightful and provocative and shows how one can combine the structural and the poststructural in important ways."

Michael W. Apple, John Bascom Professor of Curriculum and Instruction
and Educational Policy Studies, University of Wisconsin, Madison

"A tantalizing, thoughtful, and provocative book concerning music and popular culture. This analysis of aspects of the cultural politics of music education suggests solutions to important issues facing classroom teachers today."

Estelle R. Jorgensen, Professor of Music, Indiana University
and Editor of Philosophy of Music Education Review

"Julia Eklund Koza has written a thoughtful, passionate book about corporate influence over popular culture. She makes clear the importance of understanding how and to what effect our experience of the everyday world of schools, music, theater, and even our bodies is shaped by others in the service profit and power. *Stepping Across* is an eye opener and a call to action that I hope will be read, argued about, and acted on by teachers, parents, and anyone interested in wrestling control of their destiny from the 'powers that be.'"

Alex Molnar, Professor and Director of Education Policy Studies Laboratory,
Arizona State University

stepping across

Intersections
in Communications
and Culture

Cameron McCarthy and Angharad N. Valdivia
General Editors

Vol. 6

PETER LANG
New York • Washington, D.C./Baltimore • Bern
Frankfurt am Main • Berlin • Brussels • Vienna • Oxford

julia eklund koza

stepping across

four interdisciplinary studies
of education and cultural politics

PETER LANG
New York • Washington, D.C./Baltimore • Bern
Frankfurt am Main • Berlin • Brussels • Vienna • Oxford

Library of Congress Cataloging-in-Publication Data

Koza, Julia Eklund.
Stepping across: four interdisciplinary studies
of education and cultural politics / Julia Eklund Koza.
p. cm. — (Intersections in communications and culture; vol. 6)
Includes bibliographical references.
1. Critical pedagogy—United States. 2. Music—Instruction and study—
Social aspects—United States. 3. Mass media and education—United States.
4. Sexism in mass media—United States—Case studies. 5. Racism in
mass media—United States—Case studies. 6. Interdisciplinary approach
in education—United States. I. Title. II. Series.
LC196.5 .K67   370.11'5—dc21   2002152129
ISBN 0-8204-6165-2
ISSN 1528-610X

Bibliographic information published by DIE DEUTSCHE BIBLIOTHEK
Die Deutsche Bibliothek lists this publication
in the Deutsche Nationalbibliografie; detailed bibliographic data
are available in the Internet at http://dnb.ddb.de.

Cover design by Lisa Barfield

The paper in this book meets the guidelines for permanence and durability
of the Committee on Production Guidelines for Book Longevity
of the Council of Library Resources.

Royalties from this book are being donated
to *Citizens for Tax Justice.*

———

To my beloved daughter, Katherine,
who brings me immeasurable joy

"Girls grow quicker than books."
— C. S. Lewis

———

TABLE OF CONTENTS

———

ACKNOWLEDGMENTS

I wish to thank my dear partner, James Koza, for traveling on this long journey with me; my friend and former colleague, Ann DeVaney, who assured me that I would publish again; Carl Grant and Michael W. Apple, for their generous and unflagging support; the library staff in the Grainger School of Business and Arlen Christenson, for their assistance in interpreting some of the legal documents I cite in "No Hero of Mine"; my beloved cousin, the late Joel Swandby, who introduced me to *Once on This Island* and taught me that there are ways of being healed even when there is no cure; Mariamne Whatley, for her helpful suggestions concerning "To Shave or Not to Shave"; and students in my graduate seminars, for their thoughtful discussions of these studies.

Portions of "No Hero of Mine: Disney, Popular Culture, and Education" were read as a paper at the 2000 annual meeting of the American Educational Research Association (New Orleans, Louisiana); and at the CIC Music Education Research Symposium (Madison, Wisconsin, October 2001). Portions of "Rap Music: The Cultural Politics of Official Representation" were presented as a paper at the 1993 annual meeting of the American Educational Research Association (Atlanta, Georgia). Portions of "Unhappy Happy Endings: Cultural Politics in the Broadway Musical Hit *Once on This Island*" were read as a paper at the 1994 annual meeting of the American Educational Research Association (New Orleans, Louisiana).

Excerpts of "No Hero of Mine: Disney, Popular Culture, and Education" were published in "A Realm Without Angels: MENC's Partnerships with Disney and Other Major Corporations," *Philosophy of Music*

Education Review 10, no. 2 (Fall 2002): 72–79, and are reprinted with permission of the publisher. All rights reserved.

I gratefully acknowledge the copyright holder Taylor and Francis AS for granting the following permissions:

"Rap Music: The Cultural Politics of Official Representation" was published in *The Review of Education/Pedagogy/ Cultural Studies* 16, no. 2 (1994): 367–407, and is reprinted with permission of Taylor and Francis AS.

An earlier version of "Unhappy Happy Endings: Cultural Politics in the Broadway Musical Hit *Once on This Island*" appeared in *The Review of Education/Pedagogy/Cultural Studies* 19, no. 4 (1997): 367–407. This version is published with permission of Taylor and Francis AS.

PREFACE

When Cameron McCarthy offered to publish this collection, I struggled to find a title that might capture common elements among these four somewhat disparate studies. I settled on *Stepping Across* when I realized that in each case I had stepped across one or more invisible boundaries, often disciplinary, as I sought context and different perspectives on issues that had first arisen in music education. I was drawn to the title because it suggests a delicate straddling, an attempt to keep a foot in one world while simultaneously stepping into another.

One commonality of the studies is that all of them step across the threshold of the classroom door, metaphorically speaking, to explore relationships between formal schooling in the United States during the final decade of the twentieth century and the broader culture in which that schooling was nested. I go about this exploration by moving back and forth across the invisible boundaries of multiple discursive communities, drawing, for example, from music, film studies, postmodern feminist theory, and critical studies of education. Delving into a variety of genres, I locate a series of shared tropes that seems to span genres and spaces.

All of the essays simultaneously focus on interrelated constructs of race, gender, and social class. Recognizing that these are dynamic inventions, I explore their materializations at specific moments and in particular spaces, examining how the materializations tend to work in consort with each other, reinforcing each other in a living, moving, changing web. Thus, all of these are studies of privilege and power: White privilege, male privilege, heterosexual privilege, and the privileges of affluence.

The studies attend both to local mobilizations of power and to what Foucault calls hegemonic effects, i.e., major dominations. When I speak of the local, I am referring to seemingly small matters of everyday life, ranging from entertainment—including music, theater, movies, and magazines—to grooming habits. I look at these *kleine Dinge,* this little world, because I concur with Foucault's assertion that they play a significant role in power relations and that productive, reinforcing, and interdependent relationships exist between local mobilizations and major dominations. Thus, if a line of distinction *were* to exist between local mobilizations and their hegemonic effects (but Foucault said there is no such line), then these studies would step across it.

Yet another shared characteristic is that all of the studies underscore contradictions, inconsistencies, and silences in discussions and practices surrounding education. They examine, for example, corporations that claim to be concerned about schools but do not pay a fair share of taxes; a musical, ostensibly suitable for the school curriculum, that denounces racism but fails to point out the role that White colonialism plays in the construction of racial hierarchies; and calls for diversity in the teaching pool that coexist with subtle (or not-so-subtle) denunciations of difference. They consider what is not said, as well as what is said, to be part of the dynamics of power.

The first study, "No Hero of Mine: Disney, Popular Culture, and Education," grew out of my discontent with a movie, *Mr. Holland's Opus,* which was promoted through an education/business partnership between MENC, which is a national professional organization of music educators and a subsidiary of the Disney Corporation. My project began as a critique of the film's gender politics, but I soon realized that promotion of *Opus* was one small piece of a massive movement within MENC to foster partnerships with affluent and influential major corporations. Recognizing that Disney, like other major corporations, was reaping public-relations benefits from the perception that it is genuinely concerned about the future of public education in the United States, I decided to find out whether Disney's tax-paying activities were consistent with the public image it was promulgating through these films. In search of an answer to this question, I stepped into the world of corporate finance, and in the process I gained fresh perspectives on trends toward increased privatization within music education.

As I was gathering information about corporate financial practices, MENC entered into a second promotional partnership with a Disney subsidiary, this time for the film *Music of the Heart.* I was troubled by the second movie's racial politics, as well as by its masking of the significant role that racism plays in inadequate funding for public schools; thus, I decided to incorporate into the study an analysis of the racial politics of the second film.

As this book goes to press, MENC's corporate partnership activities continue unabated and apparently largely unquestioned, corporate affluence and influence molding national education policy both inside and outside of music. The second study, "Rap Music: The Cultural Politics of Official Representation," highlights particularities of the U.S. racial order at the end of the twentieth century while simultaneously exploring specific materializations of gender and class. The study was written in the early 1990's, a time when complex racial tensions were emerging surrounding the initial acquittal of four Los Angeles police officers who had been charged with using excessive force in their videotaped arrest and beating of an African American man, Rodney King. The response in Los Angeles to this acquittal was a collective outbreak of rage and violence that cost more than fifty people their lives. In addition to arguing that three major news magazines were promulgating highly racialized visions of rap music, rappers, and rap fans, my study points out that White fear, which bubbled to the surface in the days following the Los Angeles response, may have played a significant role in media discussion of the genre. I finished the essay before the Rodney King story had ended, however, and somewhat ironically, the King ending involves rap music. The four police officers were re-tried in a federal court on charges of civil rights violations; two of the four were found guilty and served prison sentences.[1] King sued the city of Los Angeles and won; although most of the $3.8 million the city paid him reportedly went to legal expenses, King used part of the money to start a rap recording business.[2] He was quoted as saying that Straight Alta-Pazz Recording was founded to give rap a boost, and his claim that the first album contained almost no profanity implies that he hoped to clean up rap's somewhat tarnished public image, an image I discuss at length in my essay.[3]

Early in my investigations, I learned that when I began to listen to the rap receiving the most attention in major news magazines, I was stepping across other boundaries than scholarly ones. As a White, middle-class, female, forty years old and relatively unacquainted with gangsta' rap, I decided that if I were going to write about it, I needed to listen to the rap causing the most controversy in the media. One scorching summer afternoon while taking in an audio shop's sidewalk sale and not finding what I was looking for, I asked the clerk for Ice-T. There was a long pause while she looked blankly at me and then replied, "Oh. You don't mean the drink." With her guidance I selected several CDs and took them to the checkout counter, where another clerk (young, White, and female, as the first had been) glanced at the titles and then asked carefully, "These aren't for *you,* are they?" I assured her they were and offered no explanation. Clearly, I did not fit the clerks' image of who listened to gangsta' rap and based on assumptions I had made large-ly from information in the media, I guessed that my age, sex, race, and social class all disqualified me. As I learned more about rap, however, I discovered that my assumption was wrong on at least two counts: the typical listener to the most violent of rap music was a White, middle-class, male teenager from the suburbs, a fact not widely published in the same magazines that excoriated rap.

The early 1990's was also a time when rap was not given serious consideration by academicians; thus, a scholar writing about rap violated an invisible boundary demarcating "worthy" topics of investigation. Long-standing scholarly silence is but one part of a larger racialized heritage that rap shares with other musical genres from the twentieth century having African American roots, notably jazz and rock-and-roll. For example, like jazz and rock-and-roll, rap's acceptance as legitimate school knowledge came late, if at all. Because definitions of legitimate school knowledge have tended to be raced, classed, and gendered, several questions implicit in my rap study bear repeating today: What is not considered worthy knowledge to be taught in school? Why is this knowledge considered unworthy? Finally, this study remains poignantly relevant not only because it explores the continuing reality of racialized responses to African American musical genres but also because racialized media coverage and the particularities of the U.S. racial order similarly seem to be playing major roles in shaping responses within the U.S. to the bombing of the New York City World Trade Center on September 11, 2001.

The third study in this collection offers a critique of the race, class, and gender politics of the musical *Once on This Island* and of the novel on which the musical is based, Rosa Guy's *My Love, My Love, or, The Peasant Girl*. Haiti is the unnamed setting for both the novel and the musical; Haiti's cultural politics are the grist from which both plots were created. I completed this essay shortly before the United States invaded Haiti in 1994 and by that time I had grown sympathetic to the assertion that U.S. policy toward Haiti often has been a self serving and racialized contributor to the political problems described in the musical and novel. The 1994 invasion, dubbed "Operation Restore Democracy" and conducted in conjunction with "coercive diplomacy,"[4] successfully returned overthrown president, Jean-Bertrand Aristide, to office. Some critics who have called the invasion a failure cite reasons that echo concerns I raised in my study. For example, former U.S. Ambassador to Algeria Ulrich S. Haynes, Jr., states that "Operation Restore Democracy" continued a long history of flawed American policy in the Caribbean Basin, some of which has supported terrorism.[5] He notes that despite the 1994 invasion, the people of Haiti wither under abject poverty, a poverty that even fuels support for the return of deposed President-for-Life Jean-Claude Duvalier.[6] He states that as part of the operation, the CIA supported Emmanuel Constant, the "head of the Haitian terrorist organization, FRAPH, that murdered and kidnapped [sic] hundreds of Haitians, and pillaged at will from 1993–1994, in violation of official US policy at the time."[7] Confirming Rosa Guy's assertion that racism has long played a role in U.S. policy toward Haiti, Haynes observes:

> Cuban boat people setting foot on American soil are allowed to stay in our country while Haitians in the same situation are summarily sent back to Haiti. Haitians, American civil rights and human rights advocates, and foreign observers latch on to this difference in treatment as evidence of American racism.[8]

Thus, Haiti, too, is an ongoing story of the effects of power, and although I probably would not stage *Once on This Island* if were teaching in a high school today, I believe the musical could form the core of a critical interdisciplinary project focusing on Haiti and incorporating social studies, literature, and music. A project such as this might be especially valuable now, given America's current political climate and its apparently unbridled optimism about its foreign policies in developing countries. The temper of the times is reflected, for example, in the results of a poll conducted in the wake of the September 11, 2001, attack on New York City's World Trade Center; according to the poll, only one-third of Americans believe that "someone who says that terrorism is the fault of how our country behaves in the world . . . should be allowed to teach in the public schools or work in the government."[9]

Like rap music, musicals have long been considered too mundane to warrant much interest from musicological circles, but as a music educator, I had more freedom to step across boundaries and to choose an unconventional topic. I was aware that in addition to playing a significant role in the school curriculum, classic musicals apparently have experienced a rebirth thanks to home video rental. According to a colleague who is also a parent, old musicals have developed something of a cult following among pre-teen girls. Thus, new generations of children are consuming for pleasure, as I once did, the cultural politics of the musicals of my childhood: *The Sound of Music, My Fair Lady, Showboat,* and *South Pacific.* I do not presume that children accept dominant understandings at face value; rather, I am intrigued by the ways in which the musicals themselves may encourage uncritical viewing.

In what was my most undisciplined and transgressive decision to date, in the final study, "To Shave or Not to Shave: The Hair Removal Imperative and Its Implications for Teachers and Teaching," I chose to say little about music or music education, even though the event prompting this essay involved a student teacher in music. "To Shave or Not to Shave" examines discourses and discursive practices surrounding women's body hair and its removal; I argue that the hair-removal imperative is a microtechnology of power—a raced, gendered, sexed, and classed governmental practice—that helps to delineate who does or does not yet constitute a good, acceptable teacher. To provide context for my assertions, I trace common thematic strands emerging in a collection of apparently disparate sources, including scientific treatises, aesthetics lectures, folk lore, and popular magazines for teenagers. Hearing shared tropes among apparently disparate voices, I add further evidence to a body of scholarship that questions the cultural neutrality and distinctiveness of scientific discourse.

Recognizing that disciplines are imagined constructs producing real effects, I have stepped across boundaries throughout my entire academic career. For example, I distinctly remember an interchange with my advisor on the day in the early 1980's that I presented him with my dissertation proposal. Ever an interloper, I had settled on a topic that involved musicology and feminist theory, in addition to music education. My advisor grumbled, "What do you want? A degree in Women's Studies or a degree in music education?" His question implicitly asked: "What are you?" and "In what slot do you belong?" My heart answered, "All of the above." Well aware of his low opinion of Women's Studies, however, and cognizant of the possible dire consequences of being completely candid, I dutifully responded, "Of course, I want a degree in music education." To his credit my advisor approved my project, although he warned me that if I included the word "feminist" in my title, I would never get hired in music education. Thus, my career as an interdisciplinarian was launched.

As I began the introduction to this collection, I realized that my dissertation portended my academic future. My appointment at UW-Madison requires that I step across boundaries. In addition to courses in music education, I also teach a graduate course on gender and sexuality issues for the Department of Curriculum and Instruction. Holding an appointment and keeping an office in each of two departments, I regularly take the ten-minute walk from one building to the other, a hike that keeps me in contact with two different academic worlds. Not wanting to leave either world, I have come to view my need to step across campus as a strength of this appointment, the accompanying frustrations notwithstanding.

UW-Madison recently instituted faculty cluster hires as a means of fostering interdisciplinarity. I applaud these initiatives, and yet as a veteran of such projects I also am concerned about potential perils to the embodied individuals involved. Undisciplined minds and bodies can be read as dangerous and disruptive. Wittingly or not, existing structures may foil attempts to step across. To step across is to run the risk of being torn apart or of being claimed and nurtured by no one. My publisher alluded to the latter risk when he advised me to take the word "interdisciplinary" out of this book's title. Speaking pragmatically from experience in the publishing industry, he explained that everyone may think "the book is for someone else."[10] This tendency, while having fiscal ramifications for a publisher, may spell disaster for an untenured professor in need of venues. Thus, supporting interdisciplinarity requires more from individuals and institutions than merely that they champion the hiring of joint appointees; yet, as I hope this volume illustrates, stepping across can produce rich rewards as we forge hybrid discourses and develop fresh perspectives.

NOTES

1. Doug Linder, "The Trials of Los Angeles Police Officers' [sic] in Connection with the Beating of Rodney King, 2001." [Online]. Available: http://www.law.umkc.edu/faculty/projects/ftrails/lapd/lapdaccount.html. 21 December 2001.

2. Ibid.; and, "People, Places & Things in the News," *NewStandard* (22 June 1997). [Online]. Available: http://www.s-t.com/daily/06-97/06-22-97/zzzwnppl.htm. 21 December 2001.

3. "People, Places & Things."

4. Paul Robyn, "The United States and Haiti (1993–1994): A Case Study in Coercive Diplomacy." (Paper, Woodrow Wilson School of Public and International Affairs, Princeton University). [Online]. Available: http://www.wws.princeton.edu/ ~ cases/papers/haiti.html. 21 December 2001.

5. Ulrich S. Haynes, Jr., "United States Foreign Policy in Haiti: A Study in Failure," *Ambassadors Review* (Fall 2000). [Online]. Available: http://www.his.com/ ~ council/haynes.htm. 21 December 2001.

6. Ibid.

7. Ibid.

8. Ibid.

9. The poll was conducted by National Public Radio, the Kaiser Family Foundation, and the Kennedy School of Government at Harvard University. See "NPR News Special Report: The NPR/Kaiser/Kennedy School Poll." [Online]. Available: http://www.npr.org. 6 December 2001.

10. Chris Myers, e-mail correspondence with author, 19 December 2001.

·1·

NO HERO OF MINE

Disney, Popular Culture, and Education (2001)

Introduction

As traditional sources of funding for public school music have disappeared and music programs have faced dramatic budget cuts, music educators have increasingly turned to corporations and to education/business partnerships as potential sources of funding. Although music education has long been connected to industry in ways other curricular areas have not, within the past decade the field's affiliations with business have grown deeper, more numerous, and increasingly complex. The promotion of education/business partnerships has become a goal of the National Association for Music Education (MENC), the national professional organization of music teachers. In March 2000, June Hinckley, then-president of MENC, set forth four visions for the organization, one of which is to build partnerships. "Without partnerships with industry, the arts and entertainment communities, and decision makers," Hinckley asserts, "we are a voice in the wind. With strong partnerships come expanded wherewithal and influence."[1] A small core of businesses, the Disney Corporation among them, has repeatedly played key roles in national ventures.

The trend in music education toward partnerships with industry is consonant with privatization initiatives elsewhere in education; however, it is a trend that has gone largely unquestioned by music educators. In particular, the effectiveness of these partnerships as a means of alleviating budgetary problems, and the issue of whose agenda will be served when industry is providing the funding for educational ventures, need further exploration.

My interest in partnerships between MENC and the Disney Corporation dates back to 1996, when I attended a complimentary premiere screening of the movie *Mr. Holland's Opus*. Held in fifty-one locations across the country and sponsored by the National Coalition for Music Education[2] in cooperation with the National Academy of Recording Arts and Sciences Foundation, the American Music Conference, and Hollywood Pictures, the promotional screening was the result of an education/business partnership forged between these entities; it was billed as an effort to mobilize the music education community around a "gift to the many dedicated teachers who have greatly inspired children over the years with the spirit and joy of music and the other arts."[3] A letter from sponsors, distributed at the screening, suggested that the movie could serve as a convincing voice when advocating for arts in the schools, and it advised previewers to "take school board members, principals, educators, administrators, civic leaders, and government representatives to see this powerful film."[4]

The movie, which was produced by the Disney Corporation's subsidiary Hollywood Pictures, chronicles the thirty-year career of a fictitious high school instrumental music teacher, Glenn Holland; promotional materials published by the Coalition provide the following synopsis: "Richard Dreyfuss portrays [a] music teacher...whose aspirations to compose have taken a back seat to the needs of his students. The film shows Holland's transformation... from 'temporary' teacher into a passionate, dedicated and beloved role model."[5] The film ends with the demise of Holland's music program, which falls victim to budget cuts.

I watched *Mr. Holland's Opus* especially carefully because at the time I was a member of MENC, one of the three organizations comprising the National Coalition for Music Education. I could not recall MENC ever having endorsed a movie, and I believed that as a member of this professional group I was participating, albeit indirectly, in the film's promotion. My intense disappointment with the film, with the reviews it received both inside and outside of education, and with MENC's decision to participate in the promotion of the movie spurred my decision to formulate a critique; it also prompted me to investigate more closely some of the players in this particular education/business partnership.

My interest redoubled in 1999 when MENC launched another promotional campaign with a Disney subsidiary, this time for the film *Music of the Heart,* starring Meryl Streep, Gloria Estefan, and Angela Bassett. In a plot reminiscent of that in *Opus,* a heroic but beleaguered music teacher attempts to save an impoverished urban school's string program. The program is saved thanks to a fund raiser at Carnegie Hall featuring performances by such luminaries as Itzhak Perlmann and Isaac Stern.

This study evolved from the events I have just described. Its first section
is a situated reading of *Mr. Holland's Opus* that analyzes the movie as a gendered text. It examines how the film both draws upon and tends to perpetuate masculinist discourses concerning teaching, heroism, and professionalism.
The second section focuses on *Music of the Heart*. I argue that the movie's
portrayal of a heroic White teacher, her Black colleagues, and the non-White
parents of her students exemplifies what Julie Kailin calls "savage liberalism,"
which she defines as "a liberal denial or ignorance or ignoring of the significance of racism and its structural roots and material basis."[6] Specifically, the
film ignores the role that racism plays in the creation and perpetuation of
funding inequities while simultaneously implying that Blacks are to blame for
current problems in urban schools. This section also interrogates the movie's
proposed solution to public schooling's budgetary problems: save select programs by holding grand-scale bake sales. Although this solution is consistent
with liberal tropes, including belief in the efficacy of heroic individualism, it
is also inadequate; exemplifying a form of selective amelioration, it suggests
that only those besieged teachers, programs, and schools that have connections with the privileged elite will be saved. Furthermore, the solution is problematic because it may draw public attention away from more fundamental
funding issues and from the idea that all children should have the opportunity to attend adequately funded schools.

In the third section I take a close look at a key player in the education/
business partnerships that were forged to promote these movies: the Disney
Corporation. I argue that the manner in which the movies were promoted
helps to create a favorable public image of the corporate world: socially
responsible and genuinely concerned both about the quality of American education and about the demise of arts education. In no way does it intimate that
corporate practices may be at least partially responsible for any declines in
the quality of public schooling. I then present counter evidence suggesting that
at least some of Disney's business practices, particularly those pertaining to
tax breaks, belie such concern. My evidence focuses on twelve specific situations and contexts. Disney, I conclude, aggressively engages in business
practices that, according to Michael Apple, Alex Molnar, and others,[7] gut
school coffers and precipitate declines in the quality of educational programs
in U.S. public schools. These practices may have an especially deleterious
effect on arts programs, given the marginalized position of the arts within the
school curriculum.

In the fourth section I briefly describe several additional education/busi-
ness partnerships between MENC and an array of other corporations, including Texaco, PepsiCo, Yamaha, Bose, and Dole. Prompted by the difficult

questions these films and the education/business partnerships raised for me, I explore some of the possible implications of business' deepening involvement in music education. Finally, I suggest political alternatives that may be more substantive and effective for music education than entering into education/ business partnerships to promote films such as *Mr. Holland's Opus* and *Music of the Heart*.

Throughout my situated reading of the two films, I use several terms—including "portrayed," "represented," and "pictured"—that may be associated with structural theories about texts and meaning making, but I am employing them in a somewhat different manner than a structuralist would. When I speak of "portrayals" and "representations," for example, I am referring to the ways in which the films position viewers such that particular readings or interpretations are likely to be made by members of specific communities of viewers, while other possible readings or interpretations are foreclosed. Rather than assuming, as a structuralist would, that meaning resides in the text (i.e., in the film) itself, I base my analysis on an American postmodern interpretation of feminist reception theory, which assumes that texts, including films, are "read and interpreted in a social context," to quote feminist educator Ann DeVaney.[8] According to this theory, a reader or viewer, rather than operating idiosyncratically, makes meaning by bringing to a specific text a familiarity with "larger unbound texts or discourses."[9] DeVaney suggests that access to discourses, as well as access to "the language and codes of communication," are by-products of group membership.[10] Meanings tend to be shared by members of the same discursive community, and, in addition, they are dynamic, constantly being negotiated and re-negotiated by the group. DeVaney states that texts are likely to be read similarly by members of the same "community of readers," a phrase she borrows from Stanley Fish, although this is not invariably the case.[11] In addition, they may be read very differently by members of a different discursive community. Thus, in DeVaney's view, the concept of dominant readings does not preclude the development of "alternative interpretations."[12] Feminist theorist Chris Weedon lists an array of factors that come into play in the process of meaning making, among them "the range and social power of existing discourses, our access to them and the political strength of the interests which they represent."[13] Several of these factors allude to a relationship between discourse and power.

In summary, while meanings are assumed to be dynamic, multiple, and contested, both within and among discursive communities, the reception theory on which my analysis of *Mr. Holland's Opus* and *Music of the Heart* is based presumes the existence, at any given moment and within specific discursive communities, of dominant meanings and dominant readings. In addition, it acknowledges the existence of dominant discourses, a concept that recognizes the social power and political investment of which Weedon speaks. The notion of the "decentered subject," central to postmodern feminist theory, also has implications for reception theory and for the reading of texts. According to Weedon, subjectivity is neither unified nor fixed, but rather, the individual is the "site of conflicting forms of subjectivity."[14] This dynamic vision of subjectivity implies that the viewer, who inevitably belongs to multiple discursive communities, may feel tugs and pulls from several sometimes conflicting discourses while watching films such as those I have analyzed. In addition, because films are polytextual, by which I mean that they are multi-stranded, simultaneously presenting visual images and music in addition to speech, the viewer may be called upon to read multiple texts simultaneously; each strand or "text" may be discursively similar to or in conflict with the others, further complicating the possibility of a definitive unified reading from anyone, myself included. Thus, while presenting a resistant reading of these films, I acknowledge that it is only one among many possible readings I or others could make. However, recognizing as did philosopher Michel Foucault the many connections that exist between discourse and power relations,[15] I have attempted to present an alternative to dominant interpretations, and in the process, to open up a conversation about connections between the dominant discourses supported by these films and power relations. The dynamic vision of subjectivity articulated by Weedon, in addition to addressing the complexity of reading texts, opens up the possibility for change both in individual and in groups.[16] With that possibility in mind, let us consider the first of the two promotional partnership films.

A Situated Reading of Mr. Hollands's Opus as Gendered Text

Mr. Holland's Opus was the first of two films to be promoted via an education/business partnership between MENC and a Disney subsidiary. When I attended the complimentary screening on January 9, 1996, I was joined by more than 25,000 music educators, administrators, and friends of the arts.[17] The local screening was a gala affair. Mike Leckrone, director of the University of Wisconsin-Madison Marching Band, was on hand to introduce the film at the Madison viewing; after the film, previewers were shown a short clip of actor Richard Dreyfuss talking about the importance of the arts. In addition to receiving a letter encouraging us to invite every influential person we know to see the film, we also were given a whole array of other promotional materials, including a cassette tape of musical excerpts from the movie, a movie poster suitable for hanging on a classroom wall, and a list of suggested ways to further the arts in local communities.[18]

Despite mixed reviews from critics, *Opus* was a huge box office success, grossing more than $80 million in U.S. theaters during the first few months following its release. [19] Shortly after it was made available for home rental, it "was ranked as number one in the rental market"[20] and has earned at least $36.5 million in home rental fees.[21] Playing to not only a national but also an international audience,[22] *Opus* generated a Golden Globe Best Actor nomination from the Hollywood Foreign Press Association and an Oscar nomination, both for actor Richard Dreyfuss.[23] The film was also nominated for a Golden Globe Award in the category "Best Screenplay."[24]

Popular acclaim is not the only measure of influence that can be applied to this film, however. In its wake, the National Academy of Recording Arts and Sciences (NARAS), one of three organizations forming the National Coalition for Music Education, created a national music teaching award named after Glenn Holland and presented it to fifty-one music teachers.[25] Eleven cities reportedly "established January 9 as 'Mr. Holland's Opus' Day,"[26] and a Mr. Holland's Opus Foundation, which provides musical instruments to school programs, was created by Michael Kamen, composer of the movie's score.[27] The movie's influence in education continues to be felt, in some cases far beyond music circles. For example, Learning Enrichment, Inc., recently created a "classroom-ready Teaching Kit" designed to help teachers from many curricular areas bring the movie into their classrooms; according to a promotional flyer, the kit will help students "reflect on their responsibilities as learners."[28]

The education/business partnership forged to promote the film was showered with accolades as well. In August 1996, the National Coalition for Music Education, along with other promotional partners in this collaboration, was presented the 1996 Summit Award, given by the American Society of Association Executives in recognition of "outstanding efforts to make America a better place to live through education, standard setting, ethics, political education, international activities, and community service."[29] Following receipt of the award, Larry Linkin, President and CEO of the National Association of Music Merchants described the *Mr. Holland's Opus* collaboration as an example of "'what is possible when we as individual organizations work collectively toward a common goal and set aside our own individual agendas for the greater good of the music community.'"[30]

Keeping these indicators of influence in mind, let us examine some of the visions of teachers, teaching, and professionalism that were supported by this film. More specifically, let us consider how these visions are gendered.

Visions of Teachers

The Constitution of the Teaching Work Force
Through utterances and silences, *Opus* contributes to an already prevalent collective forgetting concerning a significant dimension of the teaching work force: its composition by sex. Following in a Hollywood tradition of featuring heroic male teachers, the movie obscured an important reality: teaching, in general, and music teaching, in particular, are pink-collar professions. Thus, Mr. Holland is an atypical American music teacher, not because he performs heroics, but because he is male. The gendered constitution of the teaching force at large has been reported and discussed elsewhere.[31] What is less commonly known, however, is that the majority of *music* teachers are women. Unpublished statistics from Market Data Retrieval indicate that 60 percent of America's 107,559 music teachers are female.[32]

Significantly, the film featured a teacher employed in the most male-dominated (and perhaps for that reason most esteemed) of music education's many sub-specialties: secondary instrumental music. Male teachers comprise 60 percent of the nation's 13, 247 instrumental teachers, both elementary and secondary.[33] When elementary teachers are removed from the pool, however, the figures are more dramatic. Data published in 1991 reveal that 23.4 percent of instrumental music teachers in small high schools and 11.1 percent of them in large ones are women.[34] Thus, although Glenn Holland was representative of secondary instrumental teachers, he was not representative of music teachers as a whole.

Male music teachers were atypical during the time period portrayed in the movie, but male principals were the norm; significantly, the high school principal featured in the film was a woman. While creating a carnivalesque picture of a world turned upside down where women hold positional power, the movie presents a highly unlikely situation: a male high school teacher working for a female principal. In 1972, a year encompassed by the film, only 1.7 percent of all secondary school principals were women;[35] even today, the vast majority of high school principals are men.

In short, *Opus* contributes to a collective forgetting of the gendered constitution of the work force, and it erases the gendered power hierarchy that continues to structure most schools. Movies such as this one, designed for mass consumption, may play a critical role in shaping the individual and collective imagineries of vast audiences, however. What tends to be lost is the reality that every discussion about teachers and teaching, whether the topic is educational reform, regulation through mandated standards, assessment, the declining physical condition of U.S. schools, teacher competence, working conditions, or the demise of music education programs is a discussion about women, their work, and their workplaces.

Heroic Teachers: A Gendered Trope

There is little doubt but that the movie portrays the mature Holland as a hero. A pep rally, which concludes the film, is the capstone of this representation, showing us the multitudes whose lives were changed by him; the scene is accompanied by quintessentially "heroic" music, Holland's own composition. Feminist scholar Sari Knopp Biklen problematizes heroic representations of teachers, however; she identifies several characteristics of masculinist heroism, including independent rebelliousness, manifest as apart-from-the-pack individualism; single-minded commitment that crowds out family life; and inexpendability.[36] Let us consider how these heroic characteristics are reinforced by the movie.

Rebelliousness and Individualism. Arguing that heroism is characterized by rebelliousness manifest as apart-from-the-pack individualism, Biklen writes, "People are heroic in isolation from others";[37] heroic tropes tend to celebrate individual rather than collective action.[38] Holland fit this description; he was an unconventional teacher, displaying rebelliousness, for example, in his decision to focus the curriculum on popular music rather than solely on the high art canon. The unconventionality of this decision is underscored in a scene in which Holland is asked by his principal to answer to critics, portrayed as reactionary standard bearers of the dull and ordinary. The fact that Holland stood his ground and was supported by his administrator constructed his decision as heroic, rebellious, and good.

I found ample evidence both in the film and the promotional materials that Holland exhibited self-centered individualism, evidence refuting the assertion made in those same promotional materials that Holland placed his students' needs before his own. The structure of the plot, with its focus on one man, put everyone else in the background, including Holland's students, who were overshadowed as the individual teacher was glorified. Holland repeatedly monopolized the limelight, strutting during a marching band performance and publicly singing an apologetic reconciliation to his estranged son. Promotional posters for the movie similarly underscored the film's emphasis on Holland the individual; a large silhouette of him is superimposed over tiny pictures of the many students he taught and influenced. The camera angle positions viewers so that they must look up to Holland. In some of the promotional materials, the pictures of the students disappear altogether, and only Holland's imposing shadow remains.[39] Ironically, a statement about Holland's selflessness is superimposed on his solo silhouette, the visual effect conflicting with the written assertion that Holland is altruistic. Monopolizing the limelight, which may be among the rewards of heroism, tends to be inconsistent with women's work or the women who tend to do it, however.

Inexpendability. In a discussion of inexpendability, Biklen observes, "The heroic trope, by its very nature, suggests that the hero is irreplaceable and makes a unique contribution. When applied to education, the implication is that this contribution is invaluable in a way that regular teaching is not."[40] She suggests that by contrast expendability is typical of women's work, including teaching. Quoting a study by Coser and Rokoff, she writes: "In occupations sex-typed as feminine, 'each individual worker is *replaceable,* or *defined as replaceable.'*"[41]

The movie's ending, which highlights the dissolution of Holland's job, may seem to suggest that expendability is one of the film's themes, but by focusing on Holland the individual it merely supports the concept of the irreplaceable hero and overlooks expendability as a characteristic of pink-collar labor, in this case, of teaching. Prior to the job cut Holland enjoyed thirty uninterrupted years in the same school, and apparently never once was his position in jeopardy.

In contrast to Holland's one-job-for-a-lifetime path, women teachers' careers often are marked by multiple moves in and out of the profession, as well as by shifts from school to school. Arguably, teachers like Holland, who stay in one school for a lifetime and first face their expendability late in their careers, are rare.

Although Biklen acknowledges that the heroic model may offer some advantages, she questions its appropriateness for teaching, specifically arguing that "the idea of the heroic is so gendered as to be useless."[42] She later elaborates,

> Heroic tropes, even when redefined around commitment and resistance, contribute to constructing rather than deconstructing teaching as gendered activity. They do not provide insight into the rich and complex ways in which teachers' lives in schools are constrained by institutional discourses and at the same time expanded through their interaction with children. The hero is constructed against the feminine.[43]

Visions of Teaching: Problems within the Profession

The movie highlights in a superficial way problems and issues faced by teachers, including working conditions, low pay, the low status of teaching, and the marginalization of the arts within the school curriculum, but it fails to address why these problems exist. In particular, it erases the role that gender plays in their creation and perpetuation.

Working Conditions and Low Pay

Let us consider first the many working-condition issues that caused Holland to bristle. The young Holland was woefully uninformed about the expectations of the job. Time demands, including spillover and lack of free time, shocked him, as did lack of autonomy, a characteristic teaching tends to share with other pink-collar occupations.[44] He was stunned, for example, when told he was required to file lesson plans with the principal.

Holland's shock is uninterrogated, however. Apparently he felt that as a White male of a specific social class he deserved better treatment. The movie invites viewers to participate in Holland's outrage but it masks the reality that perceptions of acceptable working conditions for self or others can be gendered, raced, and classed. Biklen points out that working conditions, which tend to distinguish professions from semiprofessions, are a direct result of the constitution by sex of various occupations:

> Teaching, nursing, and social work, labeled "semiprofessions"...are differentiated from "full" professions by shorter training, a lack of control over technical knowledge, lower status, less right to privileged communication, and decreased autonomy from supervision or societal control. Teaching, like other semiprofessions, is women's work.[45]

Thus some of the very conditions that outraged Holland are direct results of the fact that the semiprofession of teaching is women's work.

The movie also addressed the issue of teacher pay but once again failed to move beyond the statement that teachers are not paid well. Holland took extra jobs to make ends meet, which suggested that teaching alone did not pay enough to support a family—at least not a White 1960's family aspiring to middle-class status. The film suggested that this inadequacy is unfortunate, but it is also presented low pay as a given; the film did not invite viewers to consider why teachers' pay would not be adequate for a male head of household. As was the case with working conditions, pay inequities within and across professions are gendered. Teaching salaries, long considered sufficient for a woman, were represented in the movie as insufficient for the "man of the house."

The Low Status of Teaching

Opus underscores Holland's ambivalence about the suitability of teaching as a career and his perception that it was a second-best option for him. Early in the film, in particular, Holland viewed teaching as a short-term choice that would enable him to accumulate the money he needed to do something more significant: compose. Throughout his teaching career he remained more or less ambivalent about his job, his dream unrealized; the movie implied that Holland's ambivalence was unfortunate. It failed to provide any indication, however, that gendered and classed perceptions about legitimate careers may have shaped Holland's views.

Holland's elevated attitude about composing, coupled with his ambivalence about teaching, are far from idiosyncratic; such perceptions thrive in American conservatories and schools of music, and they are consonant with common perceptions of teaching, regardless of the curricular area. Biklen describes a prevalent formula that equates "a teaching career with a failure of ambition."[46] She concludes that teaching's second-class status as a career is a gender issue, integrally related to the fact that it is women who teach.[47]

Significantly, not only did Holland select teaching, but he also chose a "soft," i.e., feminine, subject. Thus, in multiple ways, larger discourses call into question the suitability of music teaching as a sufficiently important and "masculine" career for a male; the film never touched upon the "why" behind Holland's ambivalence, however.

The Marginalization of Music within the School Curriculum

Draconian budget cuts resulted in the dissolution of the arts program in the high school and the loss of Mr. Holland's job; the film did not address why the arts, among the many curricular and extracurricular areas, were the primary target, however, nor did it provide any indication that such cuts principally affect females. Aside from Holland's quip to the football coach suggesting that the latter need not worry about job security, the movie and its reviews failed to address the reality that cuts to arts programs are gendered in at least four respects. First, they are cuts to programs that have been constructed as feminine and, consequently, marginalized within the public school curriculum. As I have argued elsewhere, in the United States music has long been considered a feminine domain, even though women historically have been barred from many sub-specialities.[48] This is not only because music is associated with the emotional side of a gendered rational/emotional dichotomy, but also because it was part of the sex-stereotyped curriculum offered at female academies and seminaries in the U.S. during the nineteenth century. Music's marginalization and its vulnerable position within the curriculum today are due, at least in part, to its historically gendered associations.[49] Second, studying music is generally not perceived to lead to lucrative careers; devaluing of the arts, as manifest in the selective cutting of programs in Mr. Holland's school, is the outcome of a classed, masculinist perspective that equates worth and meaning with highly paid labor outside the home. Third, cuts in arts programs are gendered because the majority of teachers affected are women. This would not be the case if cuts were to come to math, science,

or football programs. Finally, the majority of public school students participating in music are girls,[50] and thus girls constitute the student population
most likely affected.

Music educators were urged to use the film to mobilize the public around
policy issues affecting arts education; substantive change, however, requires
a deep understanding of these issues, many of which involve gender, race, and
class. *Opus* did nothing to promote such deep understanding.

Sounds and Silences: Marking the Parameters of Professionalism

By focusing on select actions taken by Holland and representing them
as honorable, good, or acceptable, the film promulgated a particular vision of
professionalism while simultaneously ignoring other visions that would have
constructed some of Hollands' actions as unacceptable, unprofessional, or
even reprehensible. The movie, I argue, reinforces a masculinist concept of
professionalism.

Commitment and Dedication: Gendered Beliefs about Professionalism

Biklen writes that commitment is one of the defining attributes of masculinist visions of a professional career, and she notes that level of commitment tends to be measured by time on the job: "Current notions of the
professional career include heavy workloads and large time commitments."[51]
She adds that a "career's tendency to spill over the nine-to-five time slot" is
one factor differentiating mere occupations from professional careers.[52]
Commitment, according to Biklen, also typically involves staying with a job
over time.[53] Thus, in masculinist scripts, professionalism is defined, in part,
as paid labor that forms the center of a person's life; according to Biklen, one
feature of heroic tropes is singlemindness that tends to crowd out family life.[54]
By contrast, placing family at the center is constructed as feminine and anti-
thetical to professionalism.

Biklen notes that some dominant discourses concerning professionalism
present women (and, I would argue, growing numbers of men) entering elite
careers with a serious dilemma: "As more women have entered professional
careers, they have had to find ways to integrate family and work life, give up
family life as they knew it, or change their workplaces (unless they drop out
of or slow down their careers)."[55] She elaborates,

> Women breaking into professional careers must understand these [workload
> and time commitment] requirements and give them priority in their lives in
> order to succeed....
> The perspective just described positions women in tension with a stable,
> coherent phenomenon called a "career" that can be described, envied, and vet-

ted. When women express and exhibit career commitment, they must reckon with these perspectives and their position (as newcomers or intruders, depending on one's point of view) and consider the implications: Their biographies rather than the structure of the career are expected to alter. How will they handle their families?[56]

Other educationists have cast a wary eye at dominant constructions of professionalism and have identified these constructions as gendered. Michael Apple, in *Teachers and Texts,* warns that intensification, i.e, unrelenting pressure to work harder in the absence of increased resources, is misrecognized as increased professionalism.[57]

Opus reinforced commitment tropes. Holland's gradual adoption of a massive work load that involved considerable time beyond the regular school day was portrayed as an act of professionalization, and his steady transformation from clock watcher into overworked but dedicated teacher was represented as good. In addition, Holland was pictured as committed because he remained uninterruptedly in one job for his entire life.

Let us consider an example of how *Opus'* vision of professionalism may undermine women teachers. Early in the movie, Holland regularly sprinted for the door at the end of the day, and these sprints were seen as a sign of his lack of commitment, a problem needing to be remedied. Similar readings of such sprints can transfer to other circumstances, however. For example, a parent who needs to dash to pick up a child at day care or to catch a child's soccer game is perhaps also read as lacking commitment. Because women still do the bulk of child care in the majority of families in the United States, regardless of whether two parents are present, those sprinters are more likely to be women—as unfair as the distribution of child-care responsibilities may be. Thus, when the movie perpetuates an understanding that links professionalism to commitment and then defines commitment as spillover time, it promotes a discourse that, in the embodied world of work, is more likely to harm women workers.

Similarly, the movie's messages about commitment tend to discredit the work record of women who need to or choose to step out of the paid work force for a time. If uninterrupted employment is a sign of commitment, then the patterns of many women's career trajectories signal something else.

Nowhere in music education are dominant discourses about commitment more evident than in the male-majority sub-speciality of secondary instrumental music, where unrelenting work is an accepted part of the culture. Spillover is especially prevalent among band directors, whose regular teaching responsibilities are augmented with an endless list of co-curricular and extra-curricular jobs (e.g., trips, contests, festivals, pep band performances at sports events, marching band appearances at parades, fund raising, and jazz band gigs at the Lions Club).

Although rarely openly discussed, the perception persists that secondary instrumental jobs are too difficult and time demanding for women. This perception can lead skeptical superintendents and principals to bypass women in job searches, can result in women being subjected to undue scrutiny once on the job, and can dissuade women from training for such careers in the first place. When women, explicitly or implicitly, are told, "If you can't stand the heat, get out of the kitchen," then women, and not the job expectations, are defined as the problem, however. Curiously, secondary instrumental jobs are not perceived to be too difficult or time demanding for men who want to raise a family, perhaps because the job expectations were established by men who expected to have stay-at-home partners and did not plan to participate equally in child care. According to Biklen, "Professional careers that carry high social status are made possible by domestic and occupational social relationships that depend on certain uses of time."[58] When women in demanding careers quip, "I need a wife," they are alluding to social relationships that historically have made the time demands of high-status professions feasible.

The movie's portrayal of job expectations for secondary instrumental teachers may have been accurate, but I question the glorification of such expectations. Holland opted for teaching and not Wall Street, but Wall Street values followed him into the classroom. In a chapter entitled "The Rebirth of Voluntary Servitude," Ann Godignon and Jean-Louis Thiriet argue that the concept of individual freedom has been interpreted in the modern era in ways that have created a new form of servitude, a servitude to unrelenting work. The "free individual," thus defined, "only exists through the continual deployment of his [sic] own capacity for nonstop work, which becomes the ultimate measure of his being."[59] *Opus* glorifies such an individual, someone who reinforces traditional visions of career and career expectations.

Finally, *Opus* glosses over some of the costs to partners and families of prevailing models of professionalism. It focuses on tensions in Holland's family but neatly resolves the conflicts. We witness the life of a man whose work habits deprived his child of a parent; hiding in his work, Holland chose for most of his career not to enter significantly into the life of his son. This is a grave matter; however, there was no divorce, no alcoholism, and no runaway son. Holland, after all, was a hero.

The movie's portrayal of professionalism invites several questions: First, who tends to benefit from this particular vision? Is the homophonic life, where centrality of career is the dominant voice, necessary for a productive career, in teaching or any other field? Is it necessarily preferable to a polyphonic vision? In a well-played fugue, for example, different voices come to the fore at different times; the best performers do not permit a single voice to dominate throughout and avoid playing all voices *fortissimo*. Does the homophonic life necessarily lead to good teaching, however defined, and to the creation of humane learning or home environments for children? In what ways might the homophonic life lead to attrition from the profession? I am not suggesting that the homophonic life should be discredited; rather, I argue that using it as the sole model for professionalism may shut many out.

The Silences: Unprofessionalism Unnoticed

Abuses of Positional Power. The movie's silences about other professional issues merit interrogation. Specifically, the film fails to suggest that abuses of the positional power accompanying teaching are unprofessional. The most serious of Holland's abuses of power surfaced in his relationship with his student Rowena, a subject I will discuss in a moment. This particular abuse, however, needs to be viewed within the larger context of the movie's representations of legitimate student-teacher power relations. Throughout the movie Holland displayed a hierarchical, patriarchal leadership style. Betty Friedan commented that this is the style many males are socialized into adopting.[60] A line delivered by the movie's football coach articulates a possible rationale for the adoption of this style: "High school is not a democracy."

Not only did Holland tend to adopt a hierarchical style, but sometimes he abused his positional power. For example, drumming on the head of what appeared to be his only African American student, criticizing an individual's musical performance in the presence of his or her peers, and publicly naming individuals who made particularly serious blunders on tests are acts of humiliation, regardless of whether they achieve a positive musical outcome. Snarling commands is not the kind of behavior that people who respect one another exhibit, and yet this was precisely how Holland sometimes responded to students, especially those he perceived to be "out of line." Due both to his sex and size, he could and did show his students "who was boss," displaying a power model that women teachers sometimes cannot and often choose not to adopt. Michel Foucault pointed out that hierarchical power models may not sufficiently convey the complexity of actual power relations in specific situations.[61] As inadequate as these power models may be, however, *Opus* seems to suggest that they are effective, appropriate, and suitable for teachers to adopt in their relationships with students. This gendered message tends to undercut other ways for students and teachers to relate to one another, ways, for example, that are based on collaboration and cooperation.

Not only did the movie reinforce abusive hierarchical models of class-room power relations, it also subtly undercut other possibilities. For exam-ple, in a rare departure Holland displayed gentleness and civility (combined with frustration) when his band could not learn to march on the football field. The football coach, who had been watching the spectacle from the sidelines while barking orders at his team, intervened. "I take it you were never in the army," the coach remarked. Thus, the army's leadership style was identified as effective, while Holland's rare show of gentleness was translated into inept bungling.

A Romantic Relationship with a Student. The most troubling issues surround-ing professionalism, however, involved portrayals of Holland's relationship with the student Rowena. Arguably, in his personal relationship with her (which included kissing) Holland stepped over the line demarcating accept-able behavior. Even though the movie's most suggestive scenes reportedly ended up on the editor's floor after previews elicited negative responses, the remaining footage clearly suggested that Holland came within a hair of hav-ing an affair with his student.[62] The stunned look on his wife's face when she realized that her husband's muse, whom Holland claimed was mythic, was none other than the teen belting out a torch song at the high school musical revue, confirmed Holland's emotional involvement with Rowena.

The manner in which Holland's relationship with this student is treat-ed in the film fails to address the gravity of Holland's actions; specifically, the relationship seemed to have had no effect on a favorable assessment of Holland as a teacher. Thus, a particular vision of professional behavior emerges from this movie: unrelenting commitment to work becomes a prima-ry marker of professionalism while romantic involvement with students is for-givable—certainly not a criterion for excluding a teacher from canonization. This concept of professionalism advantages teachers (usually males) who engage in romantic relationships or who sexually harass students while it dis-advantages students (usually females) in those same relationships. *Opus* joins a host of other movies and books suggesting that romantic student-teacher relationships are benign or even attractive. Romanticized portrayals such as this one create a climate in which allegations of coercion or abuse of power tend to be dismissed.

The film's representation of Rowena contributes to Holland's exonera-tion, implying that the teen was responsible for the relationship with her teacher. This portrayal constructs Holland's attraction as an understand-able and forgivable consequence of calculated entrapment. Through stock devices involving attire, eye contact, body language, and double entendres,

Rowena was constructed as the naughty-but-nice vamp. For example, when she sings, "I'd like to add his initial to my monograph," Rowena clearly is talking about Holland. Similarly, a doe-eyed Rowena presents Holland with the double entendre, "How was I?" By relying on traditional stereotypes of the calculating, enchanting female, Rowena's portrayal reinforces the idea that certain "types" of women gain access to power by using their beauty and sexuality as lures to snag powerful men. If inappropriate actions follow, it is deemed the woman's fault.

Holland's fascination with Rowena goes beyond physical attraction; the movie also constructs the student as holding before Holland his unfulfilled musical aspirations. Rowena is his muse, the inspiration for his creativity and compositions. Historically, one powerful belief has suggested that although women lack genius, they can effectively serve in a supporting role, inspiring the creative efforts of males. Muse or not, Rowena left for New York to become a performer, a career that supposedly requires less "genius" than composing does and is, consequently, of somewhat lower status, while Holland, inspired by his muse, achieves his somewhat higher-status goal of successfully composing.

Finally, Rowena is infantilized. Looking directly into Holland's eyes, she purrs a message of dependence: "I'm a little lamb who's lost in the woods." She concludes that she needs "Someone to Watch over Me." This scene, like the relationship as a whole, resonates with treadworn discourses: (a) women want and need older, more experienced or more powerful men to take care of them, and (b) men are attracted to women who want or need to be taken care of and find such dependence satisfying.

Thus, although pictured as somewhat foolish, Holland is forgiven for being beguiled. A cliche of males at midlife, he is enslaved to testosterone and a fragile ego, his power stolen from him by a vamp. He, not Rowena, has become the "victim."

Another way of constructing Holland would have emphasized that he, not Rowena, was a teacher and an adult; as such, he held greater positional power and should have been the more responsible of the pair. Most experienced teachers learn early in their careers how to address student crushes in a responsible manner. Many signs along the way hinted that the relationship was headed for dangerous waters, but Holland seemed oblivious to these signs (or even rejuvenated by them). If teachers are called upon to serve *in loco parentis,* however, then Holland betrayed his student and abused the power entrusted in him by her parents. Significantly, Rowena's parents and their possible response to Holland's attentions are never seen.

Professional and Unprofessional Emotions. A final gendered way that the movie marked parameters of professional behavior was through its portrayal of appropriate emotions. Holland's limited emotional repertoire, whether he was interacting with his family or students, was lamentable. One tragic example, especially given Holland's profession, was the almost complete lack of caring and affection that characterized his interactions with his deaf son. Inside or outside of the classroom, anger seemed to be Holland's only emotional recourse. Beyond the question of whether Holland's limited emotional repertoire disqualifies him for canonization, however, is the issue of what the movie presents as professional, classroom emotional behavior. The film did not suggest that emotions have no place in the classroom; instead, it reinforced a gender-laden vision of which emotions are or are not acceptable. The acceptability of various expressions of anger stands uninterrogated as do taboos against crying or otherwise appearing "weak" in professional settings. To suggest that Holland's emotional life was a professional liability rather than an asset, however, requires resisting and disrupting strong dominant constructions of masculinity and professionalism, these constructions often equating one with the other.

The Film's Appeal and Its Political Work

Clearly, the movie promoted multiple discourses and had multiple appeals. One might argue that other discourses, specifically those pertaining to the importance of the arts, spoke more loudly and compellingly than did those about gender. This argument, however, sets up a hierarchy of "first emergencies"[63] in which arts funding becomes more important than equity. Some may argue that much of the movie was set in the past, in the simpler "good old days," when actions such as Holland's wouldn't have resulted in reprimands or sexual harassment suits, and when "private" deeds did not impinge on the favorable image of public figures. I contend, however, that cultural artifacts are never politically neutral; nostalgically representing the past as desirable is a politically powerful move. In the case of this movie, the nostalgia is fully effective only for those who fail to recognize that the "good old days" were neither necessarily simple nor good for members of many groups. The postmodern premise that texts are created for specific discursive communities invites speculation about which discursive communities would be nostalgic about and derive pleasure from the gender relations served up by this film. Recognition that power plays a role in the dominance of specific discourses invites consideration of whose interests are served and which power arrangements are preserved by the perpetuation of gendered discourses about teachers, teaching, and professionalism. Thus, Foucault's suggestion that we examine the "tactical productivity" of discourses seems to be a fitting one as we examine a movie such as *Opus*.[64]

Not to be dismissed when considering the movie's appeal is the apparently calculated effort to capture the imaginations and emotions of a broad range of groups, including aging baby boomers and the deaf community, in addition to educators. Some teachers with whom I have spoken and who said they despised the film also admitted to crying at the ending, a scene in which a teacher receives well-deserved but rarely given public recognition. I wept at allusions to the war in Viet Nam. This phenomenon suggests that the movie's emotional appeal did powerful political work and may have helped to shield the film from well-deserved criticism. For me one of the more distressing points about *Opus* is how well Hollywood Pictures knew its audience; the corporation accurately predicted that the discourses informing *Opus* would be sufficiently acceptable to a wide enough audience as to make the movie a financial success. They were, and it was.

Music of the Heart: *Promotional Ventures Revisited*

Four years after *Mr. Holland's Opus* was released MENC entered into a second education/business promotional partnership with a Disney subsidiary, this time for the movie *Music of the Heart,* starring Meryl Streep, Aidan Quinn, Gloria Estefan, and Angela Bassett. Released on October 29,1999, by Miramax Films, *Music of the Heart* portrays the trials and triumphs of music teacher Roberta Guaspari (Meryl Streep) at Central Park East Elementary School in East Harlem. In a plot reminiscent of *Mr. Holland's Opus,* a heroic beleaguered music teacher institutes a successful string program in an impoverished New York City school, only to be faced, ten years later, with its possible demise due to budget cuts. Guaspari's program is saved, however, thanks to a fund raiser at Carnegie Hall featuring such luminaries as Itzhak Perlman, Isaac Stern, and Arnold Steinhardt. The film was promoted as being based on a true story. Although not as financially successful as its predecessor,[65] *Music of the Heart* received some critical acclaim; the film and its cast were nominated for a number of awards, including Golden Globe and Academy Award nominations for Streep.[66]

The roster of promotional partners for this film was similar to that for *Mr. Holland's Opus*—Miramax Films, Procter & Gamble, MENC, VH1 Save The Music Foundation, NAMM, the NARAS Foundation, AMC, and ASTA—as were the promotional strategies. Once again, music educators were invited to a complimentary preview; this one was held at the July 1999 meeting of the MENC National Assembly.[67] To coordinate with the release of the film, the cover of the October 1999 issue of MENC's trade journal *Teaching Music* featured a full-page picture of Streep in the role of Guaspari. The journal also included an 18" x 27" movie poster, which was filled on the reverse side with everything from a lesson plan based on the movie to advocacy tips ("Make certain that all the important people in your community [sic] teachers, parents, and decision-makers [sic] see Music of the Heart [sic]"). The poster instructs teachers to "place this poster [i.e., movie advertisement] in your school, school board offices, or other community gathering place where it will encourage everyone to take part in this opportunity to promote the value of music in our schools." According to the poster, the film was "proudly presented by Procter and Gamble." In turn, at the Miramax website for *Music of the Heart,* Procter and Gamble and MENC are listed among the cooperating partners in the "advocacy opportunity" created by the film; links are provided to their websites.[68]

The Film's Racialized Construction of School Problems

Promoters, including MENC, encouraged teachers to use this film as a vehicle for educational reform, but as was the case with *Mr. Holland's Opus,* I question the political and financial motives of those who made such admonitions and seriously question the appropriateness of this film as an instrument of change. Some of my reservations stem from issues similar to those I raise concerning *Opus.* For example, in both movies teaching largely is a repository for those of failed ambition or insufficient talent. Guaspari, like Holland, initially sought a career in a more high-status domain of music but settled for teaching as a pragmatic consolation prize. Similar, too, are the film's narrow focus on the individual teacher and reliance on heroic tropes. A third resemblance is the placement of the heroic teacher against a backdrop that pictures the remainder of public education as mundane and mediocre. For example, anti-public school sentiment is evident in the film's first mention of Central Park East School. In describing a possible employment opportunity, a friend of Guaspari's states that the school he has in mind is "public but alternative," a remark suggesting that alternative schools, strongly supported by proponents of privatization, are the only public schools worth considering.

My gravest reservations stem from my perception that the film, while ostensibly serving as a vehicle of reform, fails to bring to light some of the most serious issues facing education. One of the problems that a substantive reform initiative needs to address but this film ignores is the significant role that racism plays in the creation and perpetuation of inequities and inadequacies in public schooling, a topic I will discuss a bit later. In addition to ignoring racism as a contributing factor, however, *Music of the Heart* relies upon and reinforces highly problematic constructions of race that tend to blame non-Whites, Blacks, in particular, for problems in urban schools while exonerating Whites. It positions viewers such that racialized views about the problems urban public schools face are likely to be reinforced and such that simplistic visions of viable solutions to these problems seem logical and commonsensical.

Julie Kailin's analysis of White teachers' perceptions of the problem of race in their schools provided me with a useful framework for analyzing *Music of the Heart*. Kailin, who surveyed teachers in an ostensibly liberal Midwestern school district, argues that district discussions of inequity tended to manifest a form of "savage liberalism," which Kailin defines as "a liberal denial or ignorance or ignoring of the significance of racism and its structural roots and material basis."[69] Basing her conclusions on a survey that asked teachers to articulate their perceptions of racism in their school, Kailin argues that the teachers tended most often to attribute racial problems to Blacks themselves: to Black home environments, parents, teachers, staff, and students. A smaller percentage attributed problems to White teachers, staff, students, or parents; and a very small percentage (12.8 percent) cited institutional or cultural factors.[70]

In its depiction of the problems facing schools today, *Music of the Heart* underscored many of the racist perceptions that Kailin uncovered in her study. If this film is to be believed, Blacks play a major role in school problems; Whites, by and large, do not, but are valiantly trying to solve these problems; and larger cultural or institutional forces do not factor into the equation. A White teacher was portrayed as being challenged by nearly insurmountable obstacles in her job at an impoverished, predominantly non-White urban public school. Keeping Kailin's study of teachers' attributions in mind, let us look at these "problems" more closely.

Troubled Neighborhoods and Home Environment
Students' neighborhood and home environments, relentlessly pictured as dangerous, troubled, hostile, or deficient, were among the "problems" the film identified. Other portrayals evolved over time, but the negative representation of neighborhood and home remained a constant nearly throughout. With sirens wailing in the background, viewers glimpse stolen cars, drug deals on street corners, angry Black adolescents threatening a White woman in her car, abusive fathers, murdered grandmothers, single parents lacking time or money to attend to their children, families that care more about beer and baseball than about violins, incompetent ex-convict sub-contractors ripping off a gentrified White homeowner, a child killed in a drive-by shooting, and dev-

astating divorce. Significantly, these are not, by and large, White homes nor is this a White neighborhood. The school's location in East Harlem sets the scene for racialized, ethnic tropes. "Urban" has come to mean non-White, and in fact, only 7.1 percent of East Harlem's population is White and non-Hispanic.[71] Furthermore, the word "Harlem" has long been equated with African Americans, even though East Harlem, which is the setting for the film, is predominantly a Puerto Rican community where Black non-Hispanics constitute only 38.9 percent of the population.[72] The movie, while portraying what seems to be a racially and ethnically mixed neighborhood, does not clearly suggest that Puerto Ricans are in the majority. Thus, viewers not familiar with New York City might reasonably but incorrectly assume that this film is about a predominantly African American community. The only break in the film's portrayal of the community and families as troubled and troublesome comes toward the end when a few "at risk" families are miraculously "cured," turned around by the violin program. Against a background of literal and metaphorical darkness, Guaspari and her violin program emerge as salvific shining lights.

Troublesome Parents

Parents of Guaspari's students, specifically Black parents, are similarly negatively portrayed, at least until they see the error of their previously "foolish" ways and begin to back Guaspari's program. Viewers often are positioned to take sides with a White teacher against non-White parents, many of whom are Black. Consider, for example, a series of interchanges between Guaspari and the mother of Naeem, an African American boy, in which an initially hostile mother eventually comes around to supporting the program. Naeem, a model student, tells Guaspari that his mother is withdrawing him from violin class. In an encounter with Guaspari, the mother explains her logic, angrily stating, "My son has got more important things to do than learn dead White men's music." Apparently unsympathetic to the mother's concern, Guaspari chuckles and replies dismissively, "They're going to learn 'Twinkle, Twinkle, Little Star!'" The mother persists, asking Guaspari to name Black classical composers and violinists. Guaspari counters by attempting to assert that music is apolitical and that if it makes Naeem feel good, it must be alright: "It makes him feel good about himself. What does it matter who wrote it?" The scene closes with Naeem's mother questioning Guaspari's motives: "You White women come up here and think you can rescue our poor inner-city children who never asked to be rescued in the first place. No thank you." The mother walks away and commands Naeem not to look at Guaspari.

This is not the last encounter between Naeem's mother and Guaspari, however. In an apparent attempt to redeem herself, Guaspari tells the mother that saving children is the farthest thing from her mind. She describes herself as a single parent who went into teaching because she needed a job. She then lectures the mother: "You think you're protecting your son but you're not. I mean what if Arthur Ashe's mother said he couldn't play tennis because it's a White man's game? You know, the important thing is Naeem. When he plays music his whole face lights up. You should see that."

As time goes by, Guaspari's admonition begins to take effect, and a contrite mother shows up one day asking that Naeem be reinstated, an event that prompts Guaspari to cut a little jig. One of our last images of Naeem's mother features her gratefully hugging Guaspari at the Carnegie Hall benefit performance.

Let us examine this set of scenes more closely. In multiple ways the movie positions viewers to sympathize with Guaspari and to dismiss a Black mother's concerns as the misguided ranting of an illogical zealot who foolishly permits her political agenda to get in the way of her son's best interests. Dismissively wondering what fault anyone could find with the "innocent" children's song "Twinkle, Twinkle, Little Star," Guaspari never acknowledges that Naeem's mother has legitimate concerns. "Twinkle, Twinkle" was composed by a White male, Wolfgang Amadeus Mozart, and is one small part of a heavily politically invested corpus of racialized official knowledge. Guaspari only rarely departs from this corpus; she invites a country fiddler to perform at the Carnegie Hall benefit, but country music, like classical, has long been a bastion of Whiteness. The closest her music curriculum comes to acknowledging the rich cultural heritages of the non-White children at Central Park East is the inclusion, toward the end of the movie, of a lone rendition of "We Shall Overcome."

The possible cultural irrelevance of many current string programs is a serious issue meriting thoughtful consideration, but the dismissive portrayal of the parent who raised these issues suggests that her concerns were groundless and stemmed from Black supremacist narrow-mindedness. Despite Guaspari's argument to the contrary, the question of who has composed the music constituting the school curriculum is one of tremendous political importance, and yet viewers are positioned to be unsympathetic to points of view other than Guaspari's.

Similarly, the mother's questioning of Guaspari's motives for teaching in East Harlem is summarily dismissed, Guaspari, thus, apparently exonerated from any implication that she might have self-aggrandizing salvific intentions, or even that her motives might be complex. Simply needing a job is presented as preferable to envisioning oneself as a White savior; the position that neither rationale—saving children or needing a job—is particularly meritorious is never introduced, however.

Guaspari's lecture to Naeem's mother about keeping a child's best interests in mind is a racialized symbolic lesson on who best knows what constitutes good parenting. The lecture portrays Guaspari, not the mother, as the expert on the best interests of the child. Although it is always dangerous for teachers to presume that they are in a better position than a parent to know a child's best interest, this scene has racialized symbolic meaning because it resonates with discourses that construct Black parents as bad parents. A White teacher lectures a Black parent on what constitutes good parenting and the White teacher's vision wins; the Black parent concedes and reforms. Not only does she reform, but in the end she hugs the White teacher. The appreciative Black and Latino/Latina parents at the Carnegie Hall benefit applaud not only their children but also official school knowledge long linked to Whiteness. The movie sings praise to the transformative power of the high-art canon.

Troublesome Staff

Actions and attitudes of Guaspari's Black principal and of her Black teaching colleagues are presented as other problems Guaspari faces. There is, for example, the tempestuous relationship between Guaspari and the school's principal, Janet Williams (Angela Bassett), who is Black. Beautiful, impeccably dressed but consistently angry, Williams appears to have ice water in her veins, at least when it comes to Guaspari. Apparently unsupportive, she initially refuses to hire Guaspari, arguing that the violinist is unqualified and inexperienced. In response, Guaspari brings her own sons to play for Williams, after which the principal relents; for most of the film, however, Williams' interactions with Guaspari are not cordial. When some of the teachers express resentment about Guaspari pulling children out of their class to take violin lessons, Guaspari turns to Williams for support. Although promising to help, Williams snaps "but I cannot hold your hand" and appears to give no aid. At a meeting where Guaspari is told the violin program is being cut, Williams again seems cold and unsupportive. Williams' statement that she is sorry and her claim that she has been trying to save the program for days do not seem to ring true, and Guaspari slams the door in Williams' face. Confirmation of tense relations is provided when, to Guaspari's astonishment, Williams shows up at a meeting to rally grassroots support for the program. Guaspari greets Williams by remarking, " I didn't expect you to be here at all."

Guaspari's mother, seeing Williams carrying refreshments to the meeting, mutters suspiciously, "Beware of Greeks bearing you know what."

The grassroots meeting, however, marks a turning point in the film's portrayal both of the principal and of her relationship with Guaspari. As was the case with Naeem's mother, Williams receives a new and positive characterization once she begins showing support for the violin program, and in the end, it is Williams who gives a tribute to Guaspari at the Carnegie Hall benefit.

Guaspari's Black teaching colleagues are similarly represented as resentful and unsupportive. In one scene Guaspari invites several of them to join her for lunch only to have the Black teachers ignore her. Guaspari overhears one teacher say to another, "That's the sub I was talking about." Seconds later Isabel Vasquez (Gloria Estefan), one of Guaspari's Latina colleagues, sits down next to Guaspari, and inquires: "What's the matter, you got cooties or something?" Later Guaspari asks, "Is it my imagination or does everybody here hate me?" Vasquez explains that it is the marginality of specialty programs, not hatred, that prompts the other teachers to ignore her. Guaspari persists: "What about Alice?" Vasquez responds, "Cooper. She thinks the violin is a waste of time, meaning she's a bitch." The two women laugh; Guaspari has found a sympathetic friend.

Taken collectively, the portrayals of Guaspari's colleagues, specifically her Black colleagues, resonate with the perception that African Americans are a major problem in American public schools, especially if the African Americans are staff who do not subscribe to a White teacher's agenda. In addition, the tense relationship between Guaspari and Williams supports a racist stereotype: Black women will not support White women. The fact that Guaspari did lack both experience and credentials, the reality that pulling children out of class to attend a music lesson does creates extra burdens for already-strapped classroom teachers, and the observation that the violin program seemed elite both in terms of the number of students and of the subject matter taught, were ignored. In all circumstances, viewers were positioned to side with Guaspari.

The lunchtime snubbing scene, in addition to suggesting that Black teachers are unsupportive of Whites, has another layer of racial dynamics, which comes into play with the appearance of a Latina colleague to befriend Guaspari. By highlighting the amity between Guaspari and Vasquez, the film implies that Blacks, and not minorities in general, are the "problem." In addition, via this scene Guaspari is exonerated from suspicion of participating in racist or ethnocentric practices. After all, one of her best friends is a Latina. We do not find out what the African American teachers were saying about Guaspari, so we have no evidence from which to judge whether their concerns were justified; viewers are left with the impression, however, that the Black teachers were engaging in caustic but groundless sniping. Guaspari, viewers are positioned to believe, is yet another misunderstood victim of "reverse racism."

Troublesome Students

Finally, there is the film's portrayal of students, specifically of student behavior, as being among the problems Guaspari faces. Because urban children often are non-White children, there is a racialized component to portrayals of urban children as wild and uncontrollable troublemakers in need of a strong dose of discipline. Such a characterization is prominent, especially early in this film; the free-for-all that ensues when Guaspari first hands out violins, the scene in which an African American boy appears to have stolen money from his mother, and a reference to a knife-toting second grader are a few of the examples. When, at Guaspari's interview, the staff music teacher, a caricature of White racism, argues that the children at Central Park East lack the discipline needed to learn the violin, Guaspari promises that the string program will teach such discipline. Given the transformation in student behavior chronicled in the film, it appears Guaspari succeeds. What we are inclined to "learn" from these portrayals is that "urban" (read non-White) children's behavior and attitudes are among the central problems facing educators; ostensibly the solution is discipline.

Let us consider how the movie's representation of "what worked" pedagogically for Guaspari may help construct and reinforce raced and classed stereotypes about how a teacher can most effectively work with urban children. To the film's credit, Guaspari is pictured as someone who cares deeply about students and who gets excellent musical results. In addition, however, she is frequently angry, rude, and verbally abusive; at times she motivates her students by telling them that they sound terrible, stink, and will make their parents throw up at the concert. When a White presumably middle-class parent complains about Guaspari's harshness, arguing in favor of a more supportive atmosphere, Guaspari temporarily and begrudgingly changes her style. This change, however, elicits complaints from students, who say they liked the old Roberta better, and so she reverts to her old tactics. On the one hand, the student complaints may be read as support of geniuneness in teachers. On the other hand, however, the outcry from students, including the child of the complaining parent, deflates the legitimacy of the parent's concern, reducing it to middle-class progressive naivete. Supportive atmosphere is out; discipline is in. Treadworn ideas about what constitutes good "urban" teaching and about the best way to motivate "these kids" are reinforced. Discipline and toughness are effective and, judging by the children's response, are what "these kids" really want. Apparently caring teachers are so desperately needed by "these kids" that the children are willing to tolerate whatever else comes with the package.

Although Roberta's harsh behavior does not seem racially selective—she is equally rude to all her students—multiple issues of race and class enter into this portrayal of effective urban teaching. For example, the complaint from the middle-class parent raised for me the question of whether Guaspari's style, clearly portrayed as good (or good enough) for urban children and presumably better than what is delivered by her counterpart, Rausch, would be similarly celebrated or even tolerated by middle-class parents and children. A racialized, classed discourse of "tough love" for urban children fails to introduce the possibility that all children can meet high expectations in an environment of unwavering support, kindness, and respect.

Exonerated Whites

Having examined the film's characterization of non-White neighborhoods, parents, and staff, let us consider its portrayal of Whites. White characters, by and large, are pictured in a favorable light, one that assigns little or no culpability to them or to Whites, in general, for current problems in schools. Two exceptions to this exoneration are the "bad" White teacher, Mr. Rausch, and Guaspari's mother. The insertion of hyperbolic "older-generation" Whites, however, provides a contrasting backdrop against which a heroic Guaspari is sketched. Guaspari rejects Rausch's deficit model, claims that all children can be successful, and strikes out angrily against her mother, who opposes Guaspari's decision to reside in East Harlem and who disparagingly remarks that everyone in the market is speaking Spanish. Unsullied, Guaspari becomes the antithesis of racism, overcoming nearly insurmountable obstacles and bringing fame and success to children by assuming that race does not matter. By contrast to a few glaringly racist lone dogs, Guaspari is among the presumably blameless enlightened White majority. White viewers are likely to count themselves among this "blameless" band and to identify with the heroine. Therein lies a problem, however. The good White/bad White dichotomy eliminates consideration of the possibility that Guaspari, who clearly benefits from her privileged racial position, might also, through that benefitting, participate in racism, or that some of her beliefs and practices may manifest dysconscious racism. The dichotomy glosses over seemingly insignificant "details," such as the possibility, for example, that Guaspari's inclination to jettison children from the program at the slightest provocation may share roots with Rausch's elitist philosophy.

Erasure of Structural or Institutional Problems

A third indication of the film's participation in what Kailin calls savage liberal racism is the almost complete absence of reference to structural or institutional problems or to the role that structural and institutional factors, such as racism, may play in the creation of the problems Guaspari faces. The very organization of the narrative, which places the focus on an individual teacher, tends to draw attention away from larger contextual issues, as well as from substantive discussion about education and power. In a trailer preceding the film, Meryl Streep capsulizes a perspective underscored by *Music of the Heart*: "One person really can make a difference." The postmodern admonition to examine power in local and specific contexts is not a call for a retreat into the particularistic heroic individualism to which Streep's statement alludes. If, as philosopher Michel Foucault suggested, there is supportive and productive interdependence between major dominations and local mobilizations,[73] then thoughtful commentary on education and power should attend to local mobilizations *and* to the effects of these mobilizations, i.e., major dominations.

Erasure of Critical Funding Issues

Inadequate funding was one of the few school problems the film raised that seemed to have institutional or cultural causes. The shortfall was depicted as an unfortunate reality that one teacher successfully addressed and that needs to continue to be addressed if music education and children are to be saved. In its selective focus, however, the film fails to ask why schools are facing funding crises, especially during a period of relative affluence in the U.S. Who is responsible for nonsupport of public education such that all children cannot be guaranteed access to high-status knowledge? Are all children, schools, programs, and districts in equal fiscal jeopardy, and if not, why not? A probe into these larger questions, however, is likely to implicate an array of factors and players that too often remain hidden, not only in this film, but in dominant discourse about education and educational reform. Corporate abdication of tax responsibility, a subject I will discuss later, is among the critical funding factors the film does not address.

Inequitable distribution of what money is available constitutes another ignored factor. *Music of the Heart* overlooks the critical reality that racial bias is evident in current school funding inequities. Consider, for example, the results of a recent study of school funding in one U.S. urban area, Milwaukee and its surrounding suburbs. Bob Peterson, Kathy Swope, and Barbara Miner, in an executive preface to the study, state, "Race is at the core of education issues in urban areas....it is also an essential element in the widely unequal funding between schools in Milwaukee and in surrounding suburbs."[74] The report points out that as the African American population of Milwaukee has increased during the past eighteen years (from 46 percent "African American" in 1980 to 80 percent "students of color" in 1998), so has the disparity between Milwaukee and surrounding suburbs in per-student spending.[75] In 1980 the per-student spending in Milwaukee proper was 95.4 percent of the average of its surrounding suburbs, but by 1998 that amount had dropped to 81 percent.[76] The report further states that in order to meet the suburban per-student average, Milwaukee would need to significantly increase local property taxes: "Using the local property tax, Milwaukee would have to increase its school tax levy by more than 75 percent to match the suburban school funding average—in essence trading tax injustice for school funding injustice."[77] The authors of the study, Michael Barndt and Joel McNally, conclude:

> The state not only tolerates an enormous gulf between the resources provided Milwaukee's urban students of color compared to their wealthier and whiter suburban counterparts; state funding policies also allow that gap to widen every year. As a result, separate and unequal school systems based on race—outlawed in this country half a century ago—are being re-established within the Milwaukee area with the state's approval and active participation.[78]

Similarly, in a recent court decision much closer to the setting for *Music of the Heart,* New York State Justice Leland DeGrasse ruled that New York State's school funding practices are both racially discriminatory and in violation of the state constitution.[79] These practices, DeGrasse notes, have an especially deleterious effect on the children in New York City schools:

> "New York State has over the course of many years consistently violated the Education Article of the State Constitution by failing to provide the opportunity for a sound basic education to New York City public school students. In addition, the State's public school financing system has also had an unjustified disparate impact on minority students in violation of federal law."[80]

Music of the Heart tells viewers that there is a funding crisis in public education but it fails to point out that it is, in part, a crisis of equity integrally related to race and class.[81] Although the film appears to be a rallying cry for adequate school funding, its erasure of the role that racism plays in inequitable distribution of available funds is further evidence that by ignoring institutional or cultural factors, it participates in what Kailin calls savage liberal racism. Silence on the subject of the role that racism plays in current educational problems turns the public eye away from some of the gravest issues facing education. Reform initiatives, if they are to be effective, must acknowledge and address racism as a significant contributing factor. To sound the alarm that music education is in jeopardy without specifying whose music stands to be lost or for whom access to music education has become an issue is to miss an opportunity to talk substantively about educational reform.

Inadequate, Inequitable Solutions

Selective Salvation

Let us examine how Guaspari solved her budgetary woes, a solution celebrated by the film. Thanks to connections with the wife of violinist Arnold Steinhardt, Guaspari organizes a successful grand-scale "bake sale," a benefit performance at Carnegie Hall featuring a host of world-famous luminaries including Steinhardt, Itzhak Perlman, and Isaac Stern. Later, she starts her own private foundation, which generates funds to augment whatever money is provided by the district. Through individual initiative, the film suggests, heroic renegade teachers can save their jeopardized programs from the chopping block. Guaspari's is, however, a very selective salvation. While clearly consistent with other currently popular privatization tropes and with some liberal humanistic notions of agency, this highly individualistic solution is grossly insufficient and profoundly inequitable. The "bake sale" provides amelioration and relief only to those privileged few who have connections with the elite. Only access to privilege allows for access to music education. One program and a handful of children may benefit, but individualistic privatization initiatives tend to leave larger funding issues and structures untouched, even though they may make heros of the initiators.

Private initiative, much of it irreplicable, is subtly underscored throughout the film, however. First, Guaspari owns fifty violins, which she makes available to students in her school. Few teachers, especially those working in impoverished areas, are affluent enough to own and donate fifty violins. Playing a string instrument is a costly endeavor; access to instruments is an equity issue and a serious ongoing problem for string teachers who work with children in poverty. It is similarly unlikely that teachers, especially those working in impoverished schools, would have access to elite human resources such as Isaac Stern and Itzhak Perlman. Thus, Guaspari's program succeeded due in large part to some highly unusual and unlikely circumstances; the film, by celebrating the success of individual initiative, masks the spottiness of privatization and its inadequacy as a sweeping solution.

In a heartbreaking scene in *Music of the Heart,* a lottery decides which in a sea of hopeful little faces will or will not be admitted into the violin program. This scene served for me as a vivid metaphor of selective salvation, its inequity and its inadequacy. Because the violin program could afford to work with only a fraction of the number of children who wanted to study, a lottery was instituted. A great many hopeful little children were turned away. A surface appearance of fairness, brought about by an "indiscriminate" lottery, did not camouflage for me the tragic discrimination that led to the lottery in the first place. Central Park East resorted to such measures, in part, because of racialized funding. Although public schools in general may be under budgetary siege to some degree, this siege is not equitably distributed. Socio-economic status, integrally related to race and ethnicity, plays a major role in academic access. Affluent parents and schools can provide for children even in difficult economic times; poor schools and poor parents cannot. Under such circumstances, music education becomes a privilege, not a right, to be enjoyed by the children of those who can afford to provide it, within or outside of school. A failure to interrogate the relationship between school-funding impoverishment and the racial constitution of schools may lead to assumptions and solutions that tend to blame victims, and in the process, fail to provide substantive relief. In short, privatized initiatives such as Guaspari's bake sale are inadequate solutions for they are as selective in their salvation as Central Park East's violin lottery.

The Politics of "Fiddling with Facts"

Insight that may call into question the motives of *Music of the Heart's* creators is found in a critique penned by Deborah Meier, the real principal of Central Park East at the time Roberta Tzavaras (given the name Roberta "Guaspari" in the film) established the school's violin program. The film, Meier claims, is "fiddling with facts";[82] specifically, its portrayals of the neighborhood, the school, the students, and the staff, while perpetuating stereotypes about inner-city schools, were untruthful and damaging, especially because the film ostensibly told a true story and used the actual name of the school.[83] "There were no drive-by shootings of our students, or children caught on school grounds carrying concealed box cutters," Meier states.[84] She adds that rather than being a repository of the mundane and mediocre, the school was and remains successful, due largely to the collective efforts of a highly supportive staff. Meier notes that she was awarded a MacArthur Fellowship for her successful work, which she received during the time depicted in the film. She mentioned the unfairness and untruthfulness of the film's representation of the school's staff, the staff music teacher, in particular, whom she calls an "important factor in the school's eminence."[85] According to Meier, "*Music of the Heart* alters the historical meaning of the events it portrays and reinforces some destructive myths about public schools in America."[86] She also states that Roberta Tzavaras wrote an apology to Meier in which she "expressed regret over the 'controversy' aroused by *Music of the Heart* within the Central Park East community and tried to explain that she was not responsible for its untruths."[87] There is a tiny disclaimer at the end of the film, Meier observes, which states that "'some main characters have been composited or invented and a number of incidents fictionalized,'" but the disclaimer is easily overlooked.[88] I never saw it, even though I viewed the film several times and specifically looked for the disclaimer; based on advertising, introduction, and presentation, I, too, assumed the film was substantially true. Meier argues, "Real people were thus harmed in order to tell a story...confirming prejudices about public schools."[89] According to Meier, the Miramax documentary *Small Wonders,* which served as the basis for *Music of the Heart* and was nominated for an Academy Award, was far more accurate in its telling.[90] The transformation of *Small Wonders* into *Music of the Heart* apparently promised to heighten box office success by inserting sensationalism but did so at a price, not only to the school, staff, and neighborhood of the real Central Park East, but also to all are touched by such stereotypes.

In a statement at the end of the film we learn that Guaspari's private foundation is "dependent on the generosity of its donors." Although ostensibly a film about saving music in all schools, it is also, thus, an advertisement for particular private initiatives. Schools, like private foundations, are similarly dependent on their donors, however. Small philanthropic efforts, such as Proctor and Gamble's and Disney's participation in this movie, may suggest that corporations should be counted among public schooling's dependable supporters; as we shall see in the next section, though, this perception may not be accurate, at least not if sharing fairly in tax burdens constitutes public school support.

Disney: Partner in the Education/Business Partnerships

The content of Disney movies has been the subject of criticism in the past, critics ranging from the Southern Baptist church to Henry Giroux.[91] I have added my views about *Opus* and *Music of the Heart,* however, because I question MENC's participation in the promotion of these films. In this section I look more closely at Disney, the business partner in these education/business partnerships. I begin with an overview of general concerns about such partnerships.

An Overview of Concerns About Education/Business Partnerships

The coalition formed between Hollywood Pictures and the various organizations, including MENC, is a type of education/business partnership even though no money was exchanged. According to Jay Taylor, school-business partnerships have become increasingly popular; they quadrupled between 1982 and 1992 as financially strapped districts found themselves "dredging for dollars."[92] Taylor explains that "school officials find themselves scouring barren cupboards for sustenance, and some are turning to alternative sources of revenue when they don't have the stomach, the legal standing, or the headroom to raise property taxes."[93] Advocates of education/business partnerships argue that businesses should not be viewed as villainous; they point to partnerships as evidence that business takes a deep and benevolent interest in schools, families, and children.

Outside of music education, many educationists have questioned the wisdom of entering into such partnerships, however. Critics contend that on the one hand, corporations engage in much publicized acts of gift giving or school partnership, which cost the corporations relatively little (or in the case of *Opus,* result in considerable financial profit for the corporation), while on the other hand, they chisel away at the financial infrastructure of schools with unrelenting demands for special corporate tax cuts, breaks, and incentives. This practice is especially detrimental to the arts because, relegated to the feminized status of "frill," they are among the first subjects to suffer. Apple, writing about recent draconian cuts in education budgets, observes,

> Part of the situation has been caused by the intensely competitive economic conditions faced by business and industry. Their own perceived imperative to cut costs and reduce budgets (often no matter what the social consequences) has led many companies to exert considerable pressure on states and local communities to give them sizable tax breaks, thereby "cutting off money needed to finance public education."...
>
> State, city, and county governments "assemble packages that include the elimination or reduction of sales or property taxes or both, exemptions on new equipment, tax breaks for training new employees and reductions on taxes for school improvements." In some states, the rewards go further. In Florida, for example, companies even get tax breaks for fuel consumption....
>
> The issues surrounding such breaks and outright exemptions are made even more powerful when compared to the withering criticism that the business community has levelled [sic] at the schools. This is coupled with the fact that business and industry have engaged in highly publicized programs of gift-giving to specific schools and programs. Such gifts may increase the legitimacy of the business community in the eyes of some members of the public. Yet, it is clear that the amount of money involved in these public displays is considerably less than the taxes that would have been paid.[94]

Quoting Alex Molnar, Taylor points out that if the quality of public schooling has declined, business should recognize the role it has played in this demise:

> School-business partnerships can be serious, of course, Molnar says, but in too many cases, they can also be abusive. "Here you have the image of honest, public-spirited business people putting their shoulders to the wheel, rolling up their sleeves, and pitching in to save American society from the wounds that have

been inflicted on it by the disastrous failures of the political and education systems," he says. But beware: "Business people have dominated local school board policy-making from the turn of this century on and indeed during the 19th century."

Moreover says Molnar, local boards should view business involvement warily because the corporate America that offers partnerships is the same corporate America that put schools in a hard place by demanding tax concessions and abatements in the 1980s: "To the extent that public schools have been successes or failures, business people have been there creating those successes and failures."[95]

Tax breaks are but one example of what critics term "corporate welfare." John Hood, in *Policy Review,* provides a list of incentives states use to attract and keep corporations. In addition to tax abatements and tax credits, Hood mentions land giveaways, releases from infrastructure costs, the issuance of tax-exempt development bonds, offers to promote products, and job training packages. These deals are unfair to existing businesses, Hood argues, especially small ones that can never hope to receive such treatment, and he concludes that there is no clear-cut evidence these forms of corporate welfare benefit state economies.[96]

Disney's Corporate Citizenship Record

The Elusive Overall Picture

According to Robert Morrison, representing the National Association of Music Merchants, the *Opus* partnership was an unqualified success that stemmed the erosion of music education.[97] Thus, the dominant message from within and outside of music education is that this was a win-win alliance: arts in the schools were saved, Disney made money, and the public got the message that corporate America cares. Aware of the concerns raised by Taylor, Molnar, Apple, and others, however, I decided to find out more about Disney's business practices, focusing specifically on the extent to which Disney was the recipient of corporate welfare that might gut school coffers.

My initial goal was to find out whether Disney paid an equitable share of taxes. The easiest parts of this task were to establish what Disney owns and to determine what its gross revenues were in the years surrounding the release of *Opus.* According to its "Consolidated Statement of Income," the corporation's 1995 gross revenues topped $12.1 billion.[98] Carl Hiaasen, in his book *Team Rodent: How Disney Devours the World,* reports that Disney's revenues for 1997 exceeded $20 billion, up from $18.7 billion in 1996.[99] He also spells out Disney's holdings and sources of revenue:

> Walt Disney Pictures, Touchstone, Caravan, Miramax, and Hollywood Pictures; from ABC, ESPN, the Disney Channel, Arts and Entertainment, the History

Channel, and Lifetime; from Siskel and Ebert, Regis and Kathie Lee, and Monday Night Football; from nine TV stations, eleven AM radio stations, and ten FM radio stations; from home videos, stage plays, music publishing, book publishing, and seven daily newspapers; from the theme parks in Orlando, Anaheim, Tokyo, and Paris; from computer software, toys, and merchandise, from baseball and hockey franchises, from hotels, real-estate holdings, retail stores, shopping centers, housing developments, and soon even a cruise line.[100]

Since the 1998 publication of Hiaasen's book, the cruise line, Disney Magic, has materialized, now offering cruises to the Bahamas and Castaway Cay, Disney's private island. In November 1999, an agreement was reached to build a theme park in Hong Kong at an estimated cost of $3.55 billion.[101]

The next step, however, trying to ascertain whether Disney, overall, is a good tax citizen, proved to be a frustrating exercise. Disney's sheer size was the first obstacle, one that watchdog groups may increasingly face as the number of multinational conglomerates increases and corporate power is consolidated into fewer hands. Operating in many arenas, in locations around the globe, and selling diverse products meant that Disney paid a variety of taxes. This fact, combined with state variations in how public schools are funded, made my broad question seem unanswerable. How much tax a corporation pays in any given year is a matter of public record; according to its "Consolidated Statement of Income," Disney paid $736.6 million in taxes in 1995.[102] The meaning of this statistic is more elusive, however. For example, 10K statistics for one or even five years do not necessarily serve as accurate indicators, partly because corporate losses can be distributed over multiple years; during the early 1990's, Disney's European operations (i.e., Euro Disney) incurred considerable losses. Furthermore, conventional wisdom suggests that legal tax breaks may not be factored in when assessing the citizenship record of a corporation.

Trying another approach, I set out to determine what kinds of corporate social ratings Disney was receiving from research divisions affiliated with socially responsible mutual funds. If these funds were not investing in Disney, I wanted to know why. I consulted with three companies—Citizens Funds; Neuberger and Berman; and Kinder, Lydenberg, Domini. Although only one of the three companies invested in Disney, the data I gathered did little to clarify matters, largely because tax citizenship and the receipt of corporate welfare were not criteria considered by any of these firms. Neuberger and Berman's reasons for not investing were unrelated to social responsibility; Disney is considered a high-price stock and Neuberger and Berman funds focus on value stocks.[103] Kinder, Lydenberg, Domini (KLD), which is the research arm for the Domini funds, said that Domini does invest in Disney, and it provided a detailed description of Disney's social ratings. Although

KLD expressed concerns about domestic and international labor relations, overseas operations, the high salaries paid to Disney's CEOs, the effectiveness of Disney's board of directors, and Disney's treatment of animals at its theme parks, these concerns were outweighed by Disney's perceived strengths in commitment to community, diversity, the environment, and quality of product.[104] As some of its evidence of Disney's commitment to community, KLD mentioned the corporation's sponsoring of the American Teacher Awards; its planned community, Celebration, in the Reedy Creek Improvement District; and its involvement in the renovation of the New Amsterdam Theatre in New York City.[105] I mention these accolades because I will discuss tax implications of the latter two projects momentarily. The Citizens Funds did not invest in Disney, primarily because of allegations of Disney's involvement in sweatshop operations abroad and because of concerns about "environmental problems with animals on their park sites."[106] One source affiliated with socially responsible mutual funds, speaking off the record about corporate business practices, opined that there are no angels in the corporate world, adding that individual investors are faced with the difficult task of deciding which of a multiplicity of corporate offenses are least egregious to them.

Even though I was not getting clear answers, I quickly gained the sense that most sources I consulted, including watchdog groups such as Citizens for Tax Justice, view Disney warily; as a player of "legal hardball,"[107] Disney is perceived to be an extraordinarily aggressive driver of difficult bargains, exerting its considerable muscle to get exactly what it wants. Faced with this perception, I tried another approach. Instead of seeking a meta-analysis, I gathered information about Disney's corporate practices in specific instances and contexts. Using this method, I found ample evidence that Disney frequently receives the kinds of corporate welfare that deplete tax coffers. As evidence I will provide twelve examples, all of which involve public dollars.[108] I begin with a discussion of a project entailing what critics have called "overly lavish" financial concessions from governmental bodies: Disney's recent renovation of the New Amsterdam Theatre in New York City.[109]

Twelve Examples of Corporate Welfare

The Renovation of New York City's New Amsterdam Theatre. For generations Times Square's 42nd Street had been a hub of theatrical activity in New York City. By the early 1980's, however, when the area was slated for urban renewal, the street's reputation had changed.[110] The theaters had closed, the historic New Amsterdam among them, and 42nd Street teemed with sex shops, drug dealers, prostitution, and crime.[111] An ambitious renewal plan involving the construction of massive office buildings, in addition to the renovation of the theaters, never materialized, even though governments offered potential investors lucrative tax incentives.[112] In the early 1990's the district remained in disarray, its future looking grim;[113] Rebecca Robertson, president of the 42nd Street Development Project, a governmental agency created to coordinate revitalization efforts in the area, is quoted in the journal *Urban Renewal:* "'Politicians were distancing themselves from the project, which was seen as a complete debacle.'"[114]

Meanwhile, Disney's theatrical rendition of *Beauty and the Beast* had been a rousing success, and the corporation was making plans to create a theater division.[115] In 1994 as part of the plan, Disney expressed interest in the New Amsterdam; by that time, the state of New York owned the still-closed theater, which had been purchased by the 42nd Street Development Project, Inc., a state agency.[116] In the 1994 renovation agreement reached between Disney and the 42nd St. Development Project, subsidies played a role both in the leasing terms Disney received and in the financing of Disney's proposed renovations. Let us consider first the terms of the forty-nine-year lease, which could, at Disney's discretion, be extended to 100 years. As a renter, Disney pays no property taxes;[117] furthermore, because public property is tax exempt[118] and the state owns the theater, New York receives no property tax revenues from a prime piece of Manhattan real estate. The terms of the lease are particularly favorable to Disney. For the first five years, it pays $331,401 per annum in rent and is assured of no rent increases.[119] From the fifth anniversary to the fifteenth, Disney pays 103 percent per annum of the previous year's rent, a rate that increases to 104 percent in years sixteen through forty nine.[120] After the forty-ninth year, Disney may, at its discretion, exercise up to five automatic ten-year extensions; during this time, Disney would pay whichever is greater, 104 percent of the previous year's rent or eighty-five percent of fair market rental value.[121] University of Wisconsin-Madison emeritus professor of law Arlen Christenson, who confirmed my interpretations of the legal documents associated with the New Amsterdam renovation, remarked that the ten-year extensions were an especially good deal for Disney and noted that the rent increases written into the lease would not keep pace with inflation. Christenson concluded that Disney was in the driver's seat for a 100-year lease.

In addition to rent, the state would receive a small percentage of the theater's gross revenues, 2 percent of revenues equal to or less than $20 million and 3 percent of profits in excess of that amount.[122] Furthermore, because the theater is located in a Business Improvement District (BID), Disney is responsible for BID impositions (i.e., taxes or assessments), but the conditions of the lease cap those assessments at $20,000 per annum for the first five years, no more than 103 percent of the previous year's assessment for years six through fifteen, and no more than 104 percent for subsequent years.[123] Businesses located within a BID receive direct benefits from BID impositions because all revenues are funneled back into improvements for their circumscribed geographical area rather than being distributed as needed across a municipality; according to Christenson, however, this distribution arrangement has made BIDs, which have been used in other municipalities, controversial.

Government subsidies were also evident in the financing package Disney was given to facilitate the theater's renovation. According to 1995 legal documents, the corporation was to receive a $31.4 million thirty-year loan from the city and state at an interest rate of 3 percent on the first $21 million and 3.5 percent on the remainder.[124] More recent sources state that the project eventually cost $36 million, Disney receiving $28 million in loans and paying out an additional $8 million, the latter of which is being returned to the corporation in the form of state historic preservation tax credits.[125] According to Robin Stout, an attorney involved in renovation of 42nd St., Disney was the only corporation to receive such a loan.[126]

Other conditions of the agreement were similarly favorable to Disney. For example, the renovations were exempt from all city and state sales and use taxes;[127] Disney required the city to condemn and "remove sex shops from the rest of the block at a condemnation cost of $48 million";[128] and the landlord (i.e., the state) agreed to reimburse Disney for "streetscape improvements."[129] When early in the negotiations it appeared that Disney was not getting the favorable conditions it wanted, the corporation reportedly threatened to pull out.[130]

Disney opened the renovated New Amsterdam Theatre, which is flanked by a mammoth new Disney megastore, in 1997.[131] According to the Minneapolis *Star Tribune,* the renovated Times Squares district is now considered "the most sought-after 13 acres of commercial property in the world."[132]

Supporters of the agreement with Disney argue that the concessions were the only way to lure the corporation and to get the renovation of Times Square back on track. By using Disney as a "loss leader,"[133] they contend, government did not need similarly lavish packages for the corporate investors that followed Disney.[134] Prognosticators in 1998 promised that a rejuvenated Times Square will generate $328 million in tax revenues each year and they pointed to a drop in crime as a sign that the project is reaping benefits for taxpayers.[135]

Critics counter that businesses should undertake such ventures without the benefit of corporate welfare. Others point out that the concessions made to Disney did not mark the end of using tax incentives to bring development to Times Square. The list of more recent recipients of lavish Times Square tax packages includes Reuters American Holdings; Conde Nast Publications; MTV's parent company, Viacom; the Marriot Marquis Hotel; Bertelsmann AG; and Morgan Stanley.[136] One vocal critic, State Senator Franz Leichter, reportedly observed, "'The next neon sign to go up should flash dollar signs with the amount of tax breaks going to corporations that fill Times Square.'"[137]

California Adventure: The Expansion of Disneyland. Disney's protracted negotiations with the city of Anaheim over an expansion of Disneyland, the corporation's original theme park, are another study in the kinds of concessions the company often receives. Throughout the early 1990's Disney wrangled with governmental bodies over the financial details of a proposed $3 billion expansion that was to have been called "Westcot."[138] Government officials made promises and proposals involving, among other things, nearly $400 million in federal funding to finance improvements in the freeway leading to Disneyland[139] and massive tax breaks to California companies planning expansions.[140] Disney promised that no general tax revenues would be used for the expansion.[141] It also exhibited one of its signature behaviors when in 1991 it threatened to drop the plan in response to an Anaheim proposal to impose an admissions tax to help defray costs.[142] In 1995, after determining that Westcot might not be sufficiently profitable, Disney abandoned the project and one year later, introduced a scaled-down alternative, California Adventure, which will be located on a Disneyland parking lot.[143] The projected cost of the revised plan, which also includes a hotel and mall, was $1.4 billion. The revised expansion comes with its own set of tax subsidies. In 1997 Anaheim sold more than $500 million in bonds to "expand its convention center, build a giant parking garage and improve public facilities near Disneyland."[144] According to Marla Jo Fisher of the *Orange County Register,* through this act Anaheim gave Disney "$200 million in tax subsidies, including $90 million to build a parking garage and $20 million to move high-voltage power lines" located on Disney property.[145] Ronald Campbell, also of the *Register,* spelled out the city's liabilities: "Annual payments on the bonds will cost the city an estimated $23.5 million in 2002, rising to $69.5 million by 2037."[146]

Anaheim is speculating that increased tourism will make this venture profitable, and Disney is promising to help shoulder part of the bill if shortfalls occur.[147] Campbell also reported that the city is devoting "all of its hotel tax in the Disneyland area and 3 percent of the hotel tax citywide" to the venture.[148] Diverting hotel tax revenues to the Disneyland area syphons money away from less affluent parts of the city, critics have argued and, thus, widens the gap between Disneyland and Anaheim's deteriorating neighborhoods.[149] In addition to the city's subsidies, Disney will also benefit from a $1.1 billion expansion of the interstate leading to Disneyland.[150] California Adventure was scheduled to open in 2001.[151]

Tax Dollars for a Baseball Stadium. Another Disney initiative involving public monies was the 1998 renovation of the Anaheim sports stadium, home of the Disney-owned Anaheim Angels baseball team. After walking out of negotiations in 1996,[152] Disney later agreed to pay $70 million to renovate the aging stadium.[153] Conditions of the agreement included a $30 million contribution from Anaheim, $10 million of which Disney returned to the city; the remainder would be recouped through parking fees the city would collect from lots surrounding the stadium.[154] Although Anaheim agreed to receive no revenues from the sale of concessions, it was scheduled to collect a $2.00-per-head fee for every stadium admission exceeding 2.6 million, a number Disney did not expect to reach for at least ten years.[155] The *Los Angeles Times* published sports-law expert Martin Greenberg's assessment of the agreement: "'I think the taxpayers got a damn good deal.'"[156] Other sources were not as enthusiastic. In 1996 the city still reportedly owed $23 million on a 1979 renovation of the stadium.[157] Whether the new deal was a good one will depend on whether Anaheim can recoup the additional $20 million through parking fees; the question was still unanswered when Disney put the baseball franchise up for sale in 1999.[158] Rick Henderson, in a review of *Major League Losers,* Mark Rosentraub's scathing critique of sports franchises, argues that public support of these franchises "may be the most extravagant corporate welfare system in the United States today."[159] Henderson suggests that until franchise owners "who try to soak taxpayers become known as the enemies of their fans, rather than the saviors of their cities, they'll continue to get their bailouts."[160]

Timber, Cows, and the Osceola County Property Tax Appraiser. In the next example, Disney, through a two-year battle involving multiple lawsuits, attempted to retain an agricultural exemption on thousands of acres of land it owns in Osceola County, Florida.[161] The exemption permitted Disney's land to be taxed at a much-reduced rate, saving the corporation about $1 million in property taxes each year.[162]

For example, in 1988, with the agricultural exemption in effect, Disney paid $395,000 in property taxes on a parcel of land valued at $26.9 million.[163] The corporation claimed it was entitled to this exemption because it leased land "to a cattle rancher and [held] contracts with a timber company to cut down pine trees."[164] Robert Day, Osceola County's appraiser in 1989 when the battle began, argued, however, that the operations were not legitimate and no longer qualified Disney for the agricultural designation.[165] *The Orlando Sentinel Tribune* reported that Day could not find sufficient evidence that the land was being used in the manner Disney claimed.[166] Day revoked the designation, remarking, "'The taxpayers of this county have been subsidizing Disney and a lot of speculators for too long.'"[167] Representatives from the county further argued that Disney tourists constitute a drain on the county's services, roads, police, and sewers.[168] Elimination of the exemption increased the value of the property to $84 million and Disney's taxes to more than $1.4 million.[169] Disney filed suit. Tempers flared and accusations flew when the Osceola County Commissioners' early support of Day appeared to be crumbling; in the midst of the fray, newspapers reported that one of the commissioners had received campaign contributions from Disney and two of them had received contributions from the law firm representing Disney in the suits.[170] This was not the first time Disney had locked horns with an Osceola Tax Appraiser over the land's agricultural classification. The classification was challenged in 1973 by Wade Lanier, who was the Osceola Tax Appraiser at the time; a court case ensued, which Disney won.[171] The more recent battle, albeit protracted, ended somewhat differently. Amid allegations and suits, Disney agreed in May 1991 to pay $1.2 million in property taxes ($600,000 for 1989 and $600,000 for 1990) and to drop the four suits it had filed in the two previous years.[172] The compromise was reached after Disney argued that much of its Osceola property is "unbuildable swampland"; some of the land in question reportedly would later be developed into Disney's planned community, Celebration.[173]

Reedy Creek's Exemption from Development Impact Fees. Disney's exemption from development impact fees is the next example of corporate welfare. Like the agricultural classification case, this one involves the Reedy Creek Improvement District, which is where Disney's Florida land holdings are located, including Disneyworld and the planned community, Celebration. *Business Week* explains how the district came into being and how it operates:

> The Reedy Creek Improvement District, a special jurisdiction created in 1967 by the Florida legislature, accommodates Walt Disney Co.'s 28,000 acres near Orlando. Cynically called Florida's 68th county, Reedy Creek is a developer's dream. It levies taxes, sets building codes, and maintains roads. It has its own fire fighters and paramedics. It even has the authority, so far unused, to build an airport or a nuclear power plant. And Disney, whose title to 98% of the land gives it 98% of the vote in elections for board of supervisors and bond issues, can finance improvements with low-cost, tax-free Reedy Creek bonds.[174]

In this instance, Disney's receipt of corporate welfare comes in the form of exemption from impact fees, the fees developers of new ventures are almost invariably required to pay to local governments to help defray the cost of new roads and increased public services. County officials and other developers resent this special privilege, the former because they are required to foot the bill for these services, and the latter because these other developers incur costs that Disney does not. Resentment escalated in the mid-1980's when Disney began "$1 billion worth of projects, including a movie studio tour, a water park, and an evening entertainment complex called Pleasure Island."[175]

Reedy Creek's Sewage Treatment Plant. Invoking its status as a governmental arm and elbowing out all other municipalities in a six-county area, Reedy Creek garnered in 1990 "the right to issue $57.7 million in tax-free bonds,"[176] and it used those bonds to improve Disney's sewage treatment plant.[177] In doing this it took for itself "all the bonds...available for a six-county area," and as a consequence of this move, other projects, including a program that would have helped low-income families buy housing, lost out.[178] According to an editorial in the *Orlando Sentinel Tribune*, "All this happened because Reedy Creek has virtually the same powers as a local government, thanks to the Legislature's generosity."[179] In 1991, in response to complaints from Orange County officials, Reedy Creek withdrew from the bond competition.[180]

Federal Tax Credits for Affordable Housing. Again using its status as a governmental body, Reedy Creek, in 1992, purchased $13 million in "federal affordable housing tax credits that will help build 464 apartments in Winter and Kissimmee."[181] This move was a partial response to Florida's rejection of a "growth-management plan"[182] Reedy Creek had filed, the state arguing that Disney's plan "failed to adequately address affordable housing needs it has created";[183] apparently, the state felt Reedy Creek was not providing sufficient affordable housing for Disney's employees.[184] Local critics argued that although it appeared to be an altruistic act, Disney's move failed "to build homes for the neediest people while making money for an already wealthy company."[185] Another naysayer, Robert Chapman, observed, "'It's sort of like saying 'We want to help feed the hungry by buying stock in McDonald's.'"[186] Lawrence Lebowitz of the *Orlando Sentinel Times* described the purchase as a shrewd business move and enumerated Disney's financial gains: " [Disney] gets a favorable tax write-off over the next 10 years. At the end of 30 years, when the credits expire, the company also will own two valuable pieces of real estate."[187]

"America": Abandoned Plans for a Theme Park. Disney's abandoned proposal for "America," a history theme park in Prince William County, Virginia, vividly exemplifies some of the concessions the corporation garners from gov-

ernmental bodies. In 1993 Disney announced it was planning to build a
theme park near Haymarket, a town with a population of about 600, located approximately 40 miles west of Washington, D.C.[188] The initial proposal
was for a 185-acre park on 3,000 acres of land.[189] The offer looked attractive
to Prince William County, which faced shortfalls; among the touted benefits
were 3,000 new jobs, stimulation of local business, and tax revenues estimated at $1.5 billion over 30 years, which supposedly would more than pay for
the new roads and utilities needed by the park.[190] The initiative was supported by both an outgoing and an incoming governor, one a Democrat and the
other a Republican.[191] According to an article published December 11, 1993,
in the *Washington Times,* Disney promised that it would "not seek general tax
support to build a $750 million theme park," adding that "'we will pay our
own way.'"[192] The article said that "the company would seek some kind of
bond mechanism as a 'self-contained financing package' to pay for its park"
and explained that Disney's anticipated tax payments over a period of 30 years
"would pay off the bonds that would finance a highway interchange and road
and sewer improvements."[193] Less than two weeks after the publication of the
promise, the *Richmond Times-Dispatch* published an extensive list of requests
Disney announced it would be making of the state and county, all of which
involved public funding; because the list is so revealing, I quote it in its
entirety:

[from the state]
Widening of I-66 from two to three lanes in each direction between the planned
state Route 234 bypass and park site, a distance of about four miles.

Widening of state Route 15 for several hundred yards between I-66 and an
entrance to the park.

A highway ramp from I-66 into the park site.

An internal road system leading visitors to parking lots.

Signs on all major routes leading to the park, including Interstates 95 and 495
and the Dulles Toll Road.

Prominent mention in state tourism marketing campaigns and construction of
a state visitors' center on park property. The center would replace one along
I-66 that is slated for demolition.

Economic development money to train workers and relocate some equipment
from Walt Disney world in Orlando, Fla., including the well-known robotic
Hall of Presidents.

A study of extending the Virginia Railway express commuter train line to the
park site and other mass transportation options....

[from the county]
Extension of utilities to the park site, including water, sewer and gas lines.

Possible waivers or reductions in fees related to park construction, including for site plans and building permits. Disney already has received a $400,000 break in zoning application fees.

A review of the local tax code to determine whether Disney's assets deserve special consideration by assessors.[194]

The same article stated that these requests could cost the state $100 million, most of which would go to improving the highways, and it further explained Disney's bond request.[195] The corporation was asking for a "tax-increment financing scheme to pay for the [road] improvements. Under the so-called TIF plan, the state would issue bonds, to be retired with tax revenue generated by the park, to cover transportation upgrades."[196] In other words, Disney's much-touted tax revenues would be used to pay for the roads required of the theme park. Nowhere in this plan did I see discussion of the costs of educating the children of Disney's employees, nor was there mention of the increased strain the park would place on other public services.

Virginia's Governor George Allen responded with a package that promised "$141.9 million in road improvements and about $20 million in other incentives."[197] When the state Senate Finance Committee, considering the package, proposed a "dollar-a-head" admissions tax, Gov. Allen warned that Disney might walk out.[198] When Disney finally agreed to pay the $49 million in road debts created by the park should tax revenues fall short, the corporation reportedly said its move was "unprecedented" for them and cautioned the state that Disney would make no more concessions.[199] Early on, Steve Twomey, reporting for the *Washington Post*, apprised the state that Disney likes to spend public money to make private profit; he claimed that the corporation was a bully "not above threatening to walk away if they don't get what they want." [200]

In the end pressured lawmakers, conceding to Governor Allen and to Disney, approved a slightly modified package that gave Disney essentially everything for which the corporation asked.[201] Peter Baker and John F. Harris, reporting for the *Washington Post*, describe the lawmakers' dilemma:

> "We've been put in an impossible situation," said Del. Thomas M. Jackson Jr. (D-Hillsville), who had wanted to delay a final vote until spring. "The governor basically promised them the farm, and we've only got three days to fix it. We don't have any leverage. It's very frustrating. I hate being in a fight when I can't hit."
>
> Several lawmakers said Allen was applying pressure to Democrats by holding hostage the appointments of as many as 10 judges for new judicial posts. If Allen waited until after the General Assembly left town, he and circuit judges would make the appointments, not legislators.[202]

From early on, critics listed an array of reasons for opposing the theme park; some resented a Disney-fied "replica" of history served up on the land that is home to multiple Civil War sites, including Manassas National Battlefield; others were dismayed by the potential environmental and aesthetic impact of the park.[203] The bulk of concerns, however, focused on Disney's possible overestimation of the fiscal benefit the park would bring, coupled with a possible underestimation of the potential costs. Pointing to Euro Disney's shaky performance, critics argued that there were no guarantees the park would generate increased tax revenues for the state.[204] Lawmakers were also concerned that one of the amendments in the compromise package would require the state to pay any road improvement shortfalls not covered by Disney's $49 million guarantee.[205] A powerful force opposing the park was the "Disney-Take A Second Look" campaign, which was organized by the Piedmont Environmental Council (PEC), an organization reportedly receiving substantial financial support from wealthy estate owners in nearby counties.[206] A study funded by PEC reportedly stated that Disney's fiscal surplus projections were inflated; the surplus, PEC estimated, would be $2.43 million per year, considerably less than the $15.6 million calculated by the corporation.[207] According to the *Washington Times*, the study concluded that Disney's presence would not provide the property tax relief promised by Prince William County officials.[208] Richard Squires, in a *Washington Post* article entitled "Disney's Trojan Mouse," offered his views on possible financial outcomes for the state should it embark on the Prince William project:

> Disney's proposal is part of the national and global trend toward corporate colonization, and Disney is a master of this new phenomenon. In a style reminiscent of the British East India company centuries ago, Disney sends emissaries on secret missions into foreign territory to search for the right mix of natural resources—in this case, an international airport, an interstate highway, pliable local leadership, cheap land and proximity to tourist traffic—to establish a commercial colony whose profits will be sent far, far away from the local community in which they were made.[209]

Another fiscal concern expressed by the park's critics was a possible underestimation of the infrastructure costs to be shouldered by state and county governments. Squires describes those infrastructure needs: "schools, roads, water, sewage, utilities, police, jails, solid waste and fire protection."[210] The PEC study, according to the *Washington Times*, claimed that Disney underestimated "the cost of providing services to its development by $3.7 million annually."[211] This statistic did not include costs to accommodate an expected migration of new employees to the area, a figure estimated at $5.6 million per year, nor did it reflect Disney's alleged $5.4 million per annum undercounting of the costs to educate the influx of children accompanying this new work force.[212] Squires, of the *Washington Post,* concludes that "Virginians face an investment of some $2.5 billion over 30 years, of which Disney's taxes would pay less than half."[213] He points out that the new-coming citizens would pay some of the forthcoming tax bills but observes that because Disney tends to offer low-paying jobs, the newcomers would likely be low-income young people with children needing schooling .[214]

Despite Disney's receipt of a plethora of incentives and concessions from the state and local governments involved, the corporation announced in September 1994 that it was abandoning the "America" theme park project. Although publicly claiming that opposition to the park prompted the move, Disney reportedly privately was concerned that the operating season would be shorter than it had anticipated, and that the opening of the park would be delayed by lawsuits.[215]

I have included the failed "America" plan because the tactics Disney used there continue to be employed elsewhere. For example, according to the *Los Angeles Times,* Disney reportedly "broke off talks [about a theme park] with the government of Queensland, Australia, after the state refused to provide $850 million in subsidies, tax breaks and other inducements. Queensland Premier Peter Beattie told the media that 'only Goofy' would have agreed to the Disney deal."[216] Hong Kong, however, has agreed to pay $1.74 billion (or nearly half of the bill) to develop the future theme park there, and like critics of Disney's plans for other spots on the globe, naysayers in Hong Kong worry that the benefits Disney claims the city will derive from the park "may not justify Hong Kong's big investment. 'We appreciate that Mickey Mouse is coming to Hong Kong....But the question is, is Hong Kong paying too much?' asked Sin Chung-kai, a lawmaker who speaks on economic matters for the opposition Democratic Party. 'I think Disney is getting a very good deal.'"[217] Clearly, it will not be the first time.

Disney's Newspaper Sales: A Morris Trust Transaction. Using a legal tax dodge called a Morris Trust transaction, in 1997 Disney reportedly saved $600 million in taxes when it sold four newspaper holdings for $1.6 billion.[218] Disney had acquired the newspapers when it purchased Capital Cities/ABC in 1996.[219] Allan Sloan, *Newsweek*'s Wall Street editor, describes how a Morris Trust transaction works: "In this long-established tax dodge, a company creates a new subsidiary to hold the businesses it wants to keep, leaving behind only the ones it wants to sell. Then the for-sale stuff is acquired in a tax-free stock-for-stock trade."[220] He also lucidly explains the Disney deal:

1. Disney has lots of great businesses, including newspapers it got last year [1996]. It wants to sell the newspapers at a fancy price without having to pay taxes.

2. Disney starts the process by borrowing about $1 billion. This isn't taxable. The borrowing gives Disney $1 billion in cash and leaves it with a $1 billion I.O.U.

3. Disney puts everything but the newspapers and the I.O.U. into a new subsidiary, Newco. Disney holders own both Newco and Disney. None of this is taxable, either.

4. The buyer swaps its shares for Disney, giving them directly to Disney stockholders tax free, and takes over the debt. Disney changes Newco's name to Disney. Bingo: Disney shareholders have $600 million in Buyer's stock; Disney has $1 billion in cash; Buyer has the newspapers and owes $1 billion. Taxes due: zero.[221]

Disney's union protested the transaction by taking out advertisements in the *New York Times* that called Disney the "Loophole King."[222] Sloan described several other mammoth Morris Trust deals and explained that the Treasury Department was advocating for legislation to end these transactions.[223]

Disney's Use of Step-Down Preferred Stock. Allan Sloan also reported that in 1997, in addition to the Morris Trust transaction, Disney used a loophole known as step-down preferred stock, which enabled it to dodge $160 million in taxes; according to Sloan, the Treasury Department considered step-downs to be a form of tax evasion, not tax avoidance.[224] Jacqueline Doherty, reporting for *Barron's,* also confirmed that the U.S. Treasury believed step-down preferred shares were "abusive and in violation of current [1997] tax laws."[225] She illustrates the step-down process:

A company like, say, Disney, could take out a $500 million mortgage on a piece of its property at a normal market rate, maybe 8%. Disney would then create a real-estate investment trust [REIT], which would buy the mortgage. The REIT funds the purchase of the mortgage by selling $250 million of common stock to the company and $250 million of preferred stock to investors. The preferred stock pays a 13% annual dividend for the first 10 years and 1% thereafter.

As a result, the company gets a tax deduction on its interest payments as well as its principal payments to the REIT. The REIT pays no taxes because it distributes all of its income to the preferred or common stockholders in the form of dividends. The issuer's annual financing cost on money raised through such deals is a mere 1% after taxes. What's more, the investors who own the step-down preferred are typically pension funds, which don't pay taxes on dividend income. In all, these folks get perhaps $100 million a year extra by buying the step-downs.[226]

The *Houston Chronicle* reported in January 2000 that the Internal Revenue Service had taken the final steps on a journey, begun in 1997, to close the step-down loophole.[227] The IRS' decision to act in 1997 was made in response to the issuance of these securities by "companies such as Federal Home Loan Mortgage Corp., Time Warner and Walt Disney"; the *Chronicle* stated that more than $10 billion in securities were sold before the loophole was closed.[228] It also claimed that by using step downs, corporations pay no taxes on most of the funds for at least 10 years.[229]

Free Fireworks Research. The next example of corporate welfare is Disney's receipt in 1996 of $733,000 in the form of free use of tax-supported federal research laboratories. Disney asked the federal researchers to develop semiconductors that would ignite fireworks. According to the *Earth Island Journal,* Disney received this funding through a CRADA (Cooperative Research and Development Agreement): "One recipient of...federal largesse was Buena Vista Pictures, a subsidiary of the Walt Disney, Co., which prevailed on Sandia Labs' scientists to create a semiconductor for igniting fireworks displays."[230] The journal reports that in 1996 alone the federal government gave private industry $5.8 billion in the form of CRADAs; these industries have the right to withhold their findings "'from the public for up to five years.'"[231]

Free Airspace for Digital Television. Finally, for a period of at least nine years Disney will receive free television broadcast channels. This gift was one result of the 1996 Telecommunications Act, a project that "Senate Commerce Committee Chairman John McCain calls 'one of the great scams in American history.'"[232] The gift to Disney was part of a larger giveaway, estimated to be worth between $12 and $70 billion,[233] of channel space to be used for digital television. Lawrence K. Grossman of the *Columbia Journalism Review* called the initiative "a blatant case of corporate welfare," and added:

> Instead of making broadcasters bid for the new spectrum as the cellular phone and other communications industries have been doing (last year, the FCC raised some $20 billion auctioning off lower quality spectrum to nonbroadcasters), Congress and the White House caved in to the all-powerful broadcaster lobby, and simply gave the digital spectrum away, a windfall to needy multimedia Goliaths like GE, Westinghouse, Disney, and Rupert Murdoch's News Corporation, which spend millions on political contributions.[234]

The *New Republic* reported that broadcasters spent "$10.7 million on lobbying in the first six months of 1996 alone,"[235] a sign of broadcasters' recognition of their potential benefit from the Telecommunications Act. In addition to constituting corporate welfare, Congress' gift may have other far-reaching implications. The frequencies involved are likely to "launch the next revolution in home entertainment: digital television that promises theater-quality movies, CD-quality sound, Internet access, interactive games, paging services and a bag of goodies no one's dreamed up yet."[236]

Disney's Corporate Schizophrenia

Thus, in these instances at least, Disney appears to have exhibited what Alex Molnar, in his book *Giving Kids the Business,* refers to as "corporate schizophrenia."[237] In a speech given to the Senate in January 1992, Senator Howard Metzenbaum described the contradictory, or two-minded, elements of corporate policies and practices concerning public schools:

"In speech after speech, it is our corporate CEOs who state that an educated literate work force is the key to American competitiveness. They pontificate on the importance of education. *They point out their magnanimous corporate contributions to education in one breath, and then they pull the tax base out from under local schools in the next* [my emphasis]." [238]

One of the ironies about the movies that prompted my analysis is that they publicly decry the loss of arts programs in the schools and yet were created by a corporation with a reputation for aggressively seeking and getting corporate welfare, a practice that inevitably affects school coffers. Another irony is that in the case of *Opus* the National Coalition for Music Education, of which MENC is a member, approached Disney's subsidiary about creating a partnership to promote this film and not vice versa.[239] These movies were promoted through a partnership between Disney subsidiaries and an already-existing education/business partnership, the National Coalition for Music Education. Thus, we are talking about wheels within wheels. MENC had already entered into an education/business partnership before Disney's Hollywood Pictures and Miramax Films came on the scene.

Disney: Living in a Realm Without Angels

Let us consider Disney within the context of corporate practice at large. Although Disney may be somewhat more aggressive than some of its corporate counterparts, its evasive tax-dollar practices appear to be quite representative. An editorial by Jeff Leverich, a research coordinator for the Wisconsin Education Association Council, gives some sense of the magnitude of tax exemptions for businesses in my own state, Wisconsin:

In 1970, the residential sector paid 50.6 percent of all property taxes in Wisconsin. Today [1997] they pay 64 percent. In 1970, the manufacturing sector paid 17.7 percent of all property taxes. Today they pay 5.2 percent. Including some breaks for farmers, the Legislative Fiscal Bureau states that [in Wisconsin alone] business exemptions account for $30 billion, or about 15 percent of all taxable revenues in 1996.[240]

The shift in tax burden described by Leverich is due to a number of factors. An informational paper published by the State of Wisconsin's Fiscal Bureau offers several explanations, reporting that in the twenty-year period under discussion and due to changes in state law, some types of corporate property, including machinery, equipment, and computers, became exempt from taxes; it further states that growth, development, and property valuation have been more vigorous in the residential sector than in manufacturing.[241]

It is important to keep in mind that tax breaks, including those mentioned by Leverich, often result from expensive lobbying by powerful groups. For example, Wisconsin Manufacturers and Commerce (WMC), described as the state's "largest business group," reportedly spent more than $500,000 lobbying the state legislature in 1998, which resulted in tax exemptions projected to be valued at $76 million in 1999 and $80 million in the year 2000.[242] Among the biggest winners in a similar deal cut in 1996 were paper companies, including Consolidated Papers, Kimberly-Clark, and Fort Howard, in addition to the Miller Brewing Company, Cray Research, the General Motors Corporation, and Procter and Gamble.[243] In one of its publications, the *Wisconsin Manufacturers and Commerce 2001 Legislative Update*, the WMC proudly reports its most recent legislative "accomplishments," stating that in 1999 it defeated an "$80 million corporate income tax hike," that in 1998 it saved "Wisconsin businesses more than $60 million per year by successfully leading the fight to eliminate personal property taxes on computers and related equipment," and that in 1996 it defeated "proposed tax increases aimed at paying two-thirds of school costs."[244] Furthermore, the group cheerfully takes credit for instituting the school revenue caps that many teachers and school administrators claim are breaking the back of Wisconsin's public schools.[245] Former U.S. Congressman Scott Klug reportedly called WMC "the Godzilla of Wisconsin lobbying," a designation that the organization readily claims.[246]

Although federal tax dollars may not flow directly into school coffers, Robert S. McIntyre and T.D. Coo Nguyen's study of corporate federal income tax-paying practices, which appeared after I had completed my analysis, sheds considerable light on Disney's tax citizenship and the citizenship of 249 other major U. S. corporations.[247] Published by the Institute on Taxation and Economic Policy, the study reports the effective corporate federal income tax rates paid by 250 major U.S. corporations for the three-year period from 1996 through 1998. McIntyre and Nguyen state that the time period studied was tremendously profitable for corporations; these gains were not reflected in federal corporate tax revenues, however:

According to the U.S. Commerce Department, pretax corporate profits rose by a total of 23.5 percent over the three years. But federal corporate income tax revenues did not come close to keeping pace with growing profits—rising by only 7.7 percent from fiscal 1996 to fiscal 1999.[248]

McIntyre and Nguyen's findings paint a grim picture, overall, of corporate tax citizenship:

> Although some of the 250 corporations in our study paid federal income taxes at or near the statutory 35 percent corporate tax rate, the vast majority paid considerably less. Effective tax rates over the 1996–98 period ranged from a low of -9.9% for Goodyear to a high of 35.7 percent for Winn-Dixie and Paccar. Overall, for the 250 companies we analyzed, federal corporate income taxes over the three years averaged only 21.7 percent of U.S. pretax profits. The average effective tax rate on the 250 companies declined over the three years, from 22.9 percent in 1996 to only 20.1 percent in 1998—far below the 35 percent statutory corporate tax rate.[249]

For the period studied, the 250 companies received $98 billion in tax reductions,[250] and the size of the tax breaks rose steadily: $26.9 billion in 1996, $31.8 billion in 1997, and $39.3 billion in 1998.[251] The study reports that forty-one of the companies actually received refunds, in addition to having paid no taxes, for at least one year; profits for these forty-one totaled $25.8 billion.[252] Eleven companies had a negative tax rate for the three-year period.[253] Only eight companies paid a rate equal to or exceeding the federal statutory rate of 35 percent.[254]

Dollar-wise, almost one-half of the breaks were given to twenty-five companies, Disney among them, each of which received more than $1 billion in tax breaks.[255] Disney ranked twenty-third among the top twenty-five recipients; on profits of more than $8 billion, it received tax breaks totaling nearly $1.2 billion and cut its taxes by 42 percent.[256] Disney's federal rate of 20.5 percent was the same as that paid by Automatic Data Processing, GTE and Merck.[257] One hundred forty-six companies paid a higher rate and one hundred paid a lower one.[258] Disney's rates for each of the three years studied were 11.8 percent, 30.0 percent, and 18.9 percent, respectively.[259] Thus, although weighing in far below the statutory rate of 35 percent, Disney was about average among the corporations studied. It is important to keep in mind, however, that "average" in this instance is poor in terms of potential impact on tax coffers.

Providing a brief history of recent corporate tax legislation, McIntyre and Nguyen observe a recent upswing in tax breaks after a few years of somewhat successful attempts to close loopholes. According to them, a 1981 tax cut bill supported by President Reagan resulted in dramatic reductions in corporate tax payments; they state that from 1981–1983 "more than half of 250 corporations analyzed paid nothing or less in federal income taxes in at least one of the three years."[260] Public outcry resulted in the Tax Reform Act of 1986,[261] which ostensibly closed many loopholes, and by 1988 the "effective tax rate was back up to 26.5 percent."[262] McIntyre and Nguyen report that other loopholes were found in the 1990's, however, tax credits among them.[263] Critical of current corporate tax law, McIntyre and Nguyen conclude:

> Ordinary taxpayers have a right to be suspicious and even outraged about a tax code that seems so tilted toward politically well-connected companies. In a tax system that by necessity must rely heavily on the voluntary compliance of tens of millions of honest taxpayers, maintaining public trust is essential—and is endangered by the specter of widespread corporate tax avoidance.[264]

Issues for Educators

Who Is Responsible and What Are Our Alternatives?

If schools are experiencing fiscal difficulties that result in the cutting of arts programs, then many questions beg answers: Who is responsible for these difficulties? What can be done to help? Should fingers be pointed at MENC for arguably ineffectual acts, diverting precious time and resources to the promotion of problematic movies that may have done little to change the fiscal woes faced by school districts? Should they be directed at Disney and other corporate players, for engaging in business practices, legal or shady, that shift the tax burden onto private citizens and gut school coffers? At legislators for cutting deals with large corporations and being swayed by deep-pocketed lobbyists? At individuals for buying products or investing in mutual funds without knowing the corporate practices behind the product or fund? The picture is complex, as are possible solutions. There are individual and collective political actions that may be effective, however; MENC and its members might consider the following:

- Exerting pressure on legislatures to end the practice of making tax-coffer-depleting deals with big businesses.

- Working to reduce or eliminate the influence of lobbyists. Using legality as a measure of the acceptability of corporate business practice is unwise when laws are made under intense pressure from deep-pocketed lobbying groups funded by the same corporations those laws will govern.

- Advocating for campaign finance reform, so that questions about whether the loyalties of public officials were bought would not need to be raised. (Recall the case involving the Osceola County Commissioners.)

- Striving for legislation that requires all sectors to pay a fair share of taxes.

- Working to assure a more equitable distribution of the school funding that is available.

Leverich argues that "all taxed sectors must pay their fair share, and that all [state] spending needs to be examined in light of its long-term benefit to society."[265] If Disney and other similar corporations were paying their fair share, movies about the dire straits of arts programs in our schools might not be needed. When school coffers are relatively full, arts programs tend to do well. In less economically distressed times perhaps more of the music education community would agree with my assertion that the cost our national organization paid, in terms of the perpetuation of sexist and racist discourses, far exceeded whatever benefits the movies ostensibly provided.

The Deepening Involvement of Business in Music Education

A Long Tradition of Business Involvement in Music Education
Although education/business partnerships may be relatively new to the education scene at large, they have a long history in music education, a history not shared, for the most part, by even such close curricular relatives as the visual arts. For example, from the latter part of the nineteenth through the early twentieth century, music teachers were trained and certified at institutes sponsored by textbook publishers, who used these institutes as opportunities to emphasize the "special philosophies and methods of their own publications."[266] Music teacher Frances Clark's affiliation with the Victor Talking Machine Company (later known as RCA), launched not only the music appreciation movement in the schools, but also the sales of RCA recordings. Following World War I, when the invention of radio put many instrumentalists out of jobs and the market for musical instruments dwindled, manufacturers of these instruments turned their attention to the burgeoning school band movement; in addition to selling instruments to schools at reduced rates, these manufacturers sponsored national band contests and gave contest winners "generous money prizes."[267]

Financial drought has drawn music educators time and again to the corporate-funding well. I recently walked through the exhibit area at the state music teachers' convention, surveying the dazzling array of products being hawked. In addition to curricular materials, I saw (and, in some cases, tasted) an amazing variety of fundraising products, including cheesecakes, candy bars, pizzas, neck ties, candles, fruit, cheese, wind chimes, and tree ornaments. Music certainly is big business, I mused.

A New Era of Business Involvement

Business has long played a role in music education, but I perceive that within the past decade both the level and types of involvement have changed. Contemporary partnerships are arguably deeper and more complex than those of earlier times. Furthermore, the same corporations, names, and players repeatedly appear, often in partnership with MENC. For example, Disney has become a key player in an array of national teaching and outstanding student awards in music, including the "Disney Music Honors Academy"; designed for students, the academy is held at Disney World in Orlando and sports a "tuition package" of nearly $900, excluding airfare.[268] Several recent "World's Largest Concerts," gargantuan performances held in conjunction with MENC's "Music in Our Schools Month," have been located at Disney World; in addition, the guest conductor for the concert held in 2000 was Mike Davis, an employee of Walt Disney World Entertainment.[269] One of Disney's subdivisions, Disney Educational Productions, sells curricular materials, including the *World of Music Discovery*, which ostensibly help teachers integrate music across the curriculum. A letter accompanying the advertising brochure sent to music teachers closes with the following question: "Why not let the magic and music of Disney touch your classroom?"[270]

Partnerships with the Yamaha Corporation. Who, in addition to Disney, are among the familiar and key players? The Yamaha Corporation, the National Association of Recording Arts and Sciences (NARAS), and the National Association of Music Merchants/International Music Products Association (NAMM), to name a few. Most of these were players in the *Opus* and *Music of the Heart* partnerships. NARAS and NAMM have been participants in the National Standards for Arts Education Movement;[271] and they funded Frances Rauscher's recently disputed brain research (i.e., the so-called "Mozart effect" and the effects of keyboard training), which was also underwritten by the Yamaha Corporation, a manufacturer of keyboards.[272] In addition, the Yamaha Corporation's Project 2000 provided underwriting funds to music education research projects conducted at The Ohio State University, the University of Minnesota, and the University of Wisconsin-Madison. The interactive teleconference, "Technology in the Music Classroom," held in 1997, is another example of a collaboration between the Yamaha Corporation and MENC, one that may have had tremendous profit potential for Yamaha. The title suggested that technology in general was the topic of the teleconference. According to a MENC press release, however, a major component of the event was a demonstration of "Music in Education (MIE)," a computer-based music curriculum designed and marketed by Yamaha; the press release further states that the teleconference featured ways that teachers can use technology to implement the National Music Education Standards.[273] "Music in Education," in addition to being a prime example of a "teacher-proof" curriculum, costs $14,900, excluding shipping, handling, tax, *and* the price of the computer needed to run the sixteen musical keyboards included in the package.[274] While this was an event with tremendous profit potential for Yamaha, purchasers of MIE would necessarily come from a select, affluent audience, the price tag placing MIE out of the reach of many schools and districts.

In League with Texaco. Apparently Texaco, Inc. is another company that ranks high on MENC's list of favorite corporate partners. According to a recent Texaco press release, MENC bestowed the 2001 "Partnership of Professionals" award on the Texaco Foundation, in addition to giving similar honors to Walt Disney Entertainment and PepsiCo.[275] The press release states that educational reform through training of early childhood teachers is among the goals of the Texaco partnership:

> The award is in recognition of Texaco Foundation's grant program, "Early Notes: The Sound of Children Learning." The ongoing initiative focuses its support on the capacity of music education to advance educational reform, and seeks to infuse music learning into the early childhood curriculum and classroom. Among its recent efforts were a $50,000 grant to fund MENC's "Start the Music" Early Childhood Summit in June 2000 and a $80,000 grant to implement a national MENC teacher and child provider training program expanding access to best music education practices in early childhood learning.[276]

Statistics on Texaco's federal tax paying record suggest that the corporation is well equipped to fund such philanthropy; they also call into question the validity of the blanket claim, found in the press release, that Texaco is committed to the advancement of arts education.[277] According to McIntyre and Nguyen, Texaco's federal tax rate, -8.8 percent for the three-year period from 1996–98, was the second lowest of the 250 corporations studied.[278] Texaco received $1.5 billion in federal tax breaks and ranked thirteenth among the twenty-five corporations given the largest breaks.[279] These breaks cut the corporation's taxes on its $3.4 billion profits by 125 percent.[280] PepsiCo, another recipient of MENC's "Partnership of Professionals" award, paid a rate of 4.8 percent for the same three-year period, far below the federal corporate statutory tax rate of 35 percent.[281] It ranked fifteenth among the top twenty-five corporations receiving breaks and through breaks was able to cut taxes on its $4.8 billion profits by 86 percent.[282]

Fritos for Flutes. PepsiCo received MENC's accolades in recognition of the "Share the Joy with Music" program, another example of an education/business partnership promoted at the MENC website. In the "Share the Joy" program, school children and their families collect "Pepsi Notes" by purchasing Pepsi and Frito-Lay products that feature an eighth-note symbol on the package.[283] Schools that enroll in the program can redeem the notes for "free" musical instruments and supplies. The key, of course, is that children and their families must buy Pepsi products in order to collect the notes. Furthermore, the fine print states that PepsiCo will only honor redemption requests of 500 or more notes.[284] Small schools and schools in impoverished areas may operate at a disadvantage in such circumstances.

Let us consider what this offer costs students and parents, keeping in mind that PepsiCo may benefit both financially and in terms of its corporate image. Assume for a moment (and this is a big assumption in all such coupon redemption plans) that every symbol for every product purchased is turned in to the participating school. According to the PepsiCo website, a school would need to collect 5,000 Pepsi Notes to receive a "free" clarinet.[285] A four-ounce bag of Frito's corn chips sells in a local store for ninety-nine cents and features one note. In order for the school to receive the clarinet, students and their families would need to purchase 5,000 bags of Fritos at a cost of $4,950 (plus, in Wisconsin, $272.53 tax). Similarly, a twenty-four pack of Pepsi, which sells in a local store for $6.79 provides 10 notes. In that case, 500 twenty-four packs, at a total cost of $3395, would need to be purchased to secure the clarinet. Clearly, through this partnership, PepsiCo sells quite a bit of junk food at considerable cost to students and their families.[286]

"B Is for Banana," "D" Is for Dole. As we have already seen, some of MENC's collaborations with corporations involve the development of curricular materials. Another similar curricular collaboration is the "Dole 5 a Day for Better Health" campaign, which is a partnership between Dole Food Company and MENC.[287] "Dole 5 a Day" is a collection of curricular materials ostensibly designed to teach musical concepts through lesson plans that "meet the National Standards for Music Education"[288] while simultaneously promoting the consumption of a minimum of five servings of fruits and vegetables per day. Dole, which is among the world's major producers and growers of fruit—bananas and pineapples, in particular—has a vested interest in a curriculum promoting the consumption of fruits and vegetables, and that interest may be largely unrelated to safeguarding the health of America's school children. From MENC's website, music teachers can access a whole collection of "5 A Day" curricular materials, including CD-ROM "interactive edu-

cational modules," a live performance kit, a cookbook, "ten terrific songs that Dole has developed," and a series of teacher-proof lesson plans created by Marilyn Copeland Davidson, principal author of a recent MacMillan music textbook series.[289] The character of these lesson plans and MENC's particular commitment to national standards are alluded to in the following endorsement: "As with all MENC-developed lesson plans, you will find an outline clearly showing objectives, materials, standards, and procedures, along with challenges and interdisciplinary ideas."[290]

Given that Dole created the ten "terrific" songs, it is not surprising that one of them is about a major Dole product: bananas. "B Is for Banana," which bears a striking resemblance in tone and style to many T.V. commercials, is a cheerleading chant, embedded in and embodying a particular vision of what knowing music means, of why children should learn music, of what constitutes a worthwhile music experience, and of what counts as important knowledge; this upbeat song erases all evidence of the politics, strife, and inequities that have accompanied the transport of bananas "from Latin America to your home town":

[Verse 3]
I'm the perfect snack for your backpack (banana, go banana!)
Just peel the peel away (banana, eat 'em every day!)
Makes you feel good when you work or you play
I'm your
favorite make no mistake!

[Chorus]
B is for Banana
Costa Rica to Savannah
Ecuador to Montana
From Latin America to your home town
Sweet to your taste, a smile on your face
It's a great way to start your 5 A Day.
B is for Banana!
Oh, yeah![291]

Bose: In Harmony *with MENC.* More evidence of curricular development partnership activity between corporations and MENC is found in a MENC press release announcing a 1998 national conference in Phoenix, Arizona, the purpose of which appears to have been to introduce *In Harmony with Education.*[292] *In Harmony with Education* is a middle school curricular program designed "in collaboration with MENC"[293] by Bose Corporation, a major manufacturer of audio equipment. In the press release it is described as an "innovative interdisciplinary learning program" that includes "a multi-image show, 'Musically Speaking.'" Even though the Arizona event was called a MENC conference, the press release portrays the *In Harmony with Music* program as the centerpiece of a teacher-training initiative, no line being drawn between advertisement and MENC professional development:

> "Musically Speaking" is one of the most exciting events drawing educators to MENC's convention. A thirteen minute [sic] multi-image show, "Musically Speaking" aims to teach the scientific and mathematical basis of music through sound, color, imaging and emotional impact.... *The Bose In Harmony with Music* program, including "Musically Speaking" and the middle school curriculum of which it forms a part, have been presented to students in Dade County, Florida, and Central Valley, New York. This is the first opportunity that most teachers and press will have to review the materials.[294]

Revising History. To get a sense of how the recent turn toward partnerships and an educational agenda strongly supported by the corporate world may be shaping MENC's perceptions of itself, its history, and its goals, one need look only as far as the MENC website. The site includes general information about the ninety-four-year-old organization, including "Highlights of MENC's History."[295] The site lists seven events as being historically significant, only one of which, MENC's founding in 1907, occurred prior to 1990. Of the six remaining "highlights," three refer to the formation of education/business partnerships or to the national standards initiatives. This particular version of MENC's history, in addition to erasing all accomplishments of the organization's first eighty-three years, suggests that the only really significant things MENC has done, perhaps not coincidentally, pertain to an educational agenda in which the corporate world has invested heavily.

Setting an Educational Agenda. The same monochromatic corporate-supported educational agenda is evident in a brochure announcing MENC's new publications for spring, 2000.[296] Thirteen publications are featured; the descriptions of eleven of these thirteen refer to one or more of the following subjects: partnerships, brain research, national standards in the arts, and assessment. One of the two sources not fitting the pattern is a second edition of a classic history of music education and, thus, technically, not a new publication.[297]

The corporate world's sizable presence on MENC's National Advisory Council, which was formed in 1996 and which "provides direction to MENC," may be a sign that corporations will play an increasingly significant role in shaping MENC's future policies and platforms.[298] Four of the five members elected to the Council in 1998 are corporate executives, and they are employed by a familiar list of corporations: Michael Bennett, Vice President of the Band and Orchestra Division of the Yamaha Corporation; Larry Linkin, President and CEO of NAMM; Frances Preston, President and CEO of BMI; and Hilary Rosen, President and CEO of the Recording Industry Association of America (RIAA).[299]

Finally, a recent symposium, sponsored in part by MENC and titled Vision 2020, included papers presented by respected scholars in music education; among the respondents to the papers were business leaders, including Warrick Carter representing the Disney Corporation.[300] The long-term effects of business' deepening involvement in music education remain to be seen. Given the corporate practices I have described here, music educators may wish to ponder whether this deepening involvement is in the long-term best interest of the field. Corporations' bottom-line concern for fiscal gain may be at odds with fundamental educational goals.

Final Thoughts

Shortly after the release of *Opus,* I spoke with a state music education administrator, Michael George, who had helped coordinate the promotion of the movie's screening in Wisconsin. I told him that the film had grossed more than $80 million even prior to its release as a video. He responded rather acerbically, "Yes. And we didn't see one cent of it." Obviously, in the case of *Opus,* the "gift" that promotional materials claim teachers received never was intended to be a monetary one. Rather, the millions of dollars Disney profited from the movies analyzed here went straight into the corporation's coffers, that profit achieved, in no small part, thanks to the concerted efforts of concerned music educators who collaborated with the corporation. George's comment invited me to consider whether the "intangible" benefits *Opus* and *Music of the Heart* ostensibly offered to the music education community were worth the costs, as well as to ponder at what and whose expense those benefits came.

As business involvement in music education deepens, we need to wrestle with difficult questions. For example, what worldviews currently dominate within business communities? What practices and goals do they support? What visions of best educational practice might they tend to promote? What dissonances may exist between these worldviews and others that may help us to envision more equitable educational goals and practices?

This study has offered a critique of specific discourses that, if not interrupted, will continue to powerfully shape the public imaginary. It raises questions about who is and who should be shaping music education. Without a doubt, multiple discourses stemming from multiple sources do. I argue, however, that some of these discourses have far more shaping power than others. I recognize, for example, that as an academic who gets published I have rare and privileged access to specific venues. But I hold few illusions about the impact my writing may have on public imaginaries, and I concede that a popular film such as *Mr. Holland's Opus* or *Music of the Heart* may have far greater impact than any academic tome. This leads me to conclude that we academics should not underestimate the potential political power of entertainment. This power is rarely discussed in music education, however, unless the artifact in question openly challenges dominant discourses or public sensibilities.

The National Coalition for Music Education obviously believed that popular media can promote specific discourses and influence public policy, this belief presumably fueling the decision to help promote the films discussed here. Arguably, other political actions may be more effective, however. The music education community rallied around these films because it believed it would benefit from their success. As educators, however, we need to think deeply about whether the community did, and if so, at what, or whose, expense the perceived benefits were derived.

A Postscript: A Suppression of Information?

When I was considering submitting this manuscript to the National Association for Music Education (MENC) for publication, a supportive colleague, Harry Price, then-editor of MENC's own *Journal of Research in Music Education,* told me that he anticipated resistence from MENC, given the increasing influence of the music industry on the organization. Price, himself, has published quantitative research on business' deepening involvement with the national organization, one study appearing MENC's *Update.*[301] I sent the manuscript to MENC first because I believed that music educators, the audience I most wanted to reach, would most likely read MENC sources. In my cover letter I suggested that the manuscript become part of a much-needed monograph series on current issues in music education and even offered to edit the series. When the agreed-upon review time had elapsed and I had heard nothing, I telephoned Peggy Senko, the organization's Director of Publications. Senko informed me that MENC was not interested in publishing the work because it did not fit in with the organization's strategic publication plan.[302] When pressed for particulars about the plan, she replied that MENC will focus on publications that, among other things, advocate for partnerships, including education/business partnerships, and that assist in the implementation of national standards in music. She thus openly acknowledged that MENC's interests lay with advocating for several of the policies I critique in my manuscript. Expecting rejection but nevertheless stunned by the implications of what I was hearing, I asked Senko whether such a strategic plan might represent a suppression of information. I told her I was dismayed to learn that MENC was unwilling to provide a venue for substantive public discussion about the wisdom of its policies. I reiterated my assertion that business' deepening involvement in music education troubles me greatly and is an issue meriting thoughtful discussion in the music education community. Senko did not address my concerns. Realizing that I could no longer in good conscience remain a member of a professional organization I had first joined as an undergraduate in 1973 but that no longer seemed to reflect my interests, concerns, or views, I resigned from MENC in July 2000 in protest of its official policies.

If I had hoped that the resignation might create a few ripples, I was mistaken. A couple of months after I failed to renew my membership I received a form letter from MENC president, Mel Clayton. The letter claimed that MENC wanted me back and stated, "If you have a specific reason for not renewing your membership that you'd like to share with us, please feel free to call."[303] I took Clayton at his word and phoned the toll-free number. The telephone was answered by someone (not Clayton) who clearly had expected respondents to complain that the dues were too high and was unprepared to hear a spiel about the injustices perpetuated by official MENC policies. The voice on the line assured me that MENC cared about my concerns and told me that Mel Clayton, although out of the office for the week, would promptly call me upon his return. I am still waiting for the call.

In or out of MENC, I remain concerned about the issues I address in this study. MENC's long-held motto of "music for every child" seems fundamentally at odds with its advocacy of such highly problematic and potentially exclusionary policies as those supporting education/business partnerships and centralized generic standards in the arts. Those of us who remain committed to the value of an equitable music education for all children need to voice our concerns now, recalling Audre Lorde's words: "…When we speak we are afraid our words will not be heard nor welcomed but when we are silent we are still afraid. So it is better to speak…."[304]

NOTES

Note concerning endnotes: Online access to full-text articles sometimes creates page citation problems. In first and subsequent references I have chosen to follow the online's description of the pagination of the original source.

1. June Hinckley, "Music Matters: What Next?" *Music Educators Journal* 86, no. 5 (March 2000): 50.

2. The National Coalition for Music Education consists of the National Association for Music Education (MENC), the National Academy of Recording Arts and Sciences (NARAS), and the National Association of Music Merchants/ International Music Products Association (NAMM). Until 1998 MENC's official name was the Music Educators National Conference. In 1996 Richard Dreyfuss, star of *Mr. Holland's Opus*, was listed on the Coalition's letterhead as a member of the organization's Advisory Council. According to materials distributed at the screening, the Coalition was "founded in 1989 to turn back the erosion of music and arts in our nation's schools. One of the Coalition's crowning achievements was the successful inclusion of the arts as a core subject in the *National Educational Goals* adopted by Congress in 1994." Thus, advocating for national standards in arts education apparently has been another activity of the National Coalition.

3. Correspondence dated 9 January 1996, and co-signed by John J. Mahlmann, Executive Director of the Music Educators National Conference; Michael Greene, president and CEO of the National Academy of Recording Arts and Sciences; Larry R. Linkin, president and CEO of the National Association of Music Merchants; Robert B. Morrison, Executive Director of the American Music Conference, and James Berk, Executive Director of the National Academy of Recording Arts and Sciences Foundation. The letter was included in the promotional packet distributed at the screening.

4. Ibid.

5. "Hollywood Pictures and the National Coalition for Music Education Present: *Mr. Holland's Opus*," *Teaching Music* 3, no. 4 (February 1996): 47.

6. Julie Kailin, "How White Teachers Perceive the Problem of Racism in Their Schools: A Case Study in 'Liberal' Lakeview," *Teachers College Record* 100, no. 4 (Summer 1999): 728.

7. See, for example, Michael Apple, *Official Knowledge: Democratic Education in a Conservative Age* (New York: Routledge, 1993), 96; Alex Molnar, *Giving Kids the Business* (Boulder: Westview Press, 1996); and Jay Taylor, "Desperate for Dollars: In a Barren Budget Year, Schools Must Look Far and Wide for Alternative Funding Sources," *American School Board Journal* 179, no. 9 (September 1992): 20–25.

8. Ann DeVaney, "Reading Educational Computer Programs," in *Computers in Education: Social, Political, and Historical Perspectives*, ed. Robert Muffoletto and Nancy Knupfer (Cresskill, NJ: Hampton, 1993), 181.

9. Ibid.

10. Ibid., 183.

11. Ibid.

12. Ibid.

13. Chris Weedon, *Feminist Practice and Poststructuralist Theory* (Oxford: Basil Blackwell, 1987), 26.

14. Ibid., 32, 33.

15. Michel Foucault, *The History of Sexuality: An Introduction. Volume I*, trans. Robert Hurley (New York: Pantheon, 1978; New York: Vintage, 1990), 99–100.

16. Weedon, 33, 41.

17. The number of viewers was cited in several places, including "Hollywood Pictures," 47. According to sources quoted in an article by Stacy A. Teicher, "Arts Educators Get Mileage Out of *Mr. Holland's Opus*," *Christian Science Monitor,* 22 January 1996, Film Section, p. 13, the number actually exceeded 25,000. [Online]. Available: http://www.lexis-nexis.com/universe.

18. Viewers also received, among other things, a copy of an interview with Richard Dreyfuss about the film; a sheet of statistics showing a correlation between SAT scores and arts study; a "fact sheet" on Music/Arts Education suggesting that music study makes children smarter, along with quotations on the arts from notables such as President Bill Clinton, U.S. Secretary of Education Richard W. Riley, and futurist John Naisbitt; a reprint of a *USA Today* article suggesting that music instruction can improve math and science performance (via an increase in spatial IQ); a brochure describing the National Coalition; and a list of resources, available through the MENC, for implementing national standards in music education.

19. The $80 million statistic was provided by Ty Burr, "The Golden Guys; They Didn't Win Oscar Statuettes, But Sean Penn of *Dead Man Walking* and Richard Dreyfuss of *Mr. Holland's Opus* Proved Their Mettle with Shining Performances," *Entertainment Weekly* 28 June 1996–5 July 1996, Video Section, p. 113. [Online]. Available: http://www.lexis-nexis.com/universe. The Internet Movie Database (http://us.imdb.com) states that as of July 28, 1996, the movie had grossed $82.5 million in theater revenues.

20. "ASAE Presents 1996 Summit Award to National Coalition," *Teaching Music* 4, no. 2 (October 1996): 49.

21. Home rental revenues were reported by the Internet Movie Database (IMDB), at http://us.imdb.com. No date was given for this statistic.

22. For example, the movie reportedly was shown in South Africa. See Donald G. McNeil, Jr., "In South Africa, Bringing Theaters to the Townships," *New York Times,* 20 May 1996, sec. D, p. 11. [Online]. Available: http://www.lexis-nexis.com/universe.

23. The Golden Globe nomination is mentioned in James Ryan, "The Comeback Kid Tries Again," *New York Times,* 14 January 1996, sec. 2, p. 11. [Online]. Available: http://www.lexis-nexis.com/universe. Dreyfuss' nomination for an Oscar is listed in "The Oscars: A Scorecard," *New York Times,* 25 March 1996, section C, p. 11. [Online]. Available: http://www.lexis-nexis.com/universe.

24. Reported by the Internet Movie Database (IMDB), at http://us.imdb.com.

25. Richard Rothschild, "Music to Their Ears; *Mr. Holland's Opus* Rings True to Chicago-Area Band, Chorus Teachers," *Chicago Tribune,* 28 February 1996, Tempo Section, p. 1. [Online]. Available: http://www.lexis-nexis.com/universe.

26. Teicher, 13.

27. "'Opus' Foundation Aims to Give New, Used Instruments," *Teaching Music* 4, no. 5 (April 1997): 15.

28. The flyer was created by Learning Enrichment, Inc. P.O. Box 415, Pennington, NJ 08534-0415. It states that the kit is underwritten by the Proctor and Gamble Corporation, which will refund up to $5.00 to help defray movie rental costs.

29. "ASAE Presents 1996 Summit Award," 49.

30. Ibid.

31. See, for example, Michael Apple, *Teachers and Texts: A Political Economy of Class and Gender Relations in Education* (New York: Routledge, 1986).

32. Published statistics do not exist, so I relied upon Market Data Retrieval (telephone: 800-333-8802). Information provided 18 December 1996 by "Patty."

33. Ibid.

34. Charles Leonard, *The Status of Arts Education in American Public Schools* (Urbana, IL: Council for Research in Music Education, 1991), 116, 151, ERIC, ED 342708.

35. Joyce Hampel, "Women Administrators: Networking for Success," *NASSP Bulletin* 71 (October 1987): 44.

36. Sari Knopp Biklen, *School Work: Gender and the Cultural Construction of Teaching* (New York: Teachers College Press, 1995), 2, 3, and 5.

37. Biklen, 3.

38. Ibid., 2.

39. See, for example, the invitation to the premiere; all students have disappeared and only Holland's silhouette remains.

40. Biklen, 5.

41. Ibid.

42. Ibid., 3.

43. Ibid., 5.

44. Ibid., 27.

45. Ibid., 26-27.

46. Ibid., 22.

47. Ibid., 26-27.

48. Julia Eklund Koza, "Music and the Feminine Sphere: Images of Women as Musicians in *Godey's Lady's Book,* 1830-1877," *Musical Quarterly* 75, no. 2 (Summer 1991): 104.

49. Julia Eklund Koza, "Music Instruction in the Nineteenth Century: Views from *Godey's Lady's Book,* 1830-1877," *Journal of Research in Music Education* 38, no. 4, (Winter 1990): 254.

50. See statistics from J. Terry Gates, as quoted in Julia Eklund Koza, "The 'Missing Males,' and Other Gender Issues in Music Education: Evidence from the *Music Supervisors' Journal,* 1914-1924," *Journal of Research in Music Education* 41, no. 3 (Fall 1993): 212.

51. Biklen, 26.

52. Ibid., 25.

53. Ibid.

54. Ibid., 3.

55. Ibid., 25.

56. Ibid., 26.

57. Apple, *Teachers and Texts*, 45.

58. Biklen, 23.

59. Anne Godignon and Jean-Louis Thiriet, "The Rebirth of Voluntary Servitude," in *New French Thought: Political Philosophy*, ed. Mark Lilla (Princeton, NJ: Princeton University Press, 1994), 227.

60. Betty Friedan, *The Second Stage* (New York: Summit Books, 1981), 244.

61. Foucault, 94.

62. William Grimes, "'Mr. Holland' Succeeds, Almost Despite Itself," *New York Times* (21 February 1996), sec. C, p. 9.

63. I have borrowed the phrase "first emergency" from Polly Pagenhart. For an interesting discussion of this concept see Polly Pagenhart, "The Very House of Difference: Toward a More Queerly Defined Multiculturalism," in *Tilting the Tower*, ed. Linda Garber (New York: Routledge, 1994), 181.

64. Foucault, 102.

65. Two and one-half months after its release, the film, which had cost $27 million to produce, had grossed only $14.8 million. Profit information provided by the IMDBdatabase. Available: http://us.imdb.com/Business?0166943. 21 February 2001.

66. Nomination information gathered from the IMDB database. Available: http://us.imdb.com/Tawards?0166943. 21 February 2001.

67. According to a July 17, 1999, MENC press release available at www.menc.org/publication/press/archive.html (accessed on 9 March 2001), the National Assembly is composed of the organization's executive board and the "presidents, managers, and editors of the state affiliates of MENC."

68. The film's official website is www.musicoftheheart.com/musicoftheheart _sp_ gitxt.htm, which I accessed on 21 February 2001.

69. Kailin, 728.

70. Ibid., 731.

71. The East Harlem Information Outreach Project reports 1990 U.S. census data at www.eastharlem.org/ehstats.html. Accessed 15 March 2001.

72. The East Harlem Information Outreach Project reports 1990 U.S. census data at www.eastharlem.org/ehstats.html. Accessed 15 March 2001.

73. I am referring to Foucault's concept of "double conditioning." See pp. 99–100.

74. Bob Peterson, Kathy Swope, and Barbara Miner, "Executive Summary," in Michael Barndt and Joel McNally, *The Return to Separate and Unequal: Metropolitan Milwaukee School Funding Through a Racial Lens* (Milwaukee: Rethinking Schools, 2001). [Online.] Available: www.rethinkingschools.org/SpecPub/prrac/pracexec.pdf. 21 March 2001.

75. Michael Barndt and Joel McNally, *The Return to Separate and Unequal: Metropolitan Milwaukee School Funding Through a Racial Lens* (Milwaukee: Rethinking Schools, 2001), 4. [Online.] Available: www.rethinkingschools.org/SpecPub/prrac/ pracexec.pdf. 21 March 2001.

76. Ibid., 4–5.

77. Peterson, Swope, and Miner.

78. Barndt and McNally, 1.

79. Victoria Rivkin, "School Funding Scheme Struck; System Found to Violate Basic Education Rights; Reforms Left to Albany," *New York Law Journal,* 11 January 2001, p. 1. [Online.] Available: http://web.lexis-nexis.com/universe. 21 March 2001.

80. Quoted by Rivkin.

81. This point was eloquently made several years ago by Judith Pearson: "There is a crisis in education, but it's not nationwide and it's not found in test scores. It's found in the inner city and obscured by issues of race and class. It is undoubtedly the most difficult, pervasive, and perverse problem in education...." See *Myths of Educational Choice* (Westport, CT: Praeger, 1993), 13.

82. Deborah Meier, "Fiddling with Facts," *Brill's Content* 3 (February 2000): 63.

83. Ibid.

84. Ibid., 64.

85. Ibid.

86. Ibid., 63.

87. Ibid.

88. Ibid.

89. Ibid., 64.

90. Ibid., 63. The documentary Meier mentions is *Small Wonders* (Burbank, CA: Miramax Films, 1996).

91. For example, Southern Baptists have boycotted the content of some Disney films and television programs. See Carl Hiaasen, *Team Rodent: How Disney Devours the World* (New York: Ballantine, 1998), 12. See also, for example, Elizabeth Bell, Lynda Haas, and Laura Sells, eds., *From Mouse to Mermaid: The Politics of Film, Gender, and Culture* (Bloomington: Indiana University Press, 1995); Henry Giroux, "When You Wish Upon a Star It Makes a Difference Who You Are: Children's Culture and the Wonderful World of Disney," *International Journal of Educational Reform* 4, no. 1 (January 1995): 79–83; and Henry A. Giroux, *The Mouse That Roared: Disney and the End of Innocence* (Lanham, MD: Rowman & Littlefield, 1999).

92. Jay Taylor, 24, and 21.

93. Ibid., 21.

94. Apple, *Official Knowledge,* 96. Apple quotes William Celis.

95. Jay Taylor, 25.

96. John Hood, "Ante Freeze," *Policy Review* 68 (Spring 1994): 62. [Online]. Available: http://proquest.umi.com.

97. Robert Morrison, telephone interview by author, 22 May 1998.

98. I accessed Disney's 1995 10K information from the website www.sec.gov.

99. Hiaasen, 10.

100. Ibid., 11.

101. Information about Disney Magic was derived from Disney's website: www.disney.com. Hong Kong theme park details were discussed in Dirk Beveridge, "Disneyland in Hong Kong: Theme Park Projected as Big Boost to Tourism," *The Capital Times,* 2 November 1999, p. 4A.

102. I accessed Disney's 1995 10K information from the website www.sec.gov.

103. Peter Rosten, telephone interview by author, 24 July 1998.

104. Data derived from Socrates, a "social research database designed for investment professionals." This database is maintained by KLD; January 1998 data were provided by Sam Warren, research assistant for KLD.

105. Ibid.

106. Sheree Sanfacon, representing Citizens Fund, e-mail correspondence with author, 23 July 1998.

107. Evelyn Iritani, "Sunday Report; Entertaining China; Disneyland Talks Stir Debate in Hong Kong," *Los Angeles Times,* 13 June 1999, Business, part C, p. 1. [Online]. Available: http://www.lexis-nexis.com/universe.

108. These twelve examples should not be construed as a complete history of Disney's tax-paying and corporate-welfare practices. All twelve examples occurred within the past decade, however, and are, thus, approximately contemporaneous with the release of the two movies I discuss. Initially I sought data about Disney from published sources, including books, magazines, and newspapers; newspaper reportage, which I accessed largely with the help of online indices and databases, proved to be one of the most valuable sources. Most of the examples I discuss were considered newsworthy enough to have been reported in more than one print source. When significant discrepancies existed between published sources, which was the case with the New Amsterdam Theatre, I procured unpublished sources, in that instance, legal documents.

109. Susan S. Fainstein and Robert J. Stokes, "Spaces for Play: The Impacts of Entertainment Development on New York City," *Economic Development Quarterly* 12, no. 2 (May 1998), pp. 150–165. [Online]. Available: http://proquest.umi.com.

110. Ibid.

111. Todd W. Bressi, "Reveille for Times Square," *Planning* 62, no. 9 (September 1996): 4; and Fainstein and Stokes, 150–165. [Online]. Available: http://proquest.umi.com.

112. Fainstein and Stokes, 150–165.

113. Ibid.

114. Bressi, 4.

115. Ibid.

116. William Weathersby, Jr., "House of Disney Hits 42nd Street," *TCI* 31, no. 7 (August/September 1997): 6–7. [Online]. Available: http://proquest.umi.com.

117. Robin Stout, attorney, telephone interview by author, 17 July 1998.

118. Ibid.

119. "Agreement of Lease between 42nd St. Development Project, Inc., Landlord, and New Amsterdam Development Corporation, Tenant," 29 December 1994, p. 15.

120. Ibid.

121. Ibid., 73.

122. Ibid., 16.

123. Ibid., 24.

124. "Second Amended and Restated Promissory Note [made by New Amsterdam Development Corporation "in favor of 42nd St. Development Project, Inc."]," 20 July 1995, p. 2.

125. Alan D. Abbey, "Disney Banking on Theater to Light Up 42nd Street," *Times Union* (Albany, NY), 11 May 1997, p. H1. [Online]. Available: http://www.lexis-nexis.com/universe.

126. Stout.

127. "Agreement of Lease," p. 21.

128. Bressi, 4. See, "Agreement of Lease," p. 98, for details of this condition.

129. "Agreement of Lease," p. 33.

130. Brett Pulley, "Disney's Deal: A Special Report; A Mix of Glamour and Hardball Won Disney a Piece of 42nd Street," *New York Times,* 29 July 1995, sec. 1, p. 1. [Online]. Available: http://www.lexis-nexis.com/universe.

131. "The New New Amsterdam," *Economist* 343, no. 8020 (7 June 1997): 87–88. [Online]. Available: http://proquest.umi.com; and Fainstein and Stokes, 150–175.

132. "Disney's Magic Unlocks Renewal of Times Square," *Star Tribune,* 12 April 1998, p. 17A. [Online]. Available: http://www.lexis-nexis.com/universe. Abstract available at http://proquest.umi.com. Charles V. Bagli, "Reuters Steps Up Its Talks On Times Square Building," *New York Times,* 1 August 1997, Section B, p. 5, also confirmed the current desirability of the area. [Online]. Available: http://www.lexis-nexis.com/universe.

133. Clay Lifflander, quoted in Pulley, sec. 1, p. 1.

134. Fainstein and Stokes, 150–165.

135. John Davidson, "Times Square Revival," *Working Woman* 23, no. 3 (March 1998): 13. [Online]. Available: http://www.lexis-nexis.com/universe.

136. Charles V. Bagli, "Reuters Given Big Tax Deal for Its Project in Times Square," *New York Times,* 1 November 1997, sec. B, p. 1. [Online]. Available: http://www.lexis-nexis.com/universe.

137. Leichter was quoted in Bagli, "Reuters Given Big Tax Deal," sec. B., p. 1.

138. Marla Dickerson, "Is This Merely a Warmup for Extra Innings?" *Los Angeles Times,* 14 March 1996, part A, p. 1. [Online]. Available: http://www.lexis-nexis.com/universe.

139. Jeffrey A. Perlman and Robert W. Stewart, "Tax Money Sought for Disneyland Expansion," *Los Angeles Times,* 13 July 1991, part A, p. 1. [Online]. Available: http://www.lexis-nexis.com/universe.

140. Chris Woodyard, "Tax-Break Bill Seen as Disney Windfall," *Los Angeles Times,* 2 July 1992, part D, p. 1. [Online]. Available: http://www.lexis-nexis.com/universe.

141. Kevin Johnson and Matt Lait, "Disney Must Resort to Innovation for Expansion to Work," *Los Angeles Times,* 15 November 1992, part B, p. 1. [Online]. Available: http://www.lexis-nexis.com/universe.

142. Jeff Rowe, "Disney May Drop Plans for Anaheim Expansion in Anaheim," *Orange County Register,* 5 September 1991, p. C01. [Online]. Available: http://www.lexis-nexis.com/universe.

143. See Dickerson, part A, p. 1; Gene Sloan, "It's a Bigger World Planned for Disney in California," *USA Today,* 16 July 1996, p. D1. [Online]. Available: http://www.lexis-nexis.com/universe; and Esther Schrader, "The Price of Progress Is Building in Anaheim," *Los Angeles Times,* 23 February 1997, part A, p. 1. [Online]. Available: http://www.lexis-nexis.com/universe.

144. Ronald Campbell, "Anaheim, Calif., to Offer Bond Issue to Improve Area Near Disneyland," *Orange County Register,* 28 January 1997, no page. [Online]. Available: http://www.lexis-nexis.com/universe.

145. Marla Jo Fisher, "Anaheim Eyes Disney Tax Deal," *Orange County Register,* 1 October 1996, p. B01. [Online]. Available: http://www.lexis-nexis.com/universe.

146. Campbell.

147. Ibid.

148. Ibid.

149. John Rofe, "Troubles Encroach on Fantasyland; Urbanization Brings Crime to Disney's Door," *San Diego Union-Tribune,* 7 September 1997, p. A3. [Online]. Available: http://www.lexis-nexis.com/universe.

150. Schrader, part A, p. 1.

151. E. Scott Reckard, "O.C. Business Plus; Orange County Briefly; Mission Foods to Set Up Tortilla Factory in Disney Park...," *Los Angeles Times,* 17 August 1999, part C, p. 3. [Online]. Available: http://www.lexis-nexis.com/universe.

152. Dickerson, part A, p. 1.

153. "Sweet Deal—But for Whom?" *Los Angeles Times,* 19 May 1996, part B, p. 7. [Online]. Available: http://www.lexis-nexis.com/universe.

154. Bill Shaikin, "A New Home for the Angels: Edison International Field of Anaheim...," *Los Angeles Times,* 23 March 1998, p. 1. [Online]. Available: http://proquest. umi.com.

155. Ibid.

156. Ibid.

157. "Sweet Deal," part B, p. 7.

158. Bill Shaikin, "Angels, Mighty Ducks Put Out the For-Sale Sign Again," *Los Angeles Times,* 2 November 1999, part D, p. 3. [Online]. Available: http://www.lexis-nexis.com/universe.

159. Rick Henderson, "Edifice Complex," *Reason* 29, no. 4 (Aug/Sept 1997): 58–60. [Online]. Available: http://proquest.umi.com.

160. Ibid.

161. Reports differ in the precise number of acres involved. According to Lawrence Lebowitz, "Appraiser Claims Politics Muddles Disney Tax Fight," *Orlando Sentinel Tribune,* 28 September 1990, Local and State, p. B1. [Online]. Available: http://www.lexis-nexis.com/universe, Disney was running cattle and timber operations on more than 10,000 acres of land in Osceola County. "Property Appraiser Says It's 'Hardball' Time for Disney," United Press International Wire, 8 June 1989. [Online]. Available: http://www.lexis-nexis.com/universe, however, states that Disney's Osceola land holdings consist of 9,500 acres, only 4,500 of which received the agricultural designation. Sources are in agreement about Disney's tax savings, however.

162. "Property Appraiser Says It's 'Hardball' Time for Disney."

163. Lebowitz, "Appraiser Claims Politics," p. B1; and "County Tells Disney to Pay Up," United Press International, 31 August 1989. [Online]. Available: http://www.lexis-nexis.com/universe.

164. "County Tells Disney to Pay Up."

165. Lebowitz, "Appraiser Claims Politics," p. B1.

166. Lawrence Lebowitz, "Disney, Day Compromise on Tax Bill; The Settlement Ends a 2-Year Dispute Over Agricultural Classifications that Cut Disney's Tax Bill," *Orlando Sentinel Tribune,* 31 May 1991, p. 1. [Online]. Available: http://www.lexis-nexis.com/universe.

167. "County Tells Disney to Pay Up."

168. Ibid.

169. Ibid.

170. Lebowitz, "Appraiser Claims Politics," p. B1.

171. "Property Appraiser Says It's 'Hardball' Time for Disney."

172. Lebowitz, "Disney, Day Compromise on Tax Bill," p. 1.

173. Ibid.

174. Gail DeGeorge, "A Sweet Deal for Disney Is Souring Its Neighbors," *Business Week*, 8 August 1988, p. 48. [Online]. Available: http://www.lexis-nexis.com/universe.

175. Ibid.

176. "Disney's Tax-Free Sewers," *Orlando Sentinel Tribune*, 9 January 1990, p. A8. [Online]. Available: http://www.lexis-nexis.com/universe.

177. "Gubernatorial Candidate Files Suit Against Disney Over Bonds," United Press International, 19 January 1990. [Online]. Available: http://www.lexis-nexis.com/universe.

178. "Disney's Tax-Free Sewers," p. A8.

179. Ibid.

180. "Proposal Limits Disney's Tax-Exempt Bond Access," *Orlando Sentinel Tribune*, 29 March 1991, p. B5. [Online]. Available: http://www.lexis-nexis.com/universe.

181. Lawrence J. Lebowitz, "Disney Will Build 464 Apartments as Affordable Housing," *Orlando Sentinel Tribune*, 8 February 1992, p. B1. [Online]. Available: http://www.lexis-nexis.com/universe.

182. Ibid.

183. Lawrence J. Lebowitz, "This Disney Videotape Isn't for Kids," *Orlando Sentinel Tribune*, 22 February 1992, p. D6. [Online]. Available: http://www.lexisnexis.com/universe.

184. Lebowitz, "Disney Will Build," p. B1.

185. Lebowitz, "This Disney Videotape," p. D6.

186. Ibid.

187. Lebowitz, "Disney Will Build," p. B1.

188. Jim Mullen, "The Disney Experience," *Public Management* 77, no. 10 (October 1995): 4. [Online]. Available: http://proquest.umi.com; and Laurie Kellman, "Disney Foes Forming Fast; 'Second Look' Campaign Fears Traffic Sprawl," *Washington Times*, 2 December 1993, part C, p. C4. [Online]. Available: http://www.lexis-nexis.com/universe.

189. Kellman, p. C4.

190. Ibid.

191. Ibid.

192. "Disney Won't Need Taxpayer Money," *Washington Times*, 11 December 1993, p. A13. [Online]. Available: http://www.lexis-nexis.com/universe.

193. Ibid.

194. Paul Bradley, "Disney Seeks Aid of County and State," *Richmond Times-Dispatch*, 23 December 1993, no page. [Online]. Available: http://www.lexis-nexis.com/universe.

195. Ibid.

196. Ibid.

197. Lorraine Woellert, "Disney Offers to Guarantee Park's Road Debt," *Washington Times*, 10 March 1994, part A, p. A1. [Online]. Available: http://www.lexis-nexis.com/universe.

198. Bob Kemper, "A Head Tax for Mickey's Park?; Allen Says Panel's Proposal Could Kill the Deal," *Ledger-Star*, 11 February 1994, p. A1. [Online]. Available: http://www.lexis-nexis.com/universe.

199. Woellert, p. A1.

200. Steve Twomey, "Slipping Virginia a Mickey," *Washington Post*, 24 January 1994, Metro, p. D1. [Online]. Available: http://www.lexis-nexis.com/universe.

201. Peter Baker and John F. Harris, "Allen's Disney Plan Wins Key Support; $163 Million Subsidy Goes to Floor Today," *Washington Post*, 12 March 1994, p. A1. [Online]. Available: http://www.lexis-nexis.com/universe. This source also mentions another small concession Disney made.

202. Ibid.

203. Kellman, p. C4.

204. Squires, p. C1; and Woellert, p. A1.

205. Baker and Harris, p. A1.

206. See Kellman, p. C4, and Mullen, 4.

207. "Study Questions Disney's Tax Revenue," *Washington Times*, 12 July 1994, p. C8. [Online]. Available: http://www.lexis-nexis.com/universe.

208. Ibid.

209. Richard Squires, "Disney's Trojan Mouse; A Corporate Colony Paid for by Gullible Locals," *Washington Post*, 23 January 1994, p. C1. [Online]. Available: http://www.lexis-nexis.com/universe.

210. Ibid.

211. "Study Questions," p. C8.

212. Spencer S. Hsu, "Disney Tax Revenue Questioned; Opponents Say County Will Feel Minimal Relief," *Washington Post*, 14 July 1994, p. V1. [Online]. Available: http://www.lexis-nexis.com/universe.

213. Squires, p. C1.

214. Ibid.

215. Mullen, 4.

216. Iritani, part C, p. 1.

217. Beveridge, p. 4A.

218. Allan Sloan, "The Loophole King," *Newsweek*, 31 March 1997, p. 55. [Online]. Available: http//www.ebscohost.com. See "Academic Search."

219. George Garneau, "Biggest Deal Yet," *Editor and Publisher* 130, no. 15 (12 April 1997): 17, 40 + . [Online]. Available: http://proquest.umi.com. Garneau states that the sale took place in 1995, which was when the process began, but the deal was not finalized until 1996.

220. Allan Sloan, 55.

221. Ibid.

222. "Business Digest: Union to Protest Disney Tax Plan," *Fort Worth Star-Telegram*, 13 May 1997, Business, p. 2. [Online]. Available: http://www.lexis-nexis.com/universe. The ad appeared in the *New York Times*, 14 May 1997, sec. A, p. 17.

223. Allan Sloan, 55.

224. Ibid.

225. Jacqueline Doherty, "Trading Points: Disney, Union Carbide and Bear Stearns May Battle Treasury Over Tax-Dodging Securities," *Barron's* 77, no. 10 (10 March 1997): MW15. [Online]. Available: http://proquest.umi.com.

226. Ibid.

227. Rob Wells, "End Is Coming for Tax Loophole Arising from Real Estate Trusts," *Houston Chronicle*, 10 January 2000, p. 4. Accessed from the database "Dow Jones Interactive."

228. Ibid.

229. Ibid.

230. "The Global Marketplace," *Earth Island Journal* 12, no. 1 (Winter 1996/1997): 12. [Online]. Available: http://proquest.umi.com.

231. Ibid. "The Global Marketplace" quotes *Science News* as the source of the quotation about withholding information from the public.

232. The length of the air space loan is reported in Paul Taylor, "Superhighway Robbery," *New Republic*, 5 May 1997, 20. [Online]. Available: http://proquest.umi.com. For other details, see Lawrence K. Grossman, "How to Escape from a Highway Robbery," *Columbia Journalism Review* 36, no. 3 (Sept/Oct 1997): 58. [Online]. Available: http://proquest.umi.com.

233. Grossman, 58.

234. Ibid.

235. Paul Taylor, 20.

236. Ibid.

237. Molnar, 6.

238. Quoted in Jay Taylor, 23.

239. Grimes, sec. C, p. 9, states that targeting specific audiences was part of the marketing strategy for the film. The article notes that trailers were shown "to meetings of the American Symphony Orchestra League, the American Federation of Teachers and the National Association of Music Merchants." However, according to Robert

Morrison, in a telephone interview by the author, 22 May 1998, music educators initially were not among the targeted groups; the deaf community was. Morrison indicated that music educators became aware of the movie through a representative of NARAS who had done some work on the film.

240. Jeff Leverich, "Teachers Not Culprits in Property Tax Rise," *Wisconsin State Journal,* 24 November 1997, p. 5A.

241. Rick Olin, "Property Tax Level in Wisconsin," Informational Paper Number 13 (Madison: Wisconsin Legislative Fiscal Bureau, 2001), pp. 3–4.

242. Sharon Theimer, "WMC Gets Bang for Bucks on Lobbying," *Capital Times,* 4 February 1999, p. 1A.

243. See sidebar in "WMC: Corporate Tax Break Is Good for Entire State: Big Money Was Spent to Ensure Plan Passed," *Capital Times,* 11 October 1996, p. 8A.

244. "Recent WMC Accomplishments [sidebar]," *2001–2002 President's Report & Legislative Update* (Madison: Wisconsin Manufacturers & Commerce, 2001), p. 5. [Online]. Available: http://www.wmc.org.

245. Ibid.

246. Ibid., p. 7.

247. Robert S. McIntyre and T.D. Coo Nguyen, *Corporate Income Taxes in the 1990s* (Washington, D.C.: Institute on Taxation and Economic Policy, 2000). [Online]. Available: http://www.ctj.org/itep/corp00pr.htm. 3 May 2001.

248. Ibid.

249. Ibid., 2.

250. Ibid., 3

251. Ibid., 7.

252. Ibid., 2.

253. Ibid.

254. Ibid., 31.

255. Ibid., 3.

256. Ibid., 4.

257. Ibid., 27.

258. Ibid., 25–31.

259. Ibid., 34.

260. Ibid., 6.

261. Ibid.

262. Ibid.

263. Ibid., 7.

264. Ibid., 11.

265. Leverich, p. 5A.

266. James A. Keene, *A History of Music Education in the United States* (Hanover: University Press of New England, 1982), 212.

267. Alberta Powell Graham, *Great Bands of America* (New York: Thomas Nelson and Sons, 1951), 167–168.

268. See the advertisement, "Disney Music Honors Academy Program," *Teaching Music* 6, no. 1 (August 1998): 54–55.

269. "MENC: The National Association for Music Education's 15th Annual 'World's Largest Concert' at America Gardens Theatre, in Orlando, Florida with Host 'Kathy Mattea,'" MENC archive press release dated 26 February 1999. [Online]. Available: http://www.menc.org/publication/press/archive.html. 19 October 2000; "The 16th Annual 'World's Largest Concert' to Be Broadcast on March 9, 2000," MENC archive press release dated 14 December 1999. [Online]. Available: http://www.menc.org/publication/press/archive.html. 19 October 2000.

270. Correspondence from Catherine Wood, marketing manager for Disney Educational Productions, to Wendy Buehl, music teacher at Sherman Middle School, Madison, Wisconsin, 13 October 1997.

271. See "AMC News" in *Teaching Music* 4, no. 3 (December 1996): 43. Note, in particular, the side bar entitled "The National Coalition and AMC." See also, the AMC's website: www.amc-music.com.

272. See "Music Beats Computers at Enhancing Early Childhood Development," *Teaching Music* 4, no. 6 (June 1997): 42; also, Frances H. Rauscher, Gordon L. Shaw, et al. "Music Training Causes Long-Term Enhancement of Preschool Children's Spatial-Temporal Reasoning," *Neurological Research* 19, no. 1 (February 1997): 7.

273. "MENC and Yamaha Present an Interactive Video Teleconference: 'Technology in the Music Classroom,'" MENC archive press release dated 7 November 1997. [Online]. Available: http://www.menc.org/publication/press/archive.html. 5 May 2001.

274. The cost of the "Music in Education" program was found at the Yamaha website. [Online]. Available: http://www.yamaha.com/band/education/purchpc.html. 4 June 2001.

275. "Texaco Foundation Honored by MENC: The National Association for Music Education at Annual 'FAME' Awards Dinner," Texaco press release dated 15 March 2001. [Online]. Available: http://www.texaco.com/shared/pr/2001pr/pr3_15.html. 31 May 2001.

276. Ibid.

277. Ibid.

278. McIntyre and Nguyen, 25.

279. Ibid., 4.

280. Ibid.

281. Ibid., 25.

282. Ibid., 4.

283. Details of the program can be found at the "PepsiNotes Share the Joy with Music" website. [Online]. Available: http://www.pepsinotes.com/new/final_rules.asp. 31 May 2001.

284. Ibid.

285. See "Frequently Asked Questions" at the "PepsiNotes Share the Joy with Music" website. [Online]. Available: http://www.pepsinotes.com/new/final_faq.asp. 31 May 2001.

286. I wish to thank Carol Newland for pointing out the lack of nutritive value in the products sold through Pepsi's "Share the Joy" program.

287. For a description of the program, see MENC's website. [Online]. Available: http://www.menc.org/guides/dole/home.html. 19 October 2000.

288. "Jammin' 5 a Day Songs: Teacher's Guide, Tips." [Online]. Available: http://www.menc.org/guides/dole/tips.html. 19 October 2000.

289. "Jammin' 5 a Day Songs: Teacher's Guide, Other Resources." [Online]. Available: http://www.menc.org/guides/dole/other.html. 19 October 2000; and "Jammin' 5 a Day Songs: Teacher's Guide, Welcome." [Online]. Available: http://www.menc.org/guides/dole/home.html. 19 October 2000; and "Jammin' 5 a Day Songs: Teacher's Guide, Tips." [Online]. Available: http://www.menc.org/guides/dole/tips.html. 19 October 2000.

290. "Jammin' 5 a Day Songs: Teacher's Guide, Tips." [Online]. Available: http://www.menc.org/guides/dole/tips.html. 19 October 2000.

291. "Jammin' 5 a Day Songs: Teacher's Guide, The Songs." [Online]. Available: http://www.menc.org/guides/dole/lyrics/lyr_banana.html. 19 October 2000.

292. "Bose 'Musically Speaking' Multi-Image Show Highlights Music Educators National Conference's First-Ever National Music Education Convention," MENC archive press release dated 13 April 1998. [Online.] Available: http://www.menc.org/publication/press/archive.html. 19 October 2000.

293. Ibid.

294. Ibid.

295. "MENC at a Glance." [Online]. Available: http://www.menc.org/information/advocate/glance.html. 19 March 2001.

296. "The MENC Resources Spring Collection! 2000." Sales brochure.

297. I am referring here to the second edition of Michael L. Mark and Charles L. Gary's book *A History of American Music Education,* the first edition of which was published in 1992. The other book not fitting the pattern was Patrice D. Madura's *Getting Started with Vocal Improvisation.*

298. "Music Educators National Conference [Appoints] Five New Members to Its Advisory Council," MENC archive press release dated 27 April 1998. [Online]. Available: http://www.menc.org/publication/press/archive.html. 19 October 2000.

299. Ibid.

300. Program for "Vision 2020: The Housewright Symposium in Music Education," Florida State University, 23–26 September 1999.

301. Harry E. Price and Evelyn K. Orman, "MENC National Conferences 1984–1998: A Content Analysis," *Update* 18, no. 1 (Fall-Winter 1999): 26–32. Also, Harry E. Price and Evelyn K. Orman, "MENC 2000 National Biennial In-Service Conference: A Content Analysis," *Journal of Research in Music Education* 49, no. 3 (Fall 2001): 227–233.

302. Peggy Senko, MENC Director of Publications, telephone conversation with author, 2 May 2000.

303. Correspondence dated June 2000, signed by Mel Clayton.

304. Audre Lorde, "Litany for Survival," in *The Black Unicorn* (New York: Norton, 1978), 31–32. I wish to thank Roberta Lamb for acquainting me with this powerful poem.

·2·

RAP MUSIC

The Cultural Politics
of Official Representation (1994)

Rap music has been in existence for at least twenty years[1] and has been called "the most significant popular innovation" of the past two decades,[2] but American music educators have rarely welcomed this diverse and potentially powerful genre into official school knowledge. Instead, for many, rap epitomizes what they have dedicated their careers to opposing. According to a growing body of educators, however, a compelling case can be made for giving serious and respectful attention to many dimensions of popular culture, including rap.[3] Educators who acknowledge that rap is a significant aesthetic experience for countless American students and who recognize the merits of understanding and valuing the cultural experiences students bring with them, call for a broadened definition of legitimate school knowledge, one that recognizes rap as a significant cultural artifact. As forays into the complexities of cultural politics reveal connections between official knowledge and power, the problems resulting from unquestioned acceptance of traditional definitions of legitimate school knowledge have become clearer. Ignoring or denouncing popular culture—the culture of the people—sends elitist messages about whose understandings of the world do or do not count, both in schools and in the dominant culture. Thus, educators should care about rap because disregarding this important art form may help to perpetuate dominant power relations. Furthermore, popular culture sometimes serves as a venue for cultural critique, specifically of institutions and the power regimes that support them. Schooling is one such institution, and it is imperative that educators, ensconced as we are, seriously ponder the voices critical of this institution and the regimes of power that shape it.

The uninformed educator who seeks to better understand rap music quickly discovers that the genre has received scant attention in scholarly circles, particularly in music. This silence is a commentary on whose knowledge is deemed most legitimate in academe. More importantly, however, it enlarges the role of the general media as educators of educators on rap. Because the general media may be playing a central role in shaping educators' understandings and attitudes, the manner in which the media represent rap and hip hop culture is of considerable importance.

In the process of becoming more rap literate, I became intrigued by media coverage of the genre and decided to embark on an exploration of this coverage. To that end, I did a close reading of all rap related-articles that appeared in three American weekly news magazines during the ten-year period from January 1983 through December 1992; the three magazines I examined were *Newsweek, Time Magazine,* and *U.S. News and World Report.* In the following analysis, I will uncover some of the ways that discourses of domination, including inside/outside binaries that construct the outside as the undesirable other, speak through these texts, reinforcing and reinscribing unequal power relations along lines of race, social class, and gender. I will argue that in their representations of rap, rappers, and rap fans, these news magazines participated in a construction and commodification of otherness, integrally related to the perpetuation of hegemony. Construction of otherness was accomplished not only through specific textual content but also by means of what television media specialist John Fiske calls "generic characteristics" or "conventions" of news reporting.[4]

Representation and Power

This analysis is based on the assumption that representations are social constructs and on the premise that mass media representations are commodities designed to be marketed to and consumed by vast audiences. The significance of representation, specifically mass media representation, lies in its relationship to power, a relationship that bell hooks explores in her books *Yearning: Race, Gender, and Cultural Politics,* and *Black Looks: Race and Representation.* hooks discusses the critical role media representations play in shaping people's perceptions of themselves and others,[5] and she ties specific representations of race to the perpetuation of unequal power relations: "There is a direct and abiding connection between the maintenance of white supremacist patriarchy in this society and the institutionalization via mass media of specific images, representations of race, of blackness that support and maintain the oppression, exploitation, and overall domination of all black people."[6] She calls for "radical interventions," for "fierce critical interrogation" of representations, and for "revolutionary attitudes about race and representation."[7] Hooks' observations about the relationship between power and representation, and her call for new attitudes, are relevant not only in discussions of race, but also in those of social class and gender.

Binary Constructions and Oppression

Examining how oppressive representations are constructed can be a part of the fierce critical interrogation that hooks recommends. Some constructions use what John Fiske calls deep-structure binary oppositions, and what feminist Diana Fuss describes as inside/outside oppositions that depict the outside as the alien, excluded, lacking, or contaminated other.[8] Fiske explains that deep-structure abstract binaries, such as good/evil, are "metaphorically transformed into concrete representations," such as middle class/ lower class, order/lawlessness, light/dark, and masculine/feminine.[9] Fiske points to the theorizing of Roland Barthes, who argued that such binaries are part of a mythmaking that serves dominant classes in capitalist societies.[10] Fuss relates inside/outside rhetoric to regimes of power by stating that

> . . . the figure inside/outside, which encapsulates the structure of language, repression, and subjectivity, also designates the structure of exclusion, oppression, and repudiation. This latter model may well be more insistent to those subjects routinely relegated to the right of the virgule—to the outside of systems of power, authority, and cultural legitimacy.[11]

Fuss maintains that the inside/outside figure can never be completely eliminated, but it can be "worked on and worked over—itself turned inside out to expose its critical operations and interior machinery."[12]

Strategies of Containment and the News

In addition to relating narrative structures such as binary oppositions to the maintenance of unequal power relations, Fiske explains how "generic characteristics" or conventions of news reporting tend to reinforce dominant ideologies, specifically through controlling or limiting meaning.[13] Fiske considers news to be a commodity and news reporting a highly ideological practice, and he maintains that a myth of objectivity tends to obscure the ideological intent of such reporting.[14] He enumerates several general characteristics or conventions of news reporting that he contends are strategies of control and containment; the list includes selection, categorization, metaphor, negativity, and inoculation.[15] Selection and categorization involve decisions about what does or does not constitute news. Fiske points out that to discuss news in terms of "events" gives news an aura of naturalness; however, selection, which is the means by which events become news, is a cultural process.[16] Through selection and categorization, events are placed into the categories of news or not news; categorization also refers to sorting news into subcategories and to placing events on a "conceptual grid."[17] Fiske says that such subcategories are "normalizing agents,"[18] and as I will show later, choice of category may influence how an event is read and interpreted. Metaphor, according to him, is a sense-making mechanism; choice of metaphor affects how news is understood.[19] Negativity is the tendency for the news to focus on the negative or the "bad"; he comments on the ideological messages underlying the convention of focusing on bad news:

> What is absent from the text of the news, but present as a powerforce in its reading, are the unspoken assumptions that life is ordinarily smooth-running, rule- and law-abiding, and harmonious. These norms are of course prescriptive rather than descriptive, that is, they embody the sense of what our social life ought to be rather than what it is, and in doing this they embody the ideology of the dominant classes.[20]

Finally, inoculation is a metaphor for allowing radical voices to be heard in controlled doses. This practice surrounds the news with an aura of objectivity, but Fiske says it tends to strengthen rather than challenge "the social body."[21]

Selecting the General Media Sources

Before turning to a discussion of how narrative structures and news conventions operated in the texts I examined, let us briefly consider the magazines themselves. *Newsweek, Time,* and *U.S. News* are the three most widely circulated news magazines in the United States and Canada. According to 1991 statistics, *Time*'s paid circulation was 4,073,530; the circulation for *Newsweek* was 3,224,770; and the circulation for *U.S. News* was 2,237,009.[22] All three magazines are published weekly, all of them may be classified as information rather than entertainment magazines, and two of them, *Time* and *Newsweek,* regularly feature a music/arts column. As Fiske has noted in regard to television, information and entertainment are "leaky" classifications.[23] He points out, however, that in spite of this leakiness there are "very real differences" in the approaches and understandings that audiences and producers bring to these genres.[24] Information magazines were chosen for this study because of the understandings that audiences likely would bring to such texts.

Rap and rap-related subject headings in *Readers' Guide Abstracts,* which indexed articles for the ten-year period from January 1983 through December

1992, were used to find pertinent articles. Thirty-nine articles were located and read. During subsequent readings, as part of my analytical strategy, excerpts were placed in one or more thematic categories. I acknowledge that my against-the-grain readings are situated and, thus, partial and incomplete. Furthermore, I recognize that as a White, middle-class, female, I hold multiple positions, and I realize that these positions helped shape what I did or did not see.

Selection and Silence

One way to begin to understand how rap was represented is to examine patterns of coverage in the three magazines (table 1). Clearly, *Newsweek* provided the most consistent and extensive coverage while *U.S. News,* which did not have an arts/music section, spoke only rarely about the subject. Although the magazines are independent from each other, table 1 shows that they displayed remarkably similar patterns of decision making regarding when rap was or was not considered newsworthy. During the seven years prior to 1990, the magazines were nearly silent on the subject, and no articles were published during the years 1984, 1985, or 1988. Two sudden increases in coverage occurred during the same years in all three magazines, and those were the only years when *U.S. News* published any rap articles. Perhaps the most dramatic revelation from this portion of my analysis is that one-third of the thirty-nine articles published during the ten-year period appeared in the four months in 1992 immediately following the Rodney King verdict and the Los Angeles response to that verdict.[25] After those four months, coverage disappeared completely in *U.S. News* and dropped dramatically in the other two magazines. I will discuss the foci of some of these articles a bit later; but for now, let us consider the silences, particularly the silences in the two magazines featuring an arts/music column.

TABLE 1. FREQUENCY OF RAP ARTICLE PUBLICATION, BY YEAR

Year by Magazine Title	Time	Newsweek	U.S. News	Total
1983	1	1	0	2
1984	0	0	0	0
1985	0	0	0	0
1986	1	1	0	2
1987	0	1	0	1
1988	0	0	0	0
1989	0	1	0	1

(table continued on next page)

(table continued)

1990	3	7	2	12
1991	2	3	0	5
1992	7	6	3	16
Total	14	20	5	39
Arts Section?	Yes	Yes	No	

Patterns of coverage can reveal what Fiske calls the strategies of selection and categorization—in this instance, the categorization of rap music as news or not news. As I indicated earlier, Fiske maintains that these strategies are based in ideology. For many years, even those magazines featuring a music/arts column did not think rap was newsworthy; perhaps they did not think rap was art, at least not art of sufficient merit to deserve their attention. Silences and sparse coverage indicate that the magazines were in doubt about whether rap was "socially *legitimate*" cultural capital, to use Michael Apple's phrase.[26] The lengthy span when these widely read magazines relegated rap to the right of the virgule in the news/not news or art/not art binary is a reflection of whose knowledge was deemed worth knowing, and thus, indirectly, a commentary on power relations. In this instance, the role of race and social class as influential factors in the selection and categorization processes should not be overlooked.

Subcategorization: Rap as a Cultural Artifact

Another pattern emerged when I examined which news subcategory was selected when information about rap was published. Rap was more frequently discussed in the music/arts section than in any other single news category in the two magazines that featured such a section. However, in both of these magazines, articles about rap appeared *outside* the music/arts section *in the majority of cases* (e.g., in "Lifestyle," "Nation," "Living," "Sports," etc.).[27] In *U.S. News,* the magazine not featuring a music/arts section, rap articles appeared most often under the "Society" heading.

As Fiske has noted, choice of news category influences the ways that information is understood: "The categorization of news and its consequent fragmentation is a strategy that attempts to control and limit the meanings of social life, and to construct the interests of the western bourgeoisie into 'natural' common sense. Compartmentalization is central to news's strategy of containment."[28] Placing discussions of rap in categories other than the music/arts sections contributed to a construction of rap as a sociological phenomenon, as political discourse, or as reportage rather than as an art form, and, thus, it changed the terms in which rap was discussed. Regardless of whether articles appeared in or out of the arts/music section, however, there was very little discussion of the music itself, aside from its lyrics. Little attention was paid to its history, its formal characteristics, or even to the practice of sampling, which is a rich and complex musical component of rap. These absences further contributed to rap's construction as a sociological phenomenon, subject to intense social analysis. Thus, even if the magazines recognized that rap is an art form (as opposed to "not art"), they did not discuss it as such, and certainly not in terms apparently reserved for "high art." The few journalists to compare rap and "high art" placed rap on a much lower plane. For example, in a scathing critique of N.W.A.'s explicit lyrics, Jerry Adler wrote, "The outrageous implication is that to *not* sing about this stuff would be to do violence to an artistic vision as pure and compelling as Bach's."[29] George F. Will distanced rap from "high art" music by suggesting it was ludicrous to compare negative responses to 2 Live Crew to those that followed early performances of Stravinsky's *Rite of Spring*.[30]

Of course, rap *is* a socially constructed cultural artifact, as is all music; however, a double standard appears to exist, which can be made visible by comparing the terms in which Euro-American high art music is usually discussed to those used for rap. Recent attempts to regard high art music as a sociological phenomenon have often met with sharp criticism and considerable resistance, at least from within academe.[31]

One dissimilarity between the left and right sides of the high art/popular art binary is that a myth of transcendence tends to accompany the high art position, and the myth appears to insulate high art from discussion constructing it as a cultural artifact. Thus, the myth accords high art music a measure of freedom from the intense scrutiny and sociological analysis to which rap, constructed as popular art, not art, or bad art, was frequently subjected. This myth of transcendence suggests (falsely, of course) that "high" or "great" art does not participate in the racism, misogyny, homophobia, or glorification of violence with which rap was frequently associated and for which it was harshly criticized. A handful of the magazines' discussions of attempted censorship of rap lyrics shattered this myth by pointing out that a net designed to catch rap would also snag much "high art" music. Ira Glasser, executive director of the American Civil Liberties Union, was quoted as saying that there are no words in 2 Live Crew "that have not appeared in books or in serious literature."[32] Ironically, although Glasser supported 2 Live Crew's rap, he also categorized it as not serious and, thus, relegated it to the right side of the virgule.

Of course, the myth of transcendence does not completely insulate "high
art." For example, controversy over the Mapplethorpe exhibit made the news
during the same period as discussions of 2 Live Crew's lyrics. However, the
strength of the myth of transcendence may have aided the Mapplethorpe case;
significantly, the gallery showing Mapplethorpe's pieces was acquitted of all
obscenity charges while the record store owner who sold 2 Live Crew albums
was convicted, a point not lost on Peter Plagens, who wrote about the court
decisions in a *Newsweek* article entitled "Mixed Signals on Obscenity."[33]

Pierre Bourdieu theorized about the role that distinctions between high
and popular art play in the perpetuation of unequal power relations along
social class lines.[34] These distinctions, and their relationship to power, need
to be taken into account when considering representations of rap; in addition,
however, the role that these distinctions play in perpetuating unequal power
relations along racial lines also should be examined.

Rappers, Rap Fans, and Otherness

Rappers

Now that we have considered some of the ways that strategies of selection and categorization placed rap on the right side of the virgule in inside/
outside binaries, let us turn to actual textual content, specifically to that which
constructed rappers and rap fans. Rap was generally represented as a genre
by and for Black, urban, adolescent, males who were poor or from the working class. Evidence of inside/outside binaries was in abundance in comments about rappers' race and social class, the binaries variously taking the
form of high/low, good/bad, here/there, and up/down. Rap was usually associated with the right side of the virgule, and with lack or want. For example,
Jay Cocks relied upon high/low binaries when he reported that rap "began
as a fierce and proudly insular music of the American Black underclass."[35]
David Gates, in his description of rap as "a communique from the 'underclass'—or less euphemistically, poor Blacks," equated poverty (specifically
being "under") with being Black.[36] Gates also painted a picture of want and
lack when he described athletes and rappers as "the only credible role models for inner-city kids"; since most athletes and rappers are male, his comment
has sexist overtones as well.[37] In several sources, rap was described as coming from the ghetto, a term not only suggesting a place apart, but also a place
of otherness, at least from a White, Anglo-Saxon, Protestant perspective.
This place of otherness was represented as dangerous; for example, N.W.A.'s
music was described as a "rap mural of ghetto life, spray painted with

blood."[38] One source said rap originated in the "cauldron of New York City's underclass," a phrase evoking images of simmering, poisonous brews.[39] Articles that called rap the music from the streets were connecting it to a specific social-class location; however, as a location of otherness, streets were represented as undesirable places associated with crime, poverty, offal, and moral degradation. For example, one reference explained that a "new musical culture, filled with self-assertion and anger, has come boiling up from the streets. Some people think it should have stayed there."[40] The statement not only placed streets on the low side of an up/down binary but also suggested that rap had changed social location and had moved to an unnamed "higher" ground. Finally, the headline "America's Slide into the Sewer," which George F. Will chose for his anti-rap essay, suggested that America, however defined, had participated in a downward movement to a place reserved for offal.[41] We can assume that Will was describing a moral slide; however, sewers are found in or under the streets, and streets represent a social location.

A second component in the construction of rappers was an emphasis on the meteoric rises to fame and fortune that resulted from rap's popularity and success. Rap was represented as an enormously profitable venture, but mixed messages were sent about whether such profit was good. Rap's critics argued that rappers were making fortunes on obscenity and getting rich on offensiveness. Much attention was paid to the successes of controversial groups such as N.W.A.[42] In addition, critics and proponents alike sometimes listed ways that rappers and those affiliated with the sales and promotion of rap were spending their money. For example, rap impresario Russell Simmons was described as "livin' large. His empire brings him an income of $5 million a year."[43] The article enumerated some of his possessions, including a bulletproof Rolls Royce and a triplex penthouse. Simmons, the magazine reported, buys Cristal champagne and abstract art. Sports cars, a private jet, exotic trips, a home in Hollywood, and expensive jewelry were among the other possessions associated with rappers.[44] Philanthropic efforts were reported occasionally, but more often than not, the magazines focused on rappers' predilections for luxury items. In addition to symbolizing success and wealth, however, the belongings mentioned can also represent extravagance, excess, and unprincipled spending, at least to a middle-class eye.

Another element complicating the representation of successful rappers was the implication that rap is a quasi-legal means of making money, a just-barely-legal way to acquire capital. The tone was set by references to some rappers' past criminal activities. For example, 2 Live Crew's Luther Campbell was described as an "ex-gang leader turned entrepreneur," and Ice-T was reported to have been very successful as a hustler, spending five-hundred dollars on

sneakers before he changed careers.[45] Such reports set the stage for portrayals of rap as "the safe and legal road to riches."[46] One article quoted Ice-T
lyrics indicating that friends in crime were now making more money in
music.[47] Another reported that one quarter of rap's "homeboys end up in serious trouble with the law."[48]

Some links between successful rappers and crime were more subtle.
For example, when N.W.A.'s attitude was described as "jaunty and sullen by
turns; showy but somehow furtive, in glasses as opaque as a limousine window and sneakers as white as a banker's shirt," subtle connections were made
between N.W.A., crime, and otherness.[49] The words "sullen" and "furtive"
set an ominous tone. Next, reference was made to signs of fortune that have
also come to represent criminal activity. Limousines with opaque windows
are symbols of wealth, but they also are associated with pimps and drug
dealers. Opaque glasses, long worn by highway patrol officers, also suggest
drug use and inaccessibility. White banker's shirts are a symbol of legal
acquisition of capital, but N.W.A. members were not wearing banker's shirts;
instead, they donned sneakers.

Reports indicating that some successful rappers, including impresario
Russell Simmons, Tracy Marrow (Ice-T), and members of Public Enemy, had
not come from poverty, but instead had roots in the middle class,[50] contributed to a representation of rappers as impostors and charlatans, shrewd
but unscrupulous business people, who furthered their own interests at the
expense of a long list of victims, among them women and poor Black people.
Of course, rather than recognizing that all musical performances are just performances, such arguments assumed that some are and others are not. One
critic charged that Ice-T's heavy metal single *Cop Killer* was not "an authen-
tic anguished cry of rage from the ghetto," but rather a "cynical commercial
concoction designed to titillate its audience with imagery of violence"; *Cop
Killer,* the critic claimed, is "an excellent joke [by Ice-T and Time Warner, the
parent corporation] on the white establishment."[51] Another article described
impresario Simmons as sensing the commercial potential when others thought
rap was a gimmick.[52] In a discussion of an N.W.A. album released in 1991,
N.W.A's mystique was said to pay "no attention to where criminality begins
and marketing lets off."[53] Finally, when Sister Souljah spoke at a convention
of Jesse Jackson's Rainbow Coalition in 1992, and presidential candidate
William Clinton criticized Souljah, one commentator unflatteringly represented all three figures (Jackson, Souljah, and Clinton) as self-serving, bottom-line
business people whose primary interest was furthering their own careers; the
essay was entitled "Sister Souljah: Capitalist Tool."[54] The proposition that
rappers are entrepreneurs, not artists, overlooked the possibility that they

could be both; furthermore, it did not address the reality that most, if not all, artists are by necessity entrepreneurs as well.

Ironically, stories of rappers' entrepreneurialism and success, bootstrap stories that would make Horatio Alger proud, sometimes were viewed with mistrust and suspicion. Controversial rappers, at least one of whom was a card-carrying member of the Republican party,[55] were amassing wealth by serving up conservative political fare that embraced "old-fashioned social norms (even in its take on gender roles and homosexuality . . .)."[56] Ironically, these conservative voices were being vilified and rebuked by other conservatives. Thus, rappers' acquisition of wealth and their concomitant shift in social-class status did not necessarily change the representation of these rappers as outsiders. This representation can be explained, in part, in terms of power relations. If successful Black rappers are viewed as a threat to hegemony and a challenge to some White middle-class values, specifically to beliefs about who is entitled to capital, how it should be acquired, and how it should be used, then mixed or negative portrayals of these rappers may be seen as attempts to reinforce dominant ideology and to keep Black people "in their place."

Rap Fans

As mentioned earlier, rap was represented as originating in a specific place of otherness; lines of distinction were drawn in terms of race, social class, and gender. However, as the decade advanced, the magazines indicated that some types of rap were traversing some of these lines; the race and social class of the typical fan were shifting, but the age and sex generally were not. Some articles said these shifts or expansions began in the mid-1980s, but the movement may have started several years earlier.[57] When an article published in 1990 told parents that rap can be heard booming from "your kid's bedroom," the kid in question could have been either Black or White.[58] As early as 1990, articles began recognizing that music by rap's most controversial groups, for example, Public Enemy and N.W.A., was being consumed primarily by White, middle-class, suburban, adolescent males.[59] By contrast, according to John Schecter, editor of the hip-hop journal *The Source*, N.W.A. was not liked by most Black people.[60]

Audience shift or expansion was discussed most extensively in articles appearing during the final three years I analyzed, 1990–1992; this shift may help explain the dramatic increase in 1990 of the magazines' coverage of rap. The scope of the expansion was alluded to in a statement made in 1992 by rapper Tupac Shakur, who opined that rap was no longer a Black movement but rather a youth movement.[61] Throughout the final three years, however, the perception lingered that rap was, first and foremost, by and for Black people. The term often used to describe the movement of rap's popularity from one racial and social-class group to another was "crossover," and the place to which rap crossed was often called "the mainstream." Inside/outside binaries were evident throughout these discussions. The mainstream, the inside of the binary, was White, middle class, and male. Journalists spoke of rap crossing over from Black America "into the mainstream of popular culture."[62] Impresario Russell Simmons was described as moving rap "from the streets of the inner city into the mainstream of American pop culture."[63] Journalist John Leland mentioned rap's "trip to the white mainstream,"[64] and Jay Cocks talked about "why ghetto rage and the brutal abuse of women appeal to mainstream listeners."[65] Cocks later gave a profile of the typical fan that provided clues about who constituted the mainstream; fans were White, middle class, teenage and male.[66]

Inside/outside binaries took several forms in discussions of rappers and rap fans, one of which was a we/they binary to which the moral judgments good/bad were often explicitly or implicitly attached. At times, "they" were rappers, and at other times, fans. For example, an article appearing in 1990, the year when crossover began receiving substantial attention, was entitled "Polluting Our Popular Culture."[67] The article described popular culture as "the air we breathe," and 2 Live Crew was termed "a pesky new pollutant"; the journalist John Leo called for the elimination of the "2 Live Pollutants" from "our air."[68] In this we/they structure, popular culture was owned by an unspecified "us," and "they," 2 Live Crew, were a foreign contaminant. "They" were rappers and rap music from whom rap fans, constructed as "our daughters," needed to be protected. Leo, in a question that displayed a protect-the-women-and-children logic, queried, "Why should our daughters have to grow up in a culture in which musical advice on the domination and abuse of women is accepted as entertainment?"[69] Leo's question appears to be a color-blind plea to all parents; however, in an article focusing on 2 Live Crew's controversial lyrics, group leader Luther Campbell observed that he had been making similar albums for years and had received no complaints from the "decency police" until White kids starting listening.[70] Apparently, protecting daughters was not much of an issue with these watchdog groups until "our daughters" were White. Leo's question is an excellent one; however, as feminist musicians know, serving up the domination and abuse of women as entertainment is not unique to rap or to popular music; much Euro-American high art music does the same. Leo's decision to single out rap indicated that the genre was on the outside of the inside/outside binary, a position offering less protection from scrutiny.

Yet another example of the we/they binary was seen in a scathing criticism of rap fans, whom journalist Jerry Adler described as "working-class" and "underclass" youths "who forgot to go to business school in the 1980s."[71] Adler placed himself in the otherwise unspecified category of "we" and argued that "we" cannot talk to "them," the rap fans. Adler characterized fans as stupid and uninformed; he maintained that if they "had ever listened to anything except the homeboys talking trash," if they had studied and read, "*[t]hen* we might have a sensible discussion with them; but they haven't, so we can't."[72]

An especially ugly manifestation of the inside/outside binary was seen in discussions distancing rap from civilization. For example, in a diatribe focusing largely on rap, George F. Will implied that rappers are lower animals.[73] Shortly thereafter, Jerry Adler equated civilization with control and rap with chaos when he wrote, "Civilized society abhors [rap] attitude and perpetuates itself by keeping it under control."[74] A letter to the editor responded to the issue in which Adler's article appeared by chastising *Newsweek* for publishing any information about rap. Calling it a "bestial and obscene" subculture, the reader fumed, "I realize that these creatures [rappers] have the right to express themselves. . . . However, you seem to have forgotten your responsibility to your readers to keep within the bounds of decency."[75] To suggest, as these passages did, that members of a predominantly Black group such as rappers are uncivilized, low animals is to invoke a racism as old as colonialism itself.

The Other of Others

Some rap and rappers were routinely criticized for making hateful or demeaning comments about whole groups of people. The groups most frequently mentioned were women, gays, Korean immigrants, Jews, Whites, and the police; however, from time to time rap also was denounced for furthering hatred toward Blacks through the commodification of racist images of Black people. With the exception of the police, the groups mentioned were defined in terms of race, social class, gender, sexual orientation, or ethnicity. Social class was described as a separating factor when Black people were divided in opinion on the subject of rap. Discussions of Black opposition to rap shattered the myth of a unified Black voice; however, they also contributed to the perception that rap had and deserved little support from important segments of the Black community; anti-rap sentiment was thus portrayed as transcending race.[76] Paradoxically, people who may have viewed themselves as disenfranchised others—women, gays, Asian immigrants, and Jews—were summoned to join powerful dominant groups—Whites and the police—in an improbable coalition against rap. In short, not only were rappers and rap fans often represented as the others in inside/outside binaries, they also were constructed as the other of others. A quotation by bell hooks applies: "Black youth culture comes to stand for the outer limits of 'outness.'"[77]

Rap and Negativity

It would be inaccurate and misleading to say that every article openly opposed all rap. Indeed, making generalizations about the overall tone of the articles was extraordinarily difficult. It usually was impossible to simplistically categorize an article as patently pro or con, positive or negative. I can say that *U.S. News* had a prevailing attitude toward rap because anti-rap sentiments were expressed in every article; furthermore, four of the five articles were patently opposed to the rap discussed. However, when speaking about the other two magazines, especially about *Newsweek,* which presented the most extensive coverage of rap, there is an ever-present danger of being reductive. In all three magazines an image of balanced reporting, of including multiple viewpoints, was created; one way of accomplishing this was by using side-by-side pro and con arguments. The image of balance confounded attempts to analyze and generalize, and it implied that the magazines were not in the business of telling readers what to think. However, Fiske probably would describe these pro/con presentations as examples of inoculation, of allowing radical voices to speak in controlled environments.

Even though the articles were difficult to characterize and often presented the image of balance, most of them nevertheless participated in reinforcing dominant ideologies through the strategy of containment that Fiske calls negativity. Evidence of this negativity surfaced when thematic content of the articles was analyzed. The vast majority of articles made reference to at least one of the following themes: violence, obscenity, hatred, crime, gangs, and anger. Such references appeared in all *U.S. News* articles and in more than 85 percent of those published by *Time* and *Newsweek.* Thus, even when articles were sympathetic to rap, they usually reinforced a link between rap and specific negative themes. A corollary representation was that controversy is rap's constant partner. Concentrating on the negative, focusing on a circumscribed list of rap topics, and constructing rap as controversial, were means by which these magazines placed readers in a position where they likely received a skewed vision of rap, a vision that nearly obliterated its diversity. The vastness of rap and its extraordinary variety—illustrated, for example, by the existence of groups such as DC Talk, composed of students from conservative evangelist Jerry Falwell's Liberty University—was lost in a reductive wash.[78] In its relentless search for the negative and the controversial, the reporting made generalizations about the whole after looking at only a very small part. It centered on a few controversial groups rather than on the complete genre, and characteristics of the former tended to be ascribed to the latter. Coverage almost invariably obscured the reality that the rappers and rap discussed were neither necessarily representative nor the most popular with the majority of rap fans. The rare qualifying statement, such as, "The vast majority of rap is healthy," or "Rap is so vast, you can't really categorize it anymore," was barely audible amid the clatter of negativity.[79]

Negative Imagery and the Representation of Rap

Even when articles did not specifically refer to negative themes, they nevertheless sometimes constructed rap as bad in roundabout ways, for example, through use of imagery. As Fiske states, choice of image, specifically of metaphor, influences the understandings people bring to texts. There was imagery of poison and pollution. For example, one headline read "Rap Music's Toxic Fringe."[80] In a similar vein, an article suggested that the recording industry was telling consumers to "buy a gas mask or stop breathing"; it described rap as sending "venomous messages" disguised as "harmless fun."[81] There also were images of violence, anger, and fear. Ice-T's poetry, it was said, "takes a switchblade and deftly slices life's jugular."[82] A simile laced with racism described rap attitude as being "as scary as sudden footsteps in the dark."[83] Even descriptions of the music itself sometimes relied on violent imagery. For example, a journalist wrote of "the thumping, clattering scratching *assault* [my emphasis] of rap."[84] Another said that the group B.W.P served up "a vengeful brand of radical Black feminism:" in a "snarling hardcore style."[85] War metaphors were used occasionally. One passage called rap music "a series of bulletins from the front in a battle for survival," and another referred to members of Public Enemy as "racial warriors."[86] In what was perhaps the most vivid example, an image of war was evoked when conservative actor Charlton Heston likened Ice-T to Adolph Hitler, a comparison made at a Time Warner shareholders' meeting held in 1992.[87] By equating a rapper with a war figure who personifies evil of mythic proportions, Heston and the journalist who reported the event constructed Ice-T as the enemy in a battle of good against evil.

Rap, Representation, and Race

The significance of the magazines' negativity and negative representations becomes clearer when one considers that theorists have linked both negativity and negative representation to power relations. John Fiske asserted that negativity is a strategy of containment that tends to reinforce dominant ideologies. Specifically, Fiske noted, ideological practice is evident in news reporting's predisposition to construct "the bad" as an aberration in dominant culture but as normal for others.[88] Fiske commented on the relationship between "otherness," negativity, and power:

> There is, of course, a connection between elitism and negativity: the positive or "normal" actions of elite people will often be reported whereas those without social power are considered newsworthy only when their actions are disruptive or deviant. In representing the dominant as performing positive actions and the subordinate as performing deviant or negative ones the news is engaging in the same ideological practices as fictional television.[89]

Because there is a relationship between representation and power, negative representation that consistently linked a Black cultural product and Black performers to violence, obscenity, hatred, crime, gangs, and anger, and that thus represented hip hop culture as the undesirable other, must be viewed as a factor contributing to the maintenance of White supremacy. Tricia Rose, who has explored some of the complex cultural politics of rap, speaks of a "sociologically based crime discourse" that surrounds "the political economy of rap."[90] Rose asserts that opposition to rap is grounded in fear:

> Young African Americans are positioned in fundamentally antagonistic relationships to the institutions that most prominently frame and constrain their lives. The public school system, the police, and the popular media perceive and construct them as a dangerous internal element in urban America—an element that if allowed to roam about freely will threaten the social order, an element that must be policed. The social construction of rap and rap-related violence is fundamentally linked to the social discourse on Black containment and fears of a Black planet. [91]

According to Rose, this White fear, born in the days of slavery, is of loss of White control, specifically through Black uprising or revolt; the fear informs constructions of Black people, especially of young Black males, who are seen as threats "to the social order of oppression," threats that must be restrained or controlled.92

Fears of a Black Planet and the Discourse of Containment

With Rose's analysis of the cultural politics of rap music in mind, let us examine two cases from the magazines in which the negative representations of rap, rappers, and rap fans seemed clearly linked to fears of a Black planet and the social discourse of containment. I will begin with a close reading of George F. Will's essay, "America's Slide into the Sewer," in which Will stepped beyond the observation that some rap lyrics speak of violence to suggest that 2 Live Crew lyrics induce violence. In this article, Will associated rap with an actual act of violence, the brutal rape in 1989 of a Central Park jogger. 2 Live Crew, Will suggested, is where young men such as the accused rapists learn that sexual violence against women is enjoyable: "Where can you get the idea that sexual violence against women is fun? From a music store, through Walkman earphones, from boom boxes blaring forth the rap lyrics of 2 Live Crew."[93] To prove his point, Will interspersed horrifyingly graphic excerpts of courtroom testimony from the rape case with shockingly explicit rap lyrics from 2 Live Crew. He connected the rapists to rap fans by citing common characteristics of both groups: "Fact: Some members of a particular age and social cohort—the one making 2 Live Crew rich—stomped and raped the jogger to the razor edge of death, for the fun of it."[94] To bolster his argument he quoted the *Washington Post*'s Juan Williams, whom he identified as "Black and disgusted"; Williams excoriated 2 Live Crew, claiming the group is "'selling corruption—self-hate—to vulnerable young minds in a weak Black America.'"[95] Williams supported his allegation that American Black families are falling apart by citing statistics indicating that half of all Black children are raised in single-parent households headed by women.

Will charged that liberals are the tools of unscrupulous corporations, which have sold "civil pollution for profit."[96] America's priorities are wrong, Will argued, because protecting Black women receives less attention than saving endangered fish: "America today is capable of terrific intolerance about smoking, or toxic waste that threatens trout. But only a deeply confused society is more concerned about protecting lungs than minds, trout than Black women. We legislate against smoking in restaurants; singing 'Me So Horny' is a constitutional right."[97] Will's parting comments indicated that he believes protection of Black women will be accomplished by exercising more control over groups such as 2 Live Crew.

The Central Park rape was horrible and 2 Live Crew's lyrics are graphic and misogynistic; however, these realities do not change the fact that Will's argument was not only flawed, sexist, and elitist but also showed evidence of a racist fear of a Black planet. To begin to excavate the racism, sexism, and elitism implicit in Will's essay, the reader must keep in mind a critical piece of information about the Central Park rape: the jogger was White and the attackers were Black. Will made no reference to the race of either party, but this information was generally known and widely reported. Thus, Will chose as his example of crime and violence an event that was laden with prejudicial meaning and was a classic scenario for evoking White racist fears. The Central Park rape reinforced the racist perception that young Black adolescents are dangerous, out of control, and sexually violent; the event appeared to confirm the belief that uncontrolled, young Black adolescents are a threat to vulnerable (female) White America.

Next, Will linked this meaning-laden rape to a Black cultural product, even though he did not present one scintilla of evidence suggesting the accused rapists had ever listened to 2 Live Crew or to any form of rap music. Even if Will had found such evidence, he would have faced the formidable task of establishing causation. He grounded his case on the argument that the accused rapists were of the same "age and social cohort group" making 2 Live Crew rich but never articulated salient features of that cohort group. Will and Williams apparently assumed that race was one of those salient features, an assumption encountered in Williams' statement that 2 Live Crew was selling corruption to the Black community. However, as noted previously, information reported elsewhere in 1990 indicated that the typical fan of controversial rap groups was a young, White, middle-class boy from the suburbs. Thus, Will's characterization of "social cohort group" probably was flawed. Significantly, his characterization tended to perpetuate negative stereotypes of Black adolescents while it permitted members of the social cohort group most likely to listen to explicit rap—White, middle-class boys from the suburbs—to emerge unscathed.

When Will asked the question, "Where can you get the idea that sexual violence against women is fun?," he failed to list a whole array of sources unrelated to Black music, and in so doing, constructed rap music as the culprit. He did not acknowledge that young males in American society can learn misogyny from countless sources in the dominant culture, the most influential of which are probably outside the boundaries of entertainment. There is implicit racism in Will's decision to single out a Black cultural product but never to mention heavy metal, country, opera, and the classical fare typically sung in high school choirs, which often are at least as misogynistic (if perhaps not as graphic) as 2 Live Crew.

Will appears to have attempted to construct his argument as one that transcends race. For example, he included a sentence criticizing Andrew Dice Clay, whom he carefully described as a White comedian. However, that sentence was the only one to indict a White cultural product, and it was dwarfed by the extensive coverage given to 2 Live Crew. Will also appears to have tried to protect himself from the accusation of being racist by quoting a Black spokesperson. However, Juan Williams' unflattering assessment of the state of Black families and his sexist but commonly believed assumption that single-parent families headed by women are not strong, worked to reinforce White racist constructions of Black families as bad families. bell hooks has commented on similar constructions:

> . . . African-Americans need to consider whose interests are served when the predominant representation of black culture both on television news and in talk shows suggests that the black family is disintegrating and that a hostile gender war is taking place between black women and men.[98]

Finally, in a particularly patriarchal gesture, Will constructed himself as a protector of Black women; one significant aspect of this construction was that it came in response to the rape of a White woman. By placing himself in that role, Will constructed Black women as the weak or vulnerable "others" who need to be protected by the strong, more powerful White man. Protected from what? According to Will, from violence caused by Black music, his assertion simply assuming that music-induced violence exists. His unspoken, racist message is that trouble in the lives of Black people is caused by Black people, in this case, by Black musicians. Arguments such as Will's deflect attention away from real issues and substantive discussions of the kinds of change that would be necessary to alter the lived realities of many Black women's lives. Whose interests are served by such deflection? Greater control of Black discursive terrain would tend to reinforce dominant power relations; substantive change that might bring real improvement would threaten hegemony.

Some of the racial politics of Will's essay become visible when one examines the list of who looks bad in this article, that is, who is constructed as the evil, lacking, or undesirable other. First, there were the rapists, whom the newspapers had widely reported were Black. Next, there was rap music, which was generally regarded as a Black cultural product, followed by 2 Live Crew, a Black rap group. Fourth, there were 2 Live Crew fans, who were assumed to be Black (probably incorrectly). In all of these representations, negativity was achieved by linking Black people or cultural products to brutality, sexual violence, and amorality. Fifth, there were Black families, specifically those headed by women, and finally, there were unscrupulous liberals and corporations, groups whose racial constitutions were not reported. Will's superficial attempts to present himself as color blind did not mask the racism, elitism, and sexism in his constructions of Black people as dangerous, undesirable others.

Fears of a Black planet and a discourse of containment were evident not only in Will's choice of the Central Park rape as the crime to discuss and in his negative constructions of Black people and Black cultural products, but most significantly, in his cries for more regulation of Black discursive terrain. Ironically, a spurious link between rap and actual violence was the foundation for this cry. Will claimed that more control would benefit Black women, but the question of whose interests are served and who stands to benefit from

98 | Rap Music

Black containment typically elicits answers other than Black women.

Finally, Will accused liberals and corporations of participating in a pornography of violence for profit. However, news also is a marketable commodity, and an inspection of Will's article for signs of what was being sold there reveals that such accusations may also justifiably be leveled at him. For example, his decision to write about brutal violence, and to include graphic excerpts of the trial transcripts and lyrics, suggests that he himself was participating in this very commodification.

Rap coverage in the four months immediately following the Rodney King verdict and response was a second example in which representations of rap, rappers, and rap fans as the "bad other" seemed clearly linked to fears of a Black planet and the social discourse of containment. As I mentioned earlier, the three independent magazines made very similar decisions about when rap and rappers were newsworthy, and all concluded that hip hop culture was big news in the four months immediately following the Rodney King verdict and the Los Angeles response. A rapper, Sister Souljah, even made the cover of *Newsweek* in June 1992. I am not suggesting the publishers were malicious, nor do I subscribe to conspiracy theories. However, in the case of the articles appearing during that four-month period, the timing of this extensive coverage, even if it was coincidental, was of the essence. Through timing alone, rap once again was linked to controversy and violence, and was thus represented as the undesirable other.

The question of why the magazines decided to give rap such extensive coverage during those four months, and why the coverage would nearly disappear after August or September, is an interesting one. Most of the articles appearing during this period focused on (1) a comment about killing Whites that rapper Sister Souljah reportedly made at a convention of Jesse Jackson's Rainbow Coalition, or (2) Ice-T and a boycott of Time Warner proposed by police in response to the rapper's heavy-metal single *Cop Killer*. The reproaches leveled at these performers were not new: critics accused the musicians of condoning or inciting hatred and violence. In addition, several rap articles mentioned the Rodney King verdict and response. Typically such references explored the relationship between rap, the verdict, and the response.[99] Some articles spoke of rap presaging the events; others suggested it contributed to, orchestrated, or incited the insurgence. Just as George Will had done earlier, some journalists were suggesting the unlikely, namely that "bad" art was responsible for real-life events.

If we naturalize the news by saying it is merely about events and if we assume that the Souljah and Ice-T events just coincidentally happened in the wake of the verdict and response, then we lose sight of the role that the cultural process of selection plays in the reporting of news. However, if we assume that the Los Angeles response tapped the deep-seated White fears of which Tricia Rose spoke, then extensive coverage of controversies surrounding Black musicians and a Black cultural product is less puzzling, especially when the controversy included allegations of promoting or inciting hatred toward Whites and the police. A statement in *Time* by Doug Elder, a Houston police officer spearheading the boycott of Time Warner, not only reverberated with White fears but also constructed rappers (and perhaps rap fans) as the dangerous enemies, the evil outsiders in a mythic opposition of good against evil: "'You mix this [*Cop Killer*] with the summer, the violence and a little drugs, and they are going to unleash a reign of terror on communities all across this country.'"[100]

On August 4, 1992, Ice-T announced that he was withdrawing *Cop Killer*, a decision he reportedly made after employees of Warner Brothers Records, the subsidiary of Time Warner that had distributed *Cop Killer*, had received bomb or death threats.[101] If the controversy over this single is constructed as a standoff between the police and Ice-T, and if this standoff is viewed as a racist concretization of deep-structure myths, then the headlines "Ice-T Melts" and "The Ice-Man Concedeth" sent the message that "good" had prevailed over "evil."[102] The melting imagery obviously was a play on Ice-T's name; however, images of melting also send messages about power. The Wicked Witch in *The Wizard of Oz* lost her magical powers when she melted. When people melt, they are reduced, weakened, made invisible, or rendered impotent. Ice-T had not merely made a decision to withdraw a single; instead, according to the headlines, he had conceded and melted.

The *Newsweek* article reporting Ice-T's decision spoke of mounting fears that skittish corporations would exercise more internal control over future releases. The Time Warner corporate board, the article reported, "*is* demanding tighter control of what gets made."[103] Journalist John Leland expressed the concern that self censorship would stifle "controversial ideas before they can ever enter public debate."[104] Thus, limitations on discursive terrain, on published space, appeared to be a long-lasting outcome of one of the 1992 controversies. Such self censorship is significant because, as Tricia Rose maintains, control over the art form is a form of containment; self censorship is another manifestation of what Rose called the "institutional policing to which all rappers are subject."[105]

For the most part, 1992 coverage of rap ended with Ice-T's announcement. Rap once again was relegated to the "not-news" category, and the news gaze glanced elsewhere. Significantly, the tone of the two rap articles that appeared in the final months of 1992 was distinctly different from that of most others. One article constructed rap as an extraordinarily successful exportable commodity, and the other spoke largely of a new style, dancehall, that was said to be rapidly supplanting rap.[106] Both articles intimated that rap was on its way out.

When assessing whose interests were or were not served by the extensive coverage given to rap in the four months immediately following the King verdict and response, it is important to remember that news itself is a marketable commodity. Not only did these magazines link rap to violence and controversy, but the companies owning them profited from such representations, and thus, participated in their own version of what bell hooks calls "the commodification of Otherness."[107] There was potential for Time Warner to reap double benefits, first, from sales of *Cop Killer,* and, second, from sales of *Time* magazine's coverage of the controversy.

There was no indication that the magazines viewed themselves as being in any way responsible for the reduction in discursive terrain that was a promised result of the Ice-T controversy. Journalists rarely reflected on the role they, or the media in general, played in the perpetuation of specific representations of rap, rappers, or rap fans; furthermore, there was little or no discussion of the potential damage media representations may cause. Only one article, an interview with high school students, mentioned media representations of rap and hip hop culture. In this article, several high schoolers indicated that newspapers and other media, obsessed with controversy and negativity, have played a significant role in shaping rap's bad image.[108]

Theories on the Appeal of Controversial Rap to White Males

Before closing, let us consider a final related question: Why is explicit, controversial rap especially popular among White, middle-class suburban males? One theory is that stereotypical constructions of Blackness, prevalent in rap, help define Whiteness. According to this theory, consuming the "other," in this case listening to rap music, is a transgressive act, performed in defiance of dominant White norms. David Samuels writes, "Rap's appeal to Whites rested in its evocation of an age-old image of Blackness: a foreign, sexually charged, and criminal underworld against which the norms of White society are defined, and by extension, through which they may be defied."[109] Thus, for Whites, listening to rap may be an expression of adolescent rebellion and a symbol of opposition. A foray into Otherness, according to bell hooks, may be viewed by adolescents as a way out of alienation: "Masses of young people dissatisfied by U.S. imperialism, unemployment, lack of economic opportunity, afflicted by the postmodern malaise of alienation, no sense of grounding, no redemptive identity, can be manipulated by cultural strategies that offer Otherness as appeasement, particularly through commodification."[110]

Opinions have differed, however, about whether acts of transgression principally reinforce or challenge dominant power relations. Peter Stallybrass and Allon White, for example, argue that transgression tends to unravel dominant discourses: "Transgression becomes a kind of reverse or counter-sublimation, undoing the discursive hierarchies and stratifications of bodies and cultures which bourgeois society has produced as the mechanism of its symbolic dominance."[111] Another perspective is provided by hooks, who maintains that consuming otherness for pleasure is a means by which discourses of dominance are reinforced: "When race and ethnicity become commodified as resources for pleasure, the culture of specific groups, as well as the bodies of individuals, can be seen as constituting an alternative playground where members of dominating races, genders, sexual practices affirm their power over intimate relations with the Other."[112] To rebut the assumption that consuming rap is unproblematically counterhegemonic, Samuels points out that although Black music historically has been a "refuge from White middle-class boredom," in earlier times forays by Whites into Black music required face-to-face contact; with the advent of records and videos, Whites can now consume without contact.[113] One significant dimension of this no-touch mode of consumption is control; controversial rap can offer exciting, but safe, appearances of danger—semblances of street experience—to consumers who never leave the comfort of their suburban living rooms.[114] Media, to use Bakhtinian terminology, have enabled carnival to be transformed into spectacle, and this transformation alters power relations. Records and videos, thus, provide a vantage point similar to that offered by the nineteenth-century balcony, which, Stallybrass and White have observed, was a location from which the bourgeoisie "could both participate in the banquet of the streets and yet remain separated" from it and above it.[115]

Some scholars have indicated that fascination with the other is an inevitable consequence of binaries that construct otherness as evil, bad, or disgusting. For example, Stallybrass and White indicate that "disgust always bears the imprint of desire. These low domains, apparently expelled as 'Other,' return as the object of nostalgia, longing, and fascination."[116] Furthermore, these margins and sites of otherness may be viewed as growth plates, historically serving as sources of creativity from which the bourgeoisie have drawn sustenance.[117] The appeal of rap may thus be its imaginative, creative potential.

Finally, it may be argued that the text, which is what renders some rap controversial, is of little importance to many rap fans, who are drawn to the genre because of its strong, mesmerizing beat and its potential for dancing. Those who forward this explanation argue that White appeal is unrelated to rap's explicit texts and stereotypical representations of race. Perhaps no single factor accounts for rap's appeal to specific groups. However, the topic is an interesting one and merits much further consideration.

Conclusion

Through an analysis of *Time, Newsweek,* and *U.S. News,* I have explored how concretizations of deep-structure binaries and general characteristics of news reporting have constructed rap, rappers, and rap fans as the deviant, lacking, undesirable, or evil other. I have examined links between specific representations of hip hop culture and the perpetuation of dominant power relations along lines of race, social class, and gender. Specifically, I have explored how these representations were related to fears of a Black planet and to discourses of containment. Finally, I have suggested that the magazines themselves engaged in a commodification of otherness, as well as a commodification of violence, and that these news sources did not openly acknowledge their own role as participants in the construction of representations that tend to perpetuate hegemony. In revealing some of the weaknesses of these magazines' coverage of rap, I have also pointed to drawbacks of relying heavily on such media for information about the genre. Like it or not, however, the general media are educating all of us, and television, newspapers, and magazines may be the sole sources of information about rap for a large portion of the population.

Learning about rap from second-hand sources such as the general news media, given the prevalence of the myth that news reporting is objective, presents a special array of problems for educators. These problems may be particularly serious if media information substitutes for actual experience with the genre. As I mentioned at the outset, some circles are urging educators to become more rap literate and to include rap in official school knowledge. Ironically, however, current goals and conventions of news reporting appear to result in media representations that may bolster narrow beliefs about what constitutes legitimate school knowledge and fuel suspicion of popular culture. Because these magazines' representations are in many respects problematic, educators need to subject them to the "fierce critical interrogations" of which bell hooks speaks, especially as they make decisions about whether and how to include rap in the school curriculum. These fierce critical interrogations are of paramount importance, not only as an essential ingredient when consuming entertainment, but also, as we have seen here, when we consume the news.

NOTES

1. Precisely dating the inception of rap is difficult, especially because the genre has many closely related antecedents; twenty years is a conservative estimate of its age. "Rap Records: Are They Fad or Permanent?" *Billboard*, 16 February 1980, 57, said rap was at least seven years old in 1980. Phil Hardy and David Lang, in "Rap," *Encyclopedia of Rock* (New York: Macmillan, 1988), 360, indicated that one of the originators of rap, D.J. Kool, moved to New York City from Jamaica in 1967.

2. John Leland, "When Rap Meets Reggae," *Newsweek*, 7 September 1992, 59.

3. For interesting work on the relationship between popular culture and education, see Henry Giroux and Peter McLaren, eds., *Critical Pedagogy, the State, and Cultural Struggle* (Albany: SUNY Press, 1989).

4. John Fiske, *Television Culture* (New York: Routledge, 1987), 282, 283.

5. See, for example, bell hooks, *Yearning: Race, Gender, and Cultural Politics* (Boston: South End Press, 1990), 73 and 220.

6. bell hooks, *Black Looks: Race and Representation* (Boston: South End Press, 1992), 2.

7. Ibid., 7, 5.

8. Fiske, 131–134. Diana Fuss, "Inside/Out," in *Inside/Out: Lesbian Theories, Gay Theories,* ed. Diana Fuss (New York: Routledge, 1991), 1–3.

9. Ibid., 132.

10. Fiske, 134.

11. Fuss, 2.

12. Ibid., 1.

13. Fiske, 282–283.

14. Ibid., 281, 285, 288.

15. Ibid., 282–293.

16. Ibid., 283.

17. Ibid., 286–287.

18. Ibid., 287.

19. Ibid., 291–293.

20. Ibid., 284.

21. Ibid., 291.

22. *Information Please Almanac: Atlas and Yearbook, 1993,* 46th ed. (Boston: Houghton Mifflin, 1993), 310.

23. Fiske, 282.

24. Ibid.

25. In *Time,* six of seven 1992 articles were published after the L.A. response, and five of seven appeared in the four-month window. This within-window count did not

include an article appearing in the May 4, 1992, issue. Although the date of the issue technically qualified the article, I assumed the issue went to press before the verdict. In *Newsweek* five of six were published after the L.A. response. All three 1992 *U.S. News* articles appeared in the window.

26. Michael W. Apple, *Ideology and Curriculum* (London: Routledge & Kegan Paul, 1979), 6.

27. In twenty-five of the thirty-nine articles, discussions appeared in a classification other than arts/music. Eleven of twenty *Newsweek* articles were not in music/arts, and nine of fourteen *Time* articles appeared elsewhere.

28. Fiske, 287.

29. Jerry Adler, "The Rap Attitude," *Newsweek,* 19 March 1990, 58.

30. George F. Will, "America's Slide into the Sewer," *Newsweek,* 30 July 1990, 64. Early performances of *Rite of Spring* prompted riots.

31. One obvious example of this resistance is negative response to feminist musicologist Susan McClary's ground-breaking analyses and deconstructions of opera and symphonic music. For a scathing assessment of McClary, see Pieter C. Van Den Toorn, "Politics, Feminism, and Contemporary Music Theory," *Journal of Musicology* 9, no. 3 (Summer 1991): 275–299.

32. "Should Dirty Lyrics Be Against the Law?" *U.S. News and World Report,* 25 June 1990, 24. See also, Adler, 57; and John Leland, "The Iceman Concedeth," *Newsweek,* 10 August 1992, 51, for discussions of this censorship dilemma.

33. Peter Plagens, "Mixed Signals on Obscenity: Mapplethorpe Passes but 2 Live Crew Doesn't," *Newsweek,* 15 October 1990, 74.

34. Pierre Bourdieu, *Distinction: A Social Critique of the Judgement of Taste,* trans. Richard Nice (Cambridge: Harvard, 1984).

35. Jay Cocks, "Rap Around the Globe," *Time,* 19 October 1992, 70.

36. David Gates, "Decoding Rap Music," *Newsweek,* 19 March 1990, 60.

37. Ibid., 60.

38. Jay Cocks, "A Nasty Jolt for the Top Pops," *Time,* 1 July 1991, 78.

39. David E. Thigpen, "Not for Men Only," *Time,* 27 May 1991, 71.

40. Adler, 56.

41. Will, 64.

42. See Adler, 56; David Gates, "The Importance of Being Nasty," *Newsweek,* 2 July 1990, 52; and John Leland, "Rap and Race," *Newsweek,* 29 June 1992, 48, for examples of discussion of success.

43. Janice L. Simpson, "The Impresario of Rap," *Time,* 4 May 1992, 69.

44. See, for example, Jay Cocks, "U Can't Touch Him," *Time,* 13 August 1990, 73; Sally B. Donnelly, "The Fire Around the Ice," *Time,* 22 June 1992, 68; Bill Barol, "The Kings of Rap, Together," *Newsweek,* 29 June 1987, 71; and Gates, "Decoding," 60.

45. Gates, "The Importance," 52; Donnelly, 68.

46. Gates, "Decoding," 61.

47. Donnelly, 68.

48. Gates, "Decoding," 60.

49. Adler, 56.

50. Simpson, 69; Donnelly, 66 and 68; and Leland, "Rap and Race," 49.

51. Michael Kinsley, " Ice-T: Is the Issue Social Responsibility . . . ," *Time,* 20 July 1992, 88.

52. Simpson, 69.

53. John Leland, "Number One with a Bullet," *Newsweek,* 1 July 1991, 63.

54. Jack E. White, "Sister Souljah: Capitalist Tool," *Time,* 29 June 1992, 88.

55. N.W.A.'s Eazy-E reportedly "contributed $1,000 to join the Republican Senatorial Inner Circle"; see Leland, "Number," 63.

56. Leland, "Rap and Race," 52.

57. For discussions indicating the shift occurred in the middle of the 1980s, see Barol, 71; and David Gates, "Play That Packaged Music," *Newsweek,* 3 December 1990, 68. Jay Cocks, "Chilling Out on Rap Flash," *Time,* 21 March 1983, 73, talked about rappers sometimes performing for mostly white audiences in 1981, and Donnelly, 68, said Ice-T held performances for "mostly white crowds" as early as 1982.

58. Gates, "Decoding," 60.

59. For discussions of the popularity of controversial rap with White audiences, see, for example, Gates, "Decoding," 61; and Cocks, "A Nasty Jolt," 78.

60. Cocks, "A Nasty Jolt," 79.

61. John Leland, "The Word on the Street Is Heard in the Beat," *Newsweek,* 11 May 1992, 53.

62. For example, Gates, "Play," 68.

63. Simpson, 69.

64. Leland, "Rap and Race," 51.

65. Cocks, "A Nasty Jolt," 78.

66. Ibid.

67. John Leo, "Polluting Our Popular Culture," *U.S. News and World Report,* 2 July 1990, 15.

68. Ibid.

69. Ibid.

70. Gates, "The Importance," 52.

71. Adler, 59.

72. Ibid.

73. Will, 64.

74. Adler, 57.

75. See correspondence from Henry C. Eichelmann in "Letters" *Newsweek*, 9 April 1990, 13. Ironically, the same issue included several letters from irate rap fans who charged that Leo had treated rap unfairly.

76. For discussions of opposition to rap from Black people, see Leo, "Polluting," 15; Gates, "The Importance," 52; John Leo, "Rap Music's Toxic Fringe," *U.S. News and World Report*, 29 June 1992, 19; Gates, "Decoding," 60; and Will, 64; shunning of rap by Black radio stations also is mentioned in Leland, "Rap and Race," 48.

77. hooks, *Black Looks*, 34.

78. DC Talk's link to Jerry Falwell is reported in Steve Rabey, "Rhymin' and Rappin' 4D King," *Christianity Today*, 24 June 1991, 13.

79. Leo, "Rap Music's," 19; and "The Lowdown on Hip-Hop: Kids Talk About the Music," *Newsweek*, 29 June 1992, 50.

80. Leo, "Rap Music's," 19.

81. Leo, "Polluting," 15.

82. Donnelly, 66.

83. Adler, 57.

84. Ibid., 56.

85. Thigpen, 72.

86. Leland, "Rap and Race," 49.

87. Leland, "Iceman," 51.

88. Fiske, 285–286.

89. Ibid., 286.

90. Tricia Rose, "'Fear of a Black Planet': Rap Music and Black Cultural Politics in the 1990s," *Journal of Negro Education* 60, no. 3 (1991), 277.

91. Ibid., 279.

92. Ibid., 283–284, 289.

93. Will, 64.

94. Ibid.

95. Ibid.

96. Ibid.

97. Ibid.

98. hooks, *Yearning*, 73.

99. For discussions of the relationship between the Los Angeles response and rap, see, for example, Leland, "The Word," 52–53; Leland, "Rap and Race," 48, 52; Leo,

"Rap Music's," 19; and Mortimer B. Zuckerman, "The Sister Souljah Affair," *U.S. News and World Report,* 29 June 1992, 80.

100. Donnelly, 66.

101. *Newsweek* said there were bomb threats (see Leland, "Iceman," 50); *Time* said there were death threats (see "Ice-T Melts," *Time,* 10 August 1992, 23).

102. "Ice-T Melts," 23; and Leland, "Iceman," 50.

103. Leland, "Iceman," 51.

104. Ibid.

105. Rose, 276.

106. Cocks, "Rap Around," 70–71; and Leland, "When Rap," 59.

107. hooks, *Black Looks,* 21.

108. "The Lowdown," 50–51.

109. David Samuels, "The Rap on Rap," *New Republic,* 11 November 1991, 25.

110. hooks, *Black Looks,* 25.

111. Peter Stallybrass and Allon White, *The Politics and Poetics of Transgression* (Ithaca: Cornell, 1986), 200–201.

112. hooks, *Black Looks,* 23.

113. Samuels, 29.

114. Hank Shocklee, quoted in Samuels, discusses the role of control in this danger-at-a-distance mentality. See Samuels, 29.

115. Stallybrass and White, 126.

116. Ibid., 191.

117. Ibid., 21.

·3·

UNHAPPY HAPPY ENDINGS

Cultural Politics in the Broadway Musical Hit
Once on This Island *(1997; revised 2001)*

While visiting San Francisco a couple of years ago, I was invited by a favorite cousin and his partner to be their guest for an evening at the theater. They suggested a musical: *Once on This Island.* I hadn't seen a musical in nearly twenty years, even though I had loved them as a child, and I jumped at the chance. As the curtain opened, childhood pleasures returned; I was transported by the beauty of the sets, the spirited dancing, and the lively music.

As the evening progressed, however, I was pulled in several directions. On the one hand, the performance was wonderful; the music and scenery invited me to indulge in sheer escapism. On the other hand, I felt increasing discomfort stemming from the politics being played out on stage, most especially the gender politics. "Twenty years have changed the way I read musicals," I thought when I realized I wasn't having quite as good a time as I had hoped. As my discomfort increased, I glanced at others in the audience, most of whom were White, well-heeled and apparently from the middle class, and wondered, "What is going on in their heads?" In particular, I (a White, middle-class, straight female) took a sidelong glance at my cousin (a White, middle-class, gay male) and his partner (a Black, middle-class, gay male); I recognize that these descriptors do not necessarily predict a person's politics, but I nevertheless found it ironic that we were three "others," consuming presumably for pleasure a glorification of oppressive values, some of the very values that contribute in complex ways to our oppression. My sense of discomfort peaked when, as we stepped out of the theater, my cousin turned to me and asked, "Well, what did you [the "expert" musician of the family] think of it?"

That night in San Francisco has haunted me. Recognizing the central and noncontroversial role that musicals tend to play in the school curriculum, I set out to better understand what it was about this musical that led to my ambivalence. What has resulted is a close, oppositional reading of *Once on This Island*. This reading compares the musical to the novel upon which it is based, Rosa Guy's *My Love, My Love, or The Peasant Girl*. I argue that through omissions, additions, and subtle changes in emphasis, the race and class politics of the novel are transformed. Furthermore, the problematic gender politics of Guy's novel are enhanced in the musical. I contend that several additional texts, both visual and auditory, assist in moving the musical onto different political turf than that occupied by the novel. These transformations do not depoliticize the musical; rather, they move it onto less controversial political terrain. Finally, I discuss a few of the issues this analysis raises for educators. I recognize that what I present is not the only viable reading of either *Once on This Island* or of *My Love, My Love;* however, I believe it is an important reading, given the central role musicals play in official school musical knowledge.

The Musical as Official School Knowledge

Musicals have a time-honored place in the school music curriculum. Although some aficionados of high art may reject all popular genres, most music teachers embrace musicals—or at the very least tolerate them—while other popular genres, such as rap and country, remain off limits as legitimate curricular content. In some elementary schools children are taught listening skills and concert etiquette through field trips to matinee performances of musicals. Secondary general music textbooks have routinely included excerpts from musicals, and some of these texts guide students though the composition and performance of their own shows. Selections from musicals are standard fare in middle and high school choruses, and the annual production of a musical is an integral part of the choral curriculum in many high schools.

Perhaps contributing to the perception that musicals warrant a place in official school knowledge is the commonsense belief that they are, for the most part, "safe" entertainment. Although flaps may arise occasionally over salty language or sexually explicit scenes, few musicals severely test middle-class sensibilities. Furthermore, the musical as a genre, unlike many other types of dramatic productions, has generally been considered apolitical, escapist entertainment. If we assume, however, that no dimension of culture is politically neutral or value free, then even the most "noncontroversial" musical draws from discourses, or systems of thought, that are based on socially constructed aesthetic, moral, and political values. Indeed, those cultural artifacts appearing to be value free, noncontroversial, or commonsensical may be the very sites where the most significant ideological work is done, including work on issues pertaining to race, social class, gender, and power.

There is little doubt but that *Once on This Island* is widely considered to be "safe" fare. One reviewer described it as good family entertainment; the *Boston Globe* called it a "syncopated kids' show."[1] When the musical came to my community, promoters capitalized on this point, newspaper advertisements claiming that *Once* is a "delightful musical for the whole family."[2] A local newspaper even sponsored an essay contest for school children, and the two children to write the best essay beginning with the phrase "Once on this island" received free tickets to the performance.[3] I noticed an unusually large number of children in the audience at the local presentation; their presence suggested that the family-entertainment promotional approach had worked.

Perhaps because musicals are often dismissed as safe "light" entertainment, more aligned with popular culture than with high art, little work examining the cultural politics of musicals has yet been undertaken either by music educators or musicologists. A few scholars, notably Susan McClary and Catherine Clément, have examined gender politics in high art musical drama, however.[4] McClary notes that for the most part critical analysis, specifically feminist criticism, has not yet made inroads into musicology.[5] Similarly, educators such as Michael Apple have explored the cultural politics of legitimate school knowledge, specifically the relationships between knowledge and power.[6] However, the work of critical sociologists in education has never been incorporated into published discussions of musicals. Thus, this essay is a beginning.

Any number of examples from the standard repertoire could have been an excellent choice for a critical analysis of cultural politics; however, I decided to focus on *Once on This Island,* not only because of my recent experiences with it, but also because it is a relatively new work. While the gender politics of the old chestnuts may, indeed, reflect dominant thinking of a past era, a recent musical, in theory, should represent someone's current thinking.

Once on This Island's *Background*

Once on This Island is a widely acclaimed Broadway hit and has been ranked among the best of recent musicals. Nominated for eight Tony Awards, including Best Musical, Book and Score, *Once* was first produced in 1990 and is listed in the Burns Mantle Theater Yearbook as one of the ten best plays of that year.[7] The plot is derived from prizewinning author Rosa Guy's novel *My Love, My Love,* which was written in 1985. Guy, in turn, fashioned her novel after Hans Christian Andersen's fairy tale "The Little Mermaid." Guy, who is Black, was born in Trinidad and raised in New York City. The musical's lyrics and book were written by Emmy-award-winner Lynn Ahrens; Stephen Flaherty composed the music. Both Ahrens and Flaherty are White.

Once on This Island is considered more overtly political than most examples from this genre because it addresses the issue of race. According to the libretto, it is "based on the cultural, religious and racial divisions found in Haiti between the mulatto ruling class and the dark-skinned, rural peasants."[8] Featuring an all-Black cast and set on an unnamed island in the Antilles, the musical tells of star-crossed lovers separated by skin color and social class. The heroine, Ti Moune, is a beautiful, dark-skinned peasant woman whose life is altered irrevocably when she happens upon an automobile accident in which a lighter-skinned young heir has been injured. She falls in love with the handsome young man, Daniel, and when it appears he will die of his injuries, she offers the gods her own life in exchange for his. As Ti Moune nurses Daniel back to health, the couple appears to fall in love; however, ultimately Daniel rejects Ti Moune, bypassing her in marriage for Andrea, a light-skinned woman of his own social class. Ti Moune briefly considers revenge, but she cannot bring herself to harm her lover. Instead, the gods guide her into the sea, where she drowns. At the end of the musical, she is magically reincarnated as a beautiful tree that shelters and blesses her lover and his new family. Her act of personal sacrifice, which is described as a triumph of love over death, breaks the island's curse of race/class division.

Race and Class Politics

Although my principal interest is to examine constructions of gender, I begin with a brief discussion of racial and class politics because I believe it will help provide a context for my gender analysis. Issues of race and class are woven into both the novel and the musical and are the most overtly political dimensions of the plot's cultural politics. In both artifacts, problems with race/class relations are attributed to a curse that the White French colonist Armand invoked upon his mulatto son, born out of wedlock, when the son fought against his father to liberate the island.[9] Both sources represent race/class barriers as formidable, and both use gates and walls to symbolize these apparently insurmountable barriers. However, decisions by lyricist Ahrens concerning which dimensions of Guy's novel to emphasize and which to ignore, together with composer Flaherty's decisions on how specific scenes would be portrayed musically, contribute to subtle but significant changes in some dimensions of the plot.

Guy is a master of detail, skillfully spelling out the differences in living conditions between the rich, lighter-skinned upper class and the poor, dark-skinned peasants. This attention to the intricate and subtle particulars of race/class relations was not incorporated into the musical, however. The latter capitalizes on the theme of different worlds coexisting on the island,[10] and it borrows some of the book's symbols of social class—for example, machines as a sign of wealth and bare feet as an indicator of poverty, but it does not underscore the misery of the oppressed.

Several reviewers point out that race/class relations are central to the plot, one critic observing, "There's a political and social subtext underlying the surface romance."[11] A few also mentioned the fact that the entire cast is Black; these reviewers may have considered this casting to be a political statement.[12] (Without a doubt, a musical's all-White cast would not receive special comment.) Michael Feingold of the *Village Voice* called the musical's portrayal of class enmity "startling."[13] However, by ignoring detail, the musical's creators failed to adequately flesh out the consequences of existing race/class relations. The reality that changes in race/class politics may have occurred in the plot's transformation from novel to musical is supported by a comment from director/choreographer Graciela Daniele, quoted in the *Chicago Tribune.* Daniele stated that from a political standpoint *Once on This Island* is categorically different from *Dangerous Games,* an earlier production on which she had worked: "'That [*Dangerous Games*] was a political show,' Daniele said. '*Once on This Island* is something else, something very innocent and beautiful.'"[14]

Representing Peasants

One significant difference between the novel and the musical can be seen in their portrayals of peasants: the musical pictures them as happy. For example, it uses a flashy upbeat opening number to quickly lay out the implications for peasants of race/class relations.[15] Unlike readers of the novel, theatergoers are not schooled in the reality that hunger drives peasants to eat the seeds that should have been reserved for planting.[16] The musical does not describe the distended bellies of poor undernourished children, nor does it tell of how peasant food crops wither in times of drought while wealthy landowners selfishly irrigate only their own rich soil.[17] Other realities slipped by quickly and were nearly obliterated beneath a glaze of upbeat "calypso-reggae" music.

Primitive, ignorant, and wild are other descriptions found in the musical but not in Guy's novel; these changes in characterization of peasantry are directly related to cultural politics surrounding class and race. Guy briefly discusses widely held religious beliefs on the island and describes how the will of the gods affects the lives of the island's people; Ahrens gives far greater emphasis to these beliefs and accents their "primitive" aspects. Religious belief, some may argue, is in itself a sign of "primitivism," especially when the belief is in non-Judeo-Christian gods. A line from the musical reinforces such a link between religious belief and primitivism; Andrea, Daniel's wealthy fiancée, reports what she has heard about Ti Moune: "Some girls are saying / She's simple as any child . . . Barefoot and praying, / And running the halls quite wild."[18]

In addition the musical's peasants worship temperamental gods. They pray often to these gods, appealing to them to grant wishes; they try to read the gods' moods and dance to appease the gods' anger.[19] Significantly, the peasants are pictured as mere pawns to the gods. Ti Moune suggests, for example, that her rescue from a storm as a child was part of the gods' divine plan or mission for her life: "Oh gods, oh gods, / You saved my life for a reason / And now, I think I know why!"[20]

Another line from the musical claims that Ti Moune was "sent on a journey by the gods . . . that would test the strength of love."[21] The helplessness of humans in the hands of the gods is underscored by a scene in the musical in which the gods decide what events will transpire in Ti Moune's future; in this scene the gods plan the initial meeting between Ti Moune and Daniel.[22] Significantly, there is no similar scene in Guy's novel. Thus, the musical, more than the novel, pictures life's events as being beyond human agency. Critic Dan Hulbert, of the *Atlanta Constitution,* confirms this characterization, claiming that "the characters are pawns in a struggle between the Goddess of Love and the Demon of Death."[23] Although the gods are not unimportant in the novel, Guy always leaves the door open to the possibility that life's events result from human action. For example, the book is never clear about whether the goddess of love, Erzulie, really intervened on Ti Moune's part or whether this intervention was a figment of Ti Moune's imagination.[24] Although in the novel Ti Moune claims that the gods sent her to Daniel, Guy adds ambiguously, "Désirée no longer knew what was real and what imagined. She no longer knew if she ascribed to the gods words plucked her from [sic] dreams. She had come to believe her desires were the command of the gods."[25] When the gods do talk among themselves in the novel, they say they will put the people of the island to a test to determine whether people "can be responsible for each other."[26] Thus, choice remains with the people; Guy's novel is not merely about Ti Moune being "sent on a journey by the gods . . . that would test the strength of love"; it is also an important story about people's responsibility for their actions toward one another. In the musical's portrayal of the powerful gods, this latter message is largely lost, however.

In addition to losing agency to the gods, the peasants of the musical also lose wisdom. Significantly, the principal source of wisdom in Guy's novel is the peasants, themselves, even though the wealthy regard them as ignorant.[27] Peasants utter profound observations and offer practical advice—survival tactics—to compeers.[28] This is not generally the case in the musical, however, where the gods are given nearly all the notable lines. David Richards of the *New York Times* confirmed my own observations: "The gods, however, most caught my fancy, perhaps because what passes for wit and wisdom in this piece falls primarily to them."[29]

In addition to sharing wisdom with one another, most of the peasants in Guy's novel show compassion toward each other. For example, on the journey to the city, Ti Moune receives generous gifts from vendors, including food and clothing.[30] This caring attitude contrasts with the grands hommes' cruel and horrifying disregard for peasants. One example of this disregard occurs when Daniel's father comes by airplane to fetch his injured son but does not invite the elderly peasant Ton Ton Julian, who has risked his life to deliver the news of the son's whereabouts, to ride along; thus, wading through thigh-deep mud, Julian makes the long and arduous trip back to his village on foot.[31] Daniel's father shows an appalling lack of gratitude, immediately blaming the peasants for his son's illness and failing to acknowledge that they probably had saved Daniel's life.[32] Ti Moune describes the inability of the rich to regard "others" as human beings as a kind of blindness. On two occasions, Daniel's father looks through Ti Moune without seeing her, once when he comes by airplane to fetch his son, and again, after she has spent the night with Daniel.[33] Daniel, himself, looks through Ti Moune without seeing her when he casts coins into the crowd immediately after his wedding.[34] The poor are deemed property to be owned by the rich and used at will. A remark from Andrea, Daniel's fiancée, concerning Ti Moune exemplifies this point: "Daniel, how lovely. Never have I seen such a beautiful black girl. Can we keep her?"[35]

The haughty contempt the wealthy show toward the poor is not completely eliminated in the musical; for example, *Once* borrows the novel's idea that the manner in which rich people recklessly pilot fast cars down peasant-filled roads shows wanton disregard for the lives of peasants.[36] By and large, however, the musical downplays the cruelty of the grands hommes, and in addition, it disregards peasant compassion.

Wildness or exoticism is yet another element of the musical's racialized characterization of peasantry. Uninhibited sexuality is one element of this exoticism. The dancing is particularly suggestive and includes sinewy hip swaying, splayed legs, and other stock movements that have come to be associated with both "primitivism" and sexuality. One critic writes, "The 11-member cast doesn't move from place to place. It undulates. No hip remains unswiveled for long, no pelvis goes unrotated."[37] Ti Moune is invited to dance at a high-society ball. Unlike the restrained upper-class women (in the words of the musical's stage directions) she "dances without inhibition. in [sic] the peasant style."[38] The throbbing drums that often accompany peasant dancing contrast with the "civilized" waltzes of the grand hotel scenes.

This element of the musical's representation of the exoticized other draws on White fantasies, fascinations, and fears concerning Black sexuality. bell hooks comments on stereotypical White perceptions of Blackness, remarking that Whites have often believed that "non-white people had more life experience, were more worldly, sensual, and sexual because they were different."[39] Toni Morrison's observations about White authors' representations of Blackness also are applicable. Morrison notes that an imagined Africanist persona has often been used by White writers "to articulate and imaginatively act out the forbidden in American culture."[40] According to Morrison, the creation of this persona "is reflexive; an extraordinary meditation on the self; a powerful exploration of the fears and desires that reside in the writerly conscious. It is an astonishing revelation of longing, of terror, of perplexity, of shame, of magnanimity."[41] In the musical *Once on This Island* the personae created by the White team of Ahrens and Flaherty are subtly but significantly different from those created by the Black author Guy; these representations of Blackness also help to construct Whiteness.

Exonerating and Exscribing Whites

In addition to presenting a somewhat muted vision of the island's race/class politics concerning peasants, the musical tends to exonerate Whites. The race/class politics are represented largely as problems among Blacks rather than as the result of White presence on the island. Both the book and the musical suggest that racial division is a critical social issue and both trace the island's curse back to White French rule. However, at least in the case of the musical, the curse is not necessarily regarded as a consequence of this rule, but rather as the result of a particular situation: a mulatto son turning his allegiance away from his White father. Thus, White participation in the creation of a racial hierarchy that values light skin over dark is not directly addressed. A statement by Ahrens and Flaherty, which says the musical deals with "prejudice *within the race* [my emphasis],"[42] exemplifies a disregard for the role played by racist White colonial values. Failing to implicate Whites may contribute to good feelings among White theatergoers, whose vision of themselves as just and equitable is likely to go unchallenged, but it paints an incomplete picture of the island's racial dynamics. Haiti's hierarchy, in which the lightest-skinned people garner the lion's share of power and wealth, is modeled after White colonialism and repeatedly has been supported by U.S. foreign policy. For example, U.S. Marine occupation of Haiti early in the twentieth century strengthened the power of the island's elite mulatto class. The reality that Whites have been key players in the creation and maintenance of the island's racial hierarchy is largely overlooked in the musical.

The musical also ignores Guy's commentary on the effects of colonial greed on the land and its resources, once again exonerating principal participants. Haiti faces hurricanes and droughts. The musical emphasizes the island's natural disasters and represents peasants as being at the mercy of them,[43] but it eliminates Guy's sensitivity to the reality that not all "natural" disasters in developing countries are natural (or at least unavoidable). Guy emphasizes the consequences for the island's poorest and darkest people of colonists' greed, as well as the deleterious effects of colonial agricultural practices.[44] It is possible that raping the land and depleting its natural resources, neither of which brought benefits to the peasants, helped to effect climatic changes that increased the severity of the so-called natural disasters. As educator Michael Apple points out, masking the role that human involvement can play in determining the severity and consequences of "natural" disasters is quite common in Western discourse concerning developing nations.[45] Communication arts specialist John Fiske states that Western news reporting tends to portray disaster as the norm in developing countries:

> Third World countries are . . . conventionally represented in western news as places of famines and natural disaster, of social revolution, and of political corruption. These events are not seen as disrupting their social norms, but as confirming ours, confirming our dominant sense that western democracies provide the basics of life for everyone. . . . When deviations from these norms occur in our own countries they are represented as precisely that, deviations from the norm: in Third World countries, however, such occurrences are represented as their norms which differ markedly from ours.[46]

Thus, through the shift in emphasis just described, the musical reinforces dominant Western understandings of life in developing countries in ways that Guy's book does not and promotes dominant Western visions both of the self and the other.

Another dimension of Guy's book that was disregarded in the musical is the role played by the police in perpetuating divisions based on race and class; a related subject—peasant fear of police brutality—also is almost completely ignored. In several places Guy's novel vividly illustrates peasant fear of the police, the centrality of the police as the enforcing arm of power, and violence against peasants at the hands of the police.[47] As we shall see later, for example, police brutality plays a significant role in the ending to Guy's novel. By contrast, the police are mentioned only once in the musical; in this instance, the peasants, upon discovering the injured Daniel, are debating whether they should intervene, and Ton Ton Julian remarks, "If this boy dies in our hands, the rich will send police!"[48] The passage slips by quickly, however, and the musical fails to explain why peasants would not want the police called in.

Before turning to the musical's constructions of gender, let us consider a final issue concerning race. In the introduction to the libretto, Ahrens and Flaherty write, "We think the power of the story has a great deal to do with the issue of prejudice within the race, as well as with issues of wealth and class."[49] They urge future companies to follow their casting directives and, presumably, to use an all-Black cast in which shades of Blackness signify social-class status. However, they also acknowledge that "casting difficulties" may arise and, thus, they allow textual alterations in order to accommodate "interracial" productions.[50] The recommended textual alterations remove all reference to race from the musical. Therefore, some performances may erase the issue of race. Indeed, at the second performance I attended, although the entire cast was Black, differences in skin color between the two classes were not marked; skin color did not serve as a constant reminder that race, specifically Whiteness or lightness, played a significant role in the creation of an unjust and cruel social hierarchy.

Constructing Gender

In many respects the musical's constructions of gender mirror those in Guy's novel. In the process of borrowing elements from "The Little Mermaid," Guy appropriated specific understandings of gender, understandings that dominate among the White middle class and play an integral role in the continued oppression of all women. In the next portion of this essay, I examine the musical's representation of female desire and analyze its construction of femininity. In addition I examine how the decision to replace the novel's tragic ending with a supposedly happier one transforms the plot's gender politics. Third, I briefly consider some possible meanings the musical may embody concerning love and responsibility; specifically, I explore how these understandings may be gendered. Finally, I discuss political implications of the attempted universalization of culturally specific constructions of gender.

Female Desire

Desire is one of the focal points of the plot; the character Ti Moune exemplifies and embodies specific dominant constructions of feminine desire. "Ti Moune" is the orphan Désirée Dieu-Donné's nickname, her given name meaning "God-given desire," and the orphan's desires are many. In the opening scenes of the musical, for example, Ti Moune is restless and desires adventure; in the song "Waiting for Life to Begin" she dreams of life's possibilities. Upward mobility, symbolized by a racing automobile that would carry her far from her peasant existence, captures her attention. The musical highlights this desire, as well as Ti Moune's longing for romance leading to true love; Ti Moune sings, "My stranger! One day you'll arrive / Your car will stop / And in I'll hop / And off we'll drive!"[51] Once she meets the injured Daniel, she is obsessed by a desire to be with him always and to care for him. In the novel she sets out to find Daniel, once he has been returned to his family, because she is concerned about his welfare and senses that he remains close to death; in the musical, however, she is portrayed as merely following her heart's desire, claiming "[M]y dreams are there."[52] Indeed, being with Daniel becomes her fondest desire: "Daniel is my happiness," Ti Moune announces;[53] knowing he is there is all she needs.[54] Because the plot focuses on Ti Moune's devotion to Daniel, Ti Moune is represented as a woman in love and not less favorably, for example, as a woman who attempts to elevate her social status via a relationship with a powerful man. As her relationship with Daniel deepens, she dreams of marriage and domesticity. Her mind fills with images of a vine-covered cottage as she explains to him, "And our little house will have pink walls, and a blue roof, and a / tree in the garden just like the one that sheltered me as a child. / And you and I will lie in the shade of the tree. And our children / will climb in it. And it will bloom for us forever."[55]

Romance, love, a monogamous relationship in marriage, settling down in a vine-covered cottage, attending to a husband, having children, and (in the bargain) raising one's social status via marriage are stock-in-trade elements of dominant understandings of female desire, understandings that are steeped in issues of race, class, and ethnicity. Indeed, Ti Moune's desires were shared by countless ideal ladies portrayed in nineteenth-century American fiction for women, as well as by a long succession of heroines from recent musicals. Significantly, however, although White heroines of musical fame, including Maria in *The Sound of Music* and Eliza Dolittle in *My Fair Lady,* successfully achieve their goals, including upward mobility through romance, Ti Moune, a Black woman, is denied her goal. The impossibility of her dreams is underscored by the musical's costuming, which contrasts sharply with descriptions of Ti Moune's attire in the novel. In the novel, Ti Moune's transformation into a lady, once she has entered into a relationship with Daniel, is complete; her appearance at a high-society ball resembles Eliza Dolittle's introduction to her new social circle in *My Fair Lady.* Guy writes, "Désirée was now a lady whom all had to admire,"[56] and gives a detailed description of the gorgeous Ti Moune in her elegant ballroom attire:

> Her dress of white satin contrasted sharply with her black skin. . . . Her glowing hair had been pulled back into an elegant bun at the back of her head. Her shoes were delicate straps strung together to encompass her wide feet and covered with rhinestones. The couturières had indeed completed the magnificent work of art that nature had intended.[57]

Like Eliza Dolittle, Ti Moune makes a dramatic grand entrance; she is adulated by the foreign guests.

In *Once on This Island,* by contrast, Ti Moune wears a dress that clearly identifies her as a peasant. In addition, she is barefoot while the other guests wear shoes; as I mentioned earlier, shoes are a sign of class status in this story. Thus, the costuming underscores the immensity of the social gap, Ti Moune's outsider status, and the impossibility of her fulfilling her fondest desires.

Feminist theorist Rosalind Coward has observed that female desires are neither natural nor inevitable.[58] Furthermore, specific constructions are closely linked to dominant power relations. The question of who tends to benefit from dominant constructions of female desire is a valid one; as Coward points out, "Our [women's] desire sustains us, but it also sustains a way of living which may not ultimately be the best and only way for women."[59] Obviously, desires are not in a woman's best interest if they lead to her death; however, many feminists would argue that had Ti Moune lived and fulfilled her dreams, her life may not have been a happy one, either, given the limited scope of her desires. The musical portrays Ti Moune's desires as appropriate and potentially beneficial, however. Ti Moune's adoptive mother offers a cautionary word to the young woman: "Choose your dreams with care,"[60] advice that many feminists would heartily applaud. Apparently, the advice fell on deaf ears.

Ideal Femininity

Ti Moune is young, beautiful, infantilized, nurturant, and self-sacrificing; thus, she exhibits characteristics consistent with dominant, White, middle-class, Euro-American ideals of femininity. Let us consider each of these characteristics more closely. First, consistent with traditional constructions of woman that emphasize physical appearance, Ti Moune is repeatedly described as beautiful.[61] In the novel one of her primary concerns about embarking on the journey to find Daniel, once he has been returned to his family, is that the rigors of travel may destroy her looks.[62] Physical beauty is thus represented as valuable capital for women; in Ti Moune's case, because race and class do not assist her, it is perhaps her most precious asset. Second, Ti Moune is infantilized. In the musical one of the gods, Asaka, calls her a "pretty little girl"; Daniel, too, refers to her in these terms.[63] A song entitled "Some Girls," which describes differences between two stereotypical categories of women, similarly infantilizes all women.[64]

A third attribute displayed by the idealized Ti Moune is nurturance. Ti Moune is the caretaker, a mother figure whose life revolves around nursing the sick Daniel back to health. Guy describes taking care of Daniel as Ti Moune's "life's work."[65] Ti Moune repeatedly acts toward Daniel as a loving mother would act toward a small child, cradling him, holding him to her breasts, bathing him, and singing to him.[66] She is both mother figure and servant, however, in the novel performing similar tasks to those undertaken by Daniel's Black nursemaid, Madame Mathilde. In both sources, she waits on him hand and foot; in the novel, for example, she fetches fruit for him and prepares his bath.[67]

Hers is a self-effacing, selfless role; her only concerns are Daniel's needs. She also is self-sacrificing. She goes without sleep or food when she is caring for the ailing Daniel, and in the novel she forgoes eating to buy a pair of shoes needed to accomplish her mission of finding her lover.[68] Promising that she would die for Daniel, she makes the ultimate sacrifice—fending off Papa Gé, the messenger of death, by offering him her life in exchange for Daniel's.[69]

One point on which the novel and musical diverge is Ti Moune's suffering, the cost in human pain that she pays for assuming the role of the ideal woman. Guy makes it clear that Ti Moune's suffering is considerable; the musical downplays the costs of virtue. A comparison of descriptions of Ti Moune's journey to find Daniel vividly exemplifies this difference. In the novel the trip to the city is long, arduous, and painful. Ti Moune travels through desolate spots and falls into holes.[70] She is terribly hungry, and during the final leg of the journey, the pain of her ill-fitting shoes, which she endures because she knows she will need shoes to be allowed into the hotel gate, is excruciating.[71]

Once on the hotel grounds, Ti Moune lives in terror that she will be discovered and thrown out.[72] Much of this misery melts away in the musical, where Ti Moune's trip to the city is described in the upbeat song "Some Say." The song features amusing dances by characters cleverly costumed as birds, frogs, and trees. "Some Say" refers to the fact that many different versions of Ti Moune's trip circulate among the peasants. Thus, some say that the trip was difficult, while others describe it far differently. The musical, unlike the novel, leaves a question unanswered: Did she suffer on her journey or didn't she? The song says, for example, that "some say her feet were bare and the road was long and cruel"; others, however, say she got a ride to town on a mule or was taken by the gods in a car.[73] Some say Ti Moune scrubbed floors when she arrived in the city, while others claim the gods simply lifted her up to Daniel's room.[74] In the musical, the gods provide all kinds of amenities to Ti Moune on her journey, and although there are allusions to bugs and fear, the theme of suffering is easily lost.[75] The musical does not completely eliminate references to suffering, however. When toward the end of the story Ti Moune pitifully cries to Daniel, "I love you," we spectators watch a woman suffer; but overall, the theme of pain is muted, especially by the cheerful affective tone set by the music.

A virgin/whore dichotomy plays a prominent role in representations of women in this musical, and race and social class help shape the two categories. Both the novel and the musical point out that the use and abuse of women as property, in particular, the widespread use of lower-class, dark women for sexual pleasure by upper-class, light-skinned men, constituted common practice. For young unmarried men of the upper class, sowing "wild oats" among dark-skinned women, while not encouraged, was a widespread male rite of passage; the young men are allowed to toy with servants and peasants, but it is understood that when the time comes to settle down, they will marry a "lady." The musical's gossipers underscore this reality when they predict that Ti Moune's role in Daniel's life will be mistress but never bride.[76] After Daniel has announced his engagement to Andrea, he promises Ti Moune, "There will always be a place for you here,"[77] which is a perceptive observation; many societies have a place for women who are deemed acceptable for sexual liaisons but not "good enough" to marry. Typically, it is a place without status, legal rights, or the protections accorded to a spouse, however.

Similarly, having a dark-skinned peasant woman "on the side" is pictured as routine for married men of the upper class. For example, according to the novel, the island's curse was brought about by one of the White French colonist Armand's many mulatto children, who were born out of wedlock. Guy describes Armand's habits: "He had, it is said, children like bush—all over the island—from concubines. But the house he built for the wife to whom he gave his name."[78]

The musical echoes this theme of sexual license and describes the privileges of upper-class White French men married to pale blond ladies: "But

Armand took his pleasure / With the women who served him / Black peasant girls from / The village beyond."[79] When Daniel's father attempts to end his son's relationship with Ti Moune, he obliquely alludes to his own enjoyment of the sexual privileges of upper-class males: "You are not the first to want a peasant / *I, too, know their appeal* [my emphasis] / But you are my son / You'll do what must be done / No matter how you feel."[80]

The song "Some Girls," which ends with the line, "Some girls you marry, some you love" clearly articulates a virgin/whore dichotomy. In it, Daniel describes two types of girls to Ti Moune: the girls you marry, who are refined, elegant, virtuous and somewhat frivolous—but not very interesting—and the girls you love, who are natural, exotic, and passionate, but not marriageable. According to the song, the girls to marry are prim, pale, concerned about their looks, and made up with nail polish and perfume; they spend their time dressing, go to European schools, and are bright and cultured. The girls to love, by contrast, are wild, dark, and deep; thus, the stereotype of fair women being virginal and dark women sexually experienced is reinforced. In addition to being passionate and sexually available, Ti Moune, the girl Daniel loves, is "childlike," the "natural" woman, not too cultivated or refined. Daniel also spells out what the two categories of women desire. The marriageable girls have somewhat self-centered, frivolous interests: small talk, shiny cars, mirrors, French cologne, and trousseaus. By contrast, Daniel compliments Ti Moune for supposedly wanting nothing, for facing the future "with no demands."[81] Of course, wanting nothing also means that Daniel can take from her without being expected to give anything in return. Perhaps the most enigmatic line of the song reads, "Some girls you learn from / Some you teach."[82] The puzzling question here is who is who? From whom do men learn in the virgin/whore dichotomy? In the text, the virgins are described first; therefore, this line may suggest that cultivated girls are influential in a man's life; the second category of girls, by contrast, is composed of naive blank slates. On the other hand, men may learn sexual knowledge from the girls they love (whores), which they then teach to the women they marry, who as virgins supposedly have had no prior access to this knowledge.

The *Village Voice* comments upon the last line of this song: "A chapter in the history of Western sexual mores: the evolution of musical theater lyrics from '*Dein ist mein ganzes Herz*' to 'Some girls you marry / Some you love.'"[83] I argue, however, that there is nothing evolutionary about the final line; rather, it reverberates with long-standing sexist mores, especially those that often come into play when liaisons are formed between individuals of different races or social classes and when the players involved come to the relationship from different positions of power.

Both the novel and the musical make it clear that Daniel and Ti Moune have sexual relations.[84] Innuendo (which elicited laughter from the audience) is one indicator in the musical of the sexual nature the couple's relationship. Word had gotten around, the gossipers remark, "[t]hat the ailing Daniel Beauxhomme had chosen a peasant as a lover. And little by little, she was . . . / *Healing* him!"[85] The final line is delivered with a provocative pelvic thrust. The gossipers once again deal in innuendo when they say of Ti Moune, "[She] Probably makes him rise like yeast!"[86] By contrast, there was no indication that Daniel's relationship with his fiancée, Andrea, is sexual. To suggest that Ti Moune is a whore rather than a virgin is to oversimplify her representation, however. On the one hand, she displays many attributes ascribed to the archetypal virtuous woman. On the other hand, she is sexually experienced, and in a twist on typical fairy tales, is the aggressive and determined pursuer and initiator. These latter behaviors are examples of what "others" may do, but good girls do not, at least according to dominant, White, middle-class standards. And of course, unlike Andrea, Ti Moune is considered unmarriageable but fair game for Daniel's unencumbered sexual liaisons. Her story may be an object lesson, describing the dire fate in store for virtuous but fallen women, and/or it may send the racist and classist message that no matter how praiseworthy a dark-skinned, poor woman may be, on the matter of virtue she will never find herself in the same league as her light-skinned upper-class sisters.

What is clear in both the musical and the novel is that revenge and retaliation are not regarded as viable options for ideal women. In both sources, Ti Moune briefly contemplates murdering Daniel when she realizes that he has abandoned her. This contemplation comes in response to a temptation from Papa Gé, the god of death. Ti Moune's internal struggle is pictured as a mythic battle between good and evil. In the musical Papa Gé tells Ti Moune that she needs to make a choice between death and love; she can have her life back and can reclaim herself, he promises, under the condition that she kill Daniel: "Prove that death is stronger than love and you can have your own life again."[87] Thus, if Ti Moune is to remain a virtuous woman and good is to prevail, she has no choice but to sacrifice herself. The lesson is clear: There is no place in a virtuous woman's world for rage, revenge, self interest or self care. As spectators, we witness a terrible thing: a woman chooses to destroy herself rather than to bring harm to someone who has used her and hurt her deeply. And the festive music plays on.

In both sources Ti Moune refrains from committing murder, but there are subtle differences between the two temptation scenes. Significantly, in the book Daniel sleeps through the incident and never realizes that he is in peril.[88] In the musical, by contrast, he sees Ti Moune after she throws down the knife; immediately after this scene she is cast out of the house. Thus, the musical may elicit more sympathy for Daniel and provide explanation for his reprehensible actions; Ti Moune's removal from the house appears justified: Daniel perceived himself to be in danger.

If we assume for a moment that Ti Moune's story is a lesson on how justice should rightfully be brought about in the face of oppression, whether the oppression is based on race, social class, or gender, then the moral of the story appears to be that the good and right responses to long-suffering and oppression, the responses that will ultimately bring justice and peace, are those of forbearance, patience, and personal sacrifice—on the part of the oppressed. This message can be a very comforting one to oppressors because it suggests that they will not be endangered by their misdeeds nor will they pay consequences. The burden of suffering remains on the oppressed, who will not only bear the brunt of the misery but also will forgive. If we turn our gaze away from gender and focus on the subject of race for a moment, and if we recognize as Tricia Rose suggests, that fear of Black revolt has played a central role in the White American psyche since the time of slavery,[89] then portraying Ti Moune as receiving rewards for choosing the path she did has significant political implications. Ti Moune's actions toward her light-skinned oppressor may suggest that revolt is not an appropriate solution to oppression, at least when the oppressed are Black, poor, or female. This is an ironic message to promulgate in a country such as the United States that gained its independence precisely through revolution. Guy herself hypothesizes that American hostility toward Haiti and U.S. reluctance to offer the country aid are racial issues directly related to the fact that slave revolt was the means by which Haiti successfully shook off colonial rule.[90] When Guy told a reviewer that Americans were afraid of Haiti because of this revolt, the critic responded, "After 'Once on This Island' they [Americans] should be considerably less so."[91] The reviewer probably was referring to the overall feel-good tone of the musical and not specifically to racial politics, but the reviewer's perception that the musical is not threatening deserves consideration as we interrogate its racial politics.

Perhaps Ahrens and Flaherty's most dramatic departure from the novel's plot is their revision of the ending, which transforms Guy's tragedy into a "happily-ever-after" fairy tale. The musical's revised ending, I argue, adds an additional layer to the already problem-ridden representations of gender appearing in the novel. Guy's ending is set at Daniel's wedding, where divisions by race and class are strictly maintained. The guests, an elite inner circle, celebrate safe inside the gates of the hotel, while the peasants are offered

a somewhat different party outside.[92] When the car carrying the bridal couple leaves the hotel and enters the city streets, and when crowds of joyful,
somewhat drunken peasants swarm around it, the police move in, swinging
truncheons. Guy writes, *"The crowd fell back* [my emphasis]. The limousine
sped on to its destination. Still, policemen kept pushing, kept swinging. . . ."[93]
The crowd, desperately trying to escape the blows, began pushing and Ti
Moune was shoved to the ground: "Weak from hunger and pain, she lacked
the strength or will to pick herself up. Then the policemen, whipped to
unreasoning fury by the cringing crowd, hammered heads with their batons,
and the fleeing peasants stampeded, trampling the girl underfoot."[94] Thus,
Ti Moune dies in the street. In the closing scene Daniel's father spies her body
outside the gates. He calls to his groundskeeper, "I don't pay you good money
to leave dead peasants in front of my hotel. Do you want to discourage my
guests?"[95] The groundskeeper then picks up the body by an arm and leg and
dumps it in a trash heap on the side of the road. Rain ushers in a storm that
has been brewing throughout the day, the first drops falling on Ti Moune's
face; Guy explains that the rain looks like tears.

   The musical ends quite differently; Daniel's wedding is the *penultimate*
scene. Outside the gates, the heartbroken Ti Moune is ignored by the groom,
who engages in the tradition of distributing coins to the peasants; not only
does he not see her but he hands her a coin along with the others. When
Daniel departs, the gods take mercy on the distraught Ti Moune, and Erzulie,
the goddess of love, "led her to the sea, / Where Agwe wrapped her in a wave
/ And laid her to her rest"; Papa Gé then gently carries her body to the
shore.[96] The tragic mood is quickly dispelled, however, when the gods sud-
denly and magically reincarnate Ti Moune as a gorgeous flowering tree. Not
only does the tree guard Daniel and his children, it also blesses peasants and
grands hommes alike; ultimately it shatters the island's curse, cracking the
walls that divide people.[97] The musical ends as joyously as it began.

   In both the musical and the novel we as spectators consume for pleasure
images of a woman dying; thus both plots are part of a long-standing misogynistic musico-dramatic tradition; as feminist scholars such as Catherine
Clément point out, this tradition is particularly evident in opera.[98] Dying or
going mad apparently are the only options available to women experiencing
difficulties; this representation, in itself, is problematic from a feminist standpoint, and doubly problematic when it is followed in short order by wild
applause from an enthusiastic audience. However, I suggest that the musical's
ending positions viewers quite differently than does the novel's and that the
final act of the musical puts the events that came before in a different light.
By replacing the novel's tragic ending with a "happier" one, the plot's gen-

der politics are altered, the revised ending suggesting what the novel does not—that women who conform to dominant, White, middle-class constructions of femininity ultimately will be rewarded. In both the musical and the novel the message is sent that strong, aggressive, and persistent "other" women foolish enough to step outside of their sphere and to risk all for an experience as an insider will meet tragic ends. However, the musical makes an additional point: If the woman is virtuous, she ultimately will receive divine blessing and honor. In the musical "good" triumphs over evil and Ti Moune's personal sacrifice, suffering, patience, and virtue are rewarded. What is that reward? The fulfillment of Ti Moune's fondest desire, which is to serve and bless Daniel and his family.

Some may argue that Ti Moune has a transformative power in the musical that she does not in the novel because she changes the race/class relations for future generations. Significantly, however, transformation is effected through her dying, and not by economic change, political activism, or revolution. Patience, self sacrifice, and love will win the day, the musical shouts. The unlikelihood of social change coming about in this manner was commented upon by only one reviewer, a critic for the *Village Voice* who noted acerbically, "[T]he narrators don't tell us whether or not a socialist redistribution of income followed."[99]

The different means by which Ti Moune dies in the musical and the novel have quite dissimilar political implications. In the novel the death of a poor, dark-skinned woman results from police brutality, from human acts over which humans have control, and these human acts are a direct result of hegemonic power relations. In the musical, the course of events is placed in the hands of the gods, the plot once again reinforcing the idea that humans (at least "primitive" humans) are pawns in the hands of supernatural powers, whether gods or fate. The musical's absence of discussion of the police, most vividly exemplified by the decision not to include the panic scene at the end, shifts the politics of the plot; the political significance of Ti Moune's death, which resulted from unjustified actions of brutal police, is thus lost.

The musical's implication that Ti Moune commits suicide (or at the very least is taken up by the gods) is another example of how plot transformation results in a subtle change in gender politics. The novel is more ambiguous on this point, one line stating that a weakened Ti Moune may have lacked either the strength or the will to stand up when she was pushed to the ground by the panicked crowd.[100] This ambiguity gives the reader the impression that to the end, a defeated but nevertheless strong-willed Ti Moune may not have capitulated. The musical more vividly portrays her as giving up or giving in. Also, although the musical's death scene is quite easily understood if one reads the libretto, in the actual production the lines are rendered so quickly that the death is downplayed; the audience may go away without a clear understanding of what happened to Ti Moune immediately prior to her transformation into a tree.

Thus, the musical offered viewers what is represented largely as a happier ending, and while it is not one of unmitigated joy, it is sufficiently upbeat to prompt a reviewer from the *New York Times* to write, "'Everyone is likely to emerge from the theatre ready to dance down the street.'"[101] Other reviewers responded similarly, Michael Kilian from the *Chicago Tribune* observing, "The ending is bittersweet, but rendered in a fable delightful enough to charm the most anxious child."[102] What is charming about this scene? The beautiful music plays on, the stage is filled with luscious colors and delightful sets, but nevertheless, a Black woman dies and her heartless lover lives happily ever after. He lives, marries, has children, and reaps the benefits of her virtuous act. Ti Moune may be virtuous, but she also is dead, and she finds happiness only in an afterlife that permits her to be a true woman—hopelessly devoted to him.

True Love and Responsibility

Let us consider briefly some meanings the musical may foster concerning love and responsibility. Ti Moune is a noble, heroic character, well deserving of emulation, whose actions exemplify true love. The final chorus confirms this: "[S]he fills us with the power and the wonder of her love,"[103] and the *New York Times* echoes this theme in its headline "A Musical Celebrates Real Love."[104]

True love as exemplified by Ti Moune has several characteristics. First, it is powerful, strong, and persistent; it can conquer all. Erzulie, the goddess of love, sings, "Love has many pow'rs / If the love is true / It can cross the earth / And withstand the storm / It can conquer even you [Papa Gé, the god of death]!"[105] Next, it is preordained and exclusive; for every person there is only one true love. Ti Moune articulates these points when she sings, "You are the one / I was intended for / Deep in your eyes / I saw the gods' design / Now my life is forever yours / And you are mine."[106] Third, commitment, loyalty, and devotion, as exemplified in the final lines of the passage just quoted, play a central role in true love. At one point Ti Moune makes a promise: "I will never leave you, Daniel."[107] Finally, true love involves self sacrifice; it motivates Ti Moune to destroy herself before laying a hand on her lover. True love is not a shifting signifier or a social construct but, rather, a universal. This understanding not only idealizes love but also wipes it clean of all marks of politics.

One question that the musical's definition of love raises is whether Daniel loves Ti Moune. Is she his lover or his pet? Guy's novel suggests the former, Guy writing that the two "had fallen deeply in love" and were the happiest of couples.[108] She further states that they "had sworn responsibility for each other"; Daniel's apparent commitment is evident in his promise that she would always be with him.[109] Daniel does not specify in what capacity, however. Further evidence of his commitment to Ti Moune comes in his statement that he, as a member of a new generation, is not bound by the childhood betrothal his parents and Andrea's family had arranged.[110] Later, when he avows that not only does he love her, but that Andrea does as well, Daniel indicates that his proposed position for Ti Moune is quite different from the one Ti Moune had envisioned.[111] Perhaps Daniel's sad eyes on his wedding day are another sign of his lingering love for Ti Moune.[112]

Daniel's relationship with Ti Moune is more ambiguous in the musical. He claims he loves her;[113] however, when the matter of his betrothal to Andrea is raised, Daniel responds, "Ti Moune, I thought you understood. We could never marry."[114] Whether or not the Daniel of the musical *really* loves her, in both the musical and the novel he obviously has a different concept of love and its concomitant responsibilities than does Ti Moune. For example, in the novel when Ti Moune is thrown out, Daniel makes no effort to go looking for her.[115] In both novel and musical Daniel ducks distasteful tasks involving Ti Moune, handing the responsibility for delivering unpleasant messages over to his maid (in the novel) and to his fiancée (in the musical).[116] In both cases women do the emotional dirty work that Daniel neatly sidesteps. Furthermore, in the musical he attempts to exonerate himself and abdicate responsibility by claiming that his marriage to Andrea is not of his choosing. "This is how things are done, Ti Moune," he explains, and adds, "It's expected."[117] He claims powerlessness when he states, "I can't change who I am or where I'm from."[118]

In both musical and novel Daniel uses Ti Moune for his own purposes. In the novel, for example, Daniel recognizes Ti Moune's instrumental role in making him well; based on his improved health he decides, "This girl must stay."[119] Later, when asked how long she will stay, he narcissistically replies, "For as long as it takes."[120] Daniel realizes that he is indebted to Ti Moune and attempts to engage in a form of exchange in which her affection is remunerated materially. When he asks her what he can give her for healing him, Ti Moune altruistically replies that she wants the island restored.[121] Although the theme of Daniel's self-centeredness is carried over into the musical, Ti Moune's altruistic desires are not.

Daniel does not comes across as a hero; David Richards of the *New York Times* calls him a dolt and adds that most fairy tale princes are precisely that.[122] Leah D. Frank, also of the *New York Times,* describes Daniel as a "character . . . so unworthy of Ti Moune's selfless love that it is painful to watch."[123] Dolt or not, however, he escapes relatively unscathed. He survives and even thrives. The gods do not strike him down on his wedding day, washing him to his death in the sea. Because there is no price exacted from Daniel, the musical sends powerful messages about males and responsibility in love relationships, especially those liaisons involving women from marginalized or oppressed groups. As honorable as true love may be, and as central as it was to Ti Moune's being, it was not required of Daniel in his relationship with Ti Moune; he, as a man of a specific social class, had a complete and happy life without reciprocating such love.

Universalizing Representations of Gender

Perhaps the most problematic dimension of the musical's gender politics is that dominant, White, Euro-American constructions of femininity are played out by a poor, Black woman from a developing country. This enactment suggests that these culturally specific constructions are not only commonsensical and natural but also universal. Statements from the musical itself, as well as comments from reviewers, make claims about the universality of Ti Moune's experiences. Universality is underscored, for example, when Erzulie, the goddess of love, sings to Ti Moune, "You are part / Part of the human heart."[124] This statement uncritically forwards the assumption that a universally shared human heart exists, which is embodied by Ti Moune. The song also speaks of "the innocence of youth" and thus universalizes a particular culture-bound perspective of childhood.[125] The musical underscores the idea that maturation inevitably and naturally is characterized by a longing for and seeking of adventure, as well as by breaking away from the family; arguably, these, too, are culturally specific elements and not universally shared components of maturation. The idea of universality was picked up by a couple of reviewers. Leah D. Frank from the *New York Times* claimed that the musical "strikes a universal chord," and Michael Kilian of the *Chicago Tribune* proposed that the plot presents a universal human myth: "It's a story that could have been set in the ancient Greece of mythology, or the Norse land of the Valkyries or among the Indians of the American plains. Indeed, the universal sense of human life's interdependence with nature and its governing deities is overpowering and the principal reason for the musical's success."[126]

Multiple Texts

At the beginning of this essay, I described my own sense of being pulled in multiple directions as a spectator, of feeling both pleasure and distress at what I was experiencing. In this section, I explore why my attempts to be a resisting reader were thwarted, to some degree, by a sense of pleasure, and I will base my explanation on the assumption that in a musical production, there are multiple layers of text that include not only lyrics but visual text and the music as well. I contend that the visual and musical texts in *Once on This Island* are placed in the foreground and work to draw audience attention away from the lyrics; through the affective tone they set, they tend to deflate whatever counter-hegemonic politics the lyrics may advance. As we have already seen, the lyrics are by no means as politically radical as the novel's text. Earlier I mentioned the role music plays in the musical's light-hearted rendition of Ti Moune's journey to the city. This is not an isolated example of such transformation, however. Let us consider another instance. The island's race/class politics are laid out at the beginning of the musical in a prologue and the upbeat number "We Dance." In rapid-fire patter, the characters quickly lay out the signs of wealth and poverty, the material conditions, and the characteristics of the two "different worlds" that coexist on the island.[127] The lines are delivered at such a rapid pace that the lyrics are easily lost; of equal or greater importance is the festive music, which plays a central role in constructing peasants' lives as happy. How do peasants respond to the conditions of their lives? The characters chirrup happily, "We dance."[128] Rather than creating a moment of irony, the upbeat mood of the music overrides the serious implications of the lyrics and tends to trivialize them. Similarly, the song at the end of the musical helps to construct a joyous celebration of the victory of love over death and tends to suppress audience inclination to think critically about the musical's politics.

Sets, costumes, lighting, and props, which are components of the visual text, work in concert with the music to move the musical onto turf that is not conducive to oppositional thinking. The visual features are gorgeous, creating a tropical paradise and helping to set a tone of exotic fantasy-island escapism. The lush visual features did not escape the notice of reviewers;[129] a *New York Times* discussion of Loy Arcenas' sets not only typifies critics' responses but also underscores the fantastic exoticism created by the visual texts: "Mr. Arcenas, whose flair for fantasy has also been seen . . . [elsewhere, uses] a floor-to-ceiling mural emblazoned with faux-primitive flora and fauna, a tropical setting imagined in the Tahitian idiom of Gauguin, with the palette expanded to the cobalt blues and iridescent fuchsias of Matisse and Bonnard."[130]

Representing Haitian Music

The question of whose understandings dominate the musical is a pertinent one as we examine the musical styles used throughout the production. Stylistically, the music has only a remote (if any) relationship to indigenous Haitian music. Indeed, it is most closely related to the popular American styles typically found in recently composed American musical theater. As Michael Kilian from the *Chicago Tribune* notes, "The music and accents have a Caribbean flavor and the dances convey a kindred verisimilitude. But the music has more in common with the contemporary stage music of Stephen Sondheim or Andrew Lloyd Webber, though it is more natural and melodic."[131] The reviewer's choice of the word "natural" suggests that some music is natural (and thus, presumably, more suitable for representing a "primitive" culture) while other music is not. A statement by Stephen Holden of the *New York Times* may help explain the lack of relationship between the music of *Once* and the indigenous music of Haiti (or even of the Caribbean region); according to Holden, Flaherty "had only a limited knowledge of third-world music" when he began composing the musical.[132] The *Chicago Tribune* further points out that choreographer and director Graciela Daniele had "no West Indian or African roots";[133] however, the ignorance of the composer, director, and choreographer did not seem to adversely affect these reviewers' opinions.

Thus, rather than incorporating indigenous music written by Caribbean composers, *Once* presents a relatively uninformed American impression of this music; it employs what musicologist Karl Wm. Neuenfeldt calls "musical shorthands," sound bites that suggest ethnicity or geographical location to American audiences,[134] who presumably are largely unfamiliar with the indigenous musics of the region. In a discussion of North American country music's representations of the Spanish Circum-Caribbean region, Neuenfeldt describes the ideological work that can be done by such shorthands:

> Shorthands . . . can be viewed as the musical icing on the ideological cake. They add a symbolic layer of meaning that is simplistic and facile; easily accessible to broadcast consumers. But sweeteners can also be bitter bastings that poison what lies beneath; especially if they serve to enhance negative and erroneous ethnic and gender characterizations as well as ethnocentric categorizations and assumptions.[135]

Frank Rich from the *New York Times* asserts that Ahrens and Flaherty did not "pretend to authenticity, choosing instead to filter the story's environment through their own sensibility"; Rich likens *Once* to Richard Rogers' "Bali Ha'i" from *South Pacific* or to the "March of the Siamese Children" from

The King and I.[136] One could argue, however, that precedent does not excuse naively unfaithful representation, especially given the ideological meanings that Neuenfeldt believes often are imputed by musical shorthands. Furthermore, although the cultural politics of "authenticity" are complex and striving for "authenticity" may be a politically suspect goal, calling music "Caribbean" when it would not be claimed by any indigenous person associated with any Caribbean musical tradition is equally problematic.

The very notion of "Caribbean flavor," alluded to by the reviewer quoted above, and characterized by others as consisting of calypso or reggae,[137] suggests that only a few musical styles constitute the music of the entire geographical area. Perpetuating the belief that Caribbean music is a static unified whole, especially via the use of musical sound bites, tends to further uninformed American perceptions while blotting out the varied musical cultures of the Caribbean region.

Flaherty's misrepresentation of the musical culture of Haiti may seem harmless until we examine relationships between representation and power. From a post-colonial perspective the questions of who may represent whom and whose representations are considered legitimate are political and critical. Quite clearly, Haitians were not involved in the creation of this music.

Whose Cultural Politics?

With few exceptions, *Once on This Island* was critically acclaimed by reviewers. The *Boston Globe* spoke of its "wonderful" music; the *New York Times* praised its "ecstatic ritual dances."[138] In addition most reviewers made it clear that *Once on This Island* is noncontroversial, escapist entertainment. Several spoke of its innocence, gentleness, or niceness.[139] David Richards, critic for the *New York Times,* observed that "its overall effect is more that of a tropical breeze that lulls and caresses but never threatens to blow off your hat."[140] Leah Frank, also of the *New York Times,* reviewed a production of *Once* at the Gateway Playhouse, a summer theater, and remarked, "'Once on This Island' is as good as they come, and is a perfect show with which to wind up another summer season."[141] Criticism, if present at all, tended to focus on the dwarfing of this intimate off-Broadway musical on larger stages, or on what was called the cloying sweetness of the plot and lyrics.[142] I was intrigued by the absence of critical analysis of the musical's gender politics. It appears that its constructions of femininity are considered so commonsensical that they raised no warning flags among reviewers; this silence may be a testimonial to the pervasiveness of specific constructions of femininity.

Judging by the warm reception the musical received from the audience at both of the performances I attended, I surmised that most theatergoers agreed with reviewers in saying that viewing the musical is an exciting, positive experience. However, at the coat check following the local performance, I overheard the following interchange:

> Woman: Did you enjoy the performance?
> Man: Yes.
> Woman: I could hear [a female friend] grumbling at the part about some girls you marry and some you love, and at the end she said, "That was not a happy ending."

Another theatergoer, whom I asked about the political dimensions of the musical, replied, "I think the political was completely lost."

It is tempting to say that the musical's additions, omissions, and changes in emphasis are depoliticizations. However, if we accept the assumption that no human endeavor is politically neutral or value free, then what we witness in the plot's transformation is a shift in political terrain; our challenge becomes that of uncovering the "hidden" cultural politics in what largely appears to be an "apolitical" cultural product. Interestingly, when the musical is described by reviewers as political, it is the somewhat mild discussions of race and class that mark it as such; unexamined representations of gender do not. Thus, "political" becomes that which stands in opposition to dominant discourses, but by contrast, that which reinforces dominant discourses is merely considered commonsensical or natural.

Musicologist Christian Mendenhall's theories on musicals may contribute to a thoughtful analysis of *Once on This Island*'s cultural politics. Mendenhall claims that integrated musicals are "secular rituals"; he describes rituals as repeatable "acts that celebrate within a particular community its meanings and self concepts."[143] Integrated musicals, which he defines as those in which a plot is the structuring element, tell "a story which mediates the myths held as sacrosanct by the dominant culture."[144]

Myth making and symbol production are powerful acts. As we attempt to untangle *Once on This Island*'s complex cultural politics we need to ask: Who is representing whom in this musical? Whose representations count? Whose visions of social reality are validated? Whose political agenda and interests are best served? If, as Mendenhall suggests, the performance of musicals is a ritual celebration of myth, then whose myths are told?

Questions concerning cultural politics are especially pertinent to an analysis of *Once on This Island* given the reality that this musical presents otherness—constructed by Whites and consumed principally by Whites. For most theatergoers attending *Once* is an experience of consuming representations of "otherness" for pleasure, an experience that deserves close scrutiny.

As I mentioned earlier, I am not suggesting that the problems I have identified are unique to this musical. For example, Puccini's *Madame Butterfly* is strikingly similar to *Once*. Both productions present stories of love between individuals of different cultures and races. In both instances a virtuous, long-suffering woman is used and abused only to be discarded for someone considered more marriageable. In both cases virtuous women die, and although Pinkerton in *Madame Butterfly* claims he will regret his actions for the remainder of his life, he, like Daniel Beauxhomme, escapes unscathed. Finally, both *Madame Butterfly* and *Once* are steeped, both textually and musically, in orientalism and cultural imperialism; in both cultural artifacts White, Euro-American, masculinist, bourgeois perspectives are transplanted into an "exotic" setting. Indeed, given its similarities to *Madame Butterfly*, we may surmise that *Once on This Island* presents some very old messages dressed up in new clothing.

Implications for Music Educators

As the introduction to this essay indicates, I can no longer completely turn off my internal critical voice, cannot go home again to the place where musicals were innocent magical fun. Occasionally students will grumble that I have spoiled their fun, too, by nurturing their skills at critique. Of course, one could argue that being a cultural critic has its own pleasures, which may or may not be as enjoyable as indulging in blissful escapism. Given the reality that acquiring skills in cultural critique may "spoil some of the fun," why do I advocate that teachers learn the art of cultural critique and encourage their students to do likewise? Practicing cultural critique can be a first step toward action. For those who have been born into privilege, it can be a way to pick up and begin to wear the mantle of responsibility that should accompany privilege. For those who have not, it can be a way to explain, affirm, and confirm. As teachers, we can abdicate our own responsibilities of privilege by claiming that students are not sheep and that they are always "free" to draw their own conclusions. That claim assumes, however, that students already possess the tools, perspectives, and familiarity with alternate discourses that are needed if one is to chisel away at school knowledge's presentations of truth.

Interrogating the assumption that school knowledge is apolitical, accurate, benign, and incontrovertible is a powerful political act, as is reflecting upon the potential ramifications of what we teach. To begin this reflection is to start on a journey filled with ethical questions, which may be particularly thorny when we ask students not merely to watch but also to *embody* musico-dramatic characters, to become Ti Moune and Daniel. We can choose to assume that music is just music and that the best music is divorced from all ties to the mundane, including politics. Doing so, however, is to refuse to take up the mantle of responsibility that accompanies the privilege of teaching.

In closing, I disagree with the *Village Voice*'s assessment of *Once on This Island;* the musical, critic Michael Feingold claims, "is, for the most part, such a cheery, skillfully made little entertainment that I can't imagine anyone taking violent exception to it."[145] A line from the musical articulates a rationale for concern; the peasants claim that they recount Ti Moune's story because, "Our lives become / The stories that we weave."[146] If this is so, then the stories we tell in school warrant special scrutiny. It is time to weave stories with happier endings for women and for men of color.

NOTES

1. A press representative for the show was quoted in the *Christian Science Monitor* as saying that the show does a "very big family business." See Tony Vellela, "A Musical Survives on Broadway," *Christian Science Monitor,* 18 October 1991, p. 14; and Kevin Kelly, "Calypso Whimsy Is Cover for a Feeble Fable," *Boston Globe,* 26 February 1991, Arts and Film Sec., p. 52.

2. See advertisement in the *Wisconsin State Journal,* 10 February 1994, p. 2E.

3. "Young Imaginations Flourish on Fictional Island," *Wisconsin State Journal,* 8 February 1994, p. 2C.

4. See, for example, Susan McClary, *Feminine Endings: Music, Gender, and Sexuality* (Minneapolis: University of Minnesota Press, 1988); and Catherine Clément, *Opera, or the Undoing of Women,* with a foreword by Susan McClary, trans. Betsy Wing (Minneapolis: University of Minnesota Press, 1988).

5. Susan McClary's forward to Clément, ix.

6. See, for example, Michael W. Apple, *Ideology and Curriculum* (London: Routledge and Kegan Paul, 1979).

7. "Program Information," in *Performing Arts, San Francisco and Bay Area Edition* 5, no. 4 (April 1992): P-5.

8. Lynn Ahrens and Stephen Flaherty, *Once on This Island, Libretto/Vocal Book* (New York: Music Theatre International, [1991]), preceding 1.

9. Rosa Guy, *My Love, My Love, or The Peasant Girl* (New York: Henry Holt and Company, 1985), 39; and Ahrens and Flaherty, 27.

10. Ahrens and Flaherty, 1 and 3, for example.

11. See Richard Christiansen, "'Island' Keeps Its Charm: Simple Tale Still Effective," *Chicago Tribune*, 3 April 1992, sec. 1, p. 20, for quotation. See Kelly, 52; and Michael Kilian, "Caribbean Tales: The Gods Make 'Island' a Simple but Profound Hit," *Chicago Tribune*, 29 March 1992, sec. 13, p. 16, for comments on race relations.

12. See Kelly, 52; Kilian, 16; and Stephen Holden, "Striving for What's Hummable," *New York Times*, 24 May 1990, sec. C, p. 17 for mentioning of the racial constitution of the cast.

13. Michael Feingold, "Island-Hopping," *Village Voice* 30 October 1990, p. 99.

14. Kilian, 16.

15. Ahrens and Flaherty, 1–4.

16. See Guy, 10, for a reference to this practice.

17. Guy, 7.

18. Ahrens and Flaherty, 44.

19. See, for example, Ahrens and Flaherty, 1, 2, 11–12, 21.

20. Ibid., 17.

21. Ibid., 5.

22. Ibid., 13–16.

23. Dan Hulbert, "Director's Boyhood Memories Live Again in 'Island,'" *Atlanta Journal and Atlanta Constitution*, 21 February 1993, sec. N, p. 2.

24. See, for example, Guy, 18.

25. Ibid., 75.

26. Ibid., 52.

27. Daniel's wealthy father remarks about the ignorance of peasants in Guy, 86.

28. See Guy, 31, 34, 39, 40, 41–42, 59, 60, 62, 65, 66, 74, 76, 87, 98, 104, and 113 for examples of this imparting of wisdom.

29. David Richards, "There Is Warmth to Be Found in 2 Gentle Fables," *New York Times*, 28 October 1990, sec. 2, p. 5.

30. See, for example, Guy, 59–60, and 75.

31. Ibid., 31, 33.

32. Ibid., 32.

33. Ibid., 32, 87.

34. Ibid., 117.

35. Ibid., 105–106.

36. See Ibid., 17; and Ahrens and Flaherty, 17.

37. Richards, 5.

38. Ahrens and Flaherty, 45.

39. bell hooks, *Black Looks: Race and Representation* (Boston: South End Press, 1992), 23.

40. Toni Morrison, *Playing in the Dark: Whiteness and the Literary Imagination* (Cambridge: Harvard University Press, 1992), 66.

41. Ibid., 17.

42. Ahrens and Flaherty, "Author's Note" (no page).

43. Ibid., 1.

44. See, for example, Guy, 38.

45. Michael W. Apple, *Official Knowledge: Democratic Education in a Conservative Age* (New York: Routledge, 1993), 104.

46. John Fiske, *Television Culture* (London: Routledge, 1987), 285.

47. See, for example, Guy, 22 and 23.

48. Ahrens and Flaherty, 18.

49. Ibid., "Author's Note" (no page).

50. Ibid.

51. Ibid., 12.

52. Ibid., 29.

53. Guy, 99.

54. Ahrens and Flaherty, 30.

55. Ibid., 43.

56. Guy, 95.

57. Ibid., 96.

58. Rosalind Coward, *Female Desires: How They Are Sought, Bought and Packaged* (New York: Grove, 1985), 14.

59. Coward, 13.

60. Ahrens and Flaherty, 29.

61. See, for example, Guy, 77 and 96; and Ahrens and Flaherty, 10, 37, and 45.

62. Guy, 58.

63. Ahrens and Flaherty, 32, 37.

64. Ibid., 43.

65. Guy, 88.

66. See Ahrens and Flaherty, 23, 38 (cradling); Guy, 27, 82, 88 (holding to breasts); Ahrens and Flaherty, 19 (bathing); Guy, 82 (singing).

67. Guy, 88, 90.

68. Ahrens and Flaherty, 19; Guy, 73.

69. See Guy, 29 and 41, for example; and Ahrens and Flaherty, 24 and 48.
70. Guy, 60.
71. Ibid., 77.
72. Ibid., 80.
73. Ahrens and Flaherty, 34.
74. Ibid., 36.
75. Ibid., 32, 33.
76. Ibid., 43.
77. Ibid., 46.
78. Guy, 38.
79. Ahrens and Flaherty, 25–26.
80. Ibid., 42.
81. Ibid., 44.
82. Ibid., 43.
83. Feingold, 99.
84. See, for example, Guy, 89.
85. Ahrens and Flaherty, 40.
86. Ibid., 42.
87. Ibid., 48.
88. Guy, 111.
89. Tricia Rose, "'Fear of a Black Planet': Rap Music and Black Cultural Politics in the 1990s," *Journal of Negro Education* 60, no. 3 (1991): 289.
90. Kilian, 17.
91. Ibid.
92. Guy, 116.
93. Ibid., 118.
94. Ibid.
95. Ibid., 118–119.
96. Ahrens and Flaherty, 51.
97. Ibid.
98. See Clément, especially the chapter entitled "Dead Women," 43–59.
99. Feingold, 99.
100. Guy, 118.

101. Quoted in Ahrens and Flaherty, back cover.

102. Kilian, 17.

103. Ahrens and Flaherty, 52.

104. Leah D. Frank, "A Musical Celebrates Real Love," *New York Times,* 27 September 1992, sec. LI, p. 11.

105. Ahrens and Flaherty, 14.

106. Ibid., 23.

107. Ibid., 41.

108. Guy, 89 and 97–98.

109. Guy, 33, 91.

110. Ibid., 103.

111. Ibid., 109.

112. Ibid., 117.

113. Ahrens and Flaherty, 42.

114. Ibid., 47.

115. See Guy, 112–113, for a description of her eviction.

116. See, for example, Guy, 104; and Ahrens and Flaherty, 46.

117. Ahrens and Flaherty, 46.

118. Ibid., 47.

119. Guy, 85.

120. Ibid., 86.

121. Ibid., 93.

122. Richards, 5.

123. Frank, 11.

124. Ahrens and Flaherty, 38.

125. Ibid.

126. Frank, 11; and Kilian, 17.

127. Ahrens and Flaherty, 3–4.

128. Ibid., 2.

129. See, for example, Kilian, 16; Kelly, 52; and Sylvia Drake, "'Once on This Island' an Undemanding Musical," *Los Angeles Times,* 24 July 1992, sec. F, p. 17.

130. Frank Rich, "'Once on This Island,' Fairy Tale Bringing Caribbean to 42nd Street," *New York Times,* 7 May 1990, sec. C, p. 12.

131. Kilian, 16.

132. Holden, 17.

133. Kilian, 16.

134. Karl Wm. Neuenfeldt, "Sun, Sea, Sex, and Senoritas: 'Shorthand' Images of Ethnicity, Ethos, and Gender in Country Songs Set in the Circum-Caribbean," *Popular Music and Society* 15, no. 2 (Summer 1991): 3.

135. Ibid., 4.

136. Rich, 12.

137. See, for example, Holden, 17; Roberta Smith, "Behind the Painted World of 'Once on This Island,'" *New York Times,* 14 October 1990, sec. 2, p. 5; and Kelly, 52.

138. Kelly, 52; Rich, 11.

139. Richards (p. 5) called it a "gentle fable"; Dan Hulbert, "Among Current N.Y. Stage Offerings, 'Six Degrees of Separation' Stands," *Atlanta Journal and Atlanta Constitution,* 11 November 1990, Sec. N, p. 3, spoke of its delightful innocence.

140. Richards, 5.

141. Frank, 11.

142. For discussions of staging problems, see Frank, 11; Drake, 17; and Hulbert, "Director's," 2. For comments on the lyrics and plot see Drake, 17, and Kelly, 52.

143. Christian Mendenhall, "American Musical Comedy as a Liminal Ritual of Woman as Homemaker," *Journal of American Culture* 13 (Winter 1990): 57.

144. Ibid.

145. Feingold, 99.

146. Ahrens and Flaherty, 54.

·4·

TO SHAVE
OR NOT TO SHAVE

*The Hair-Removal Imperative and Its Implications
for Teachers and Teaching (2001)*

"Janine," a student teacher in a music education certification program at a university in the Midwest, was having trouble at all three of her placement sites. Her difficulties came as a surprise to the faculty who knew her. Her musical skills were acceptable; she was bright, engaging, and kind. She also was unconventional in the sense that she didn't fit the typical profile of students at that university. Born in New York, Janine was Jewish, a vegetarian, and the daughter of academics who did research on radical issues. Her politics appeared to be left wing. The community into which Janine was placed for student teaching was known for its liberal views and appeared to be fairly open-minded about how teachers should look and act. When troubles surfaced, Janine's university supervisor met with the cooperating teachers, who listed several concerns; high on the list in one teacher's mind was the fact that Janine, reportedly to the horror of the high school students in her classes, did not shave her legs. Not only did she not shave them, but she didn't cover them, either. "High school students will never accept her with those legs," the cooperating teacher at the high school remarked. "I think you [the university supervisor] should tell her to shave them." The supervisor replied that he would do no such thing. Although not the only issue raised, Janine's unshaven legs were a touch point, a distillation of everything else that not merely was different but ostensibly was "wrong" with this student, the shaving issue symbolizing larger realities of difference and larger differences.

As the semester progressed it became clear that Janine would not successfully complete student teaching, and by mutual agreement the university terminated the experience. She graduated without certification and reportedly joined a human services program similar to the Peace Corps. Upon hearing Janine's story, a professor well informed about issues of social justice and equity remarked, "Student teachers need to shave their legs." When pressed, the professor explained that the practice is tied to issues of class, gender, and race.

A popular middle school teacher stated that her unshaven legs were show stoppers. She had developed a strategy for addressing the disruption: whenever her legs were creating an uproar in the classroom, she moved the focus back onto "legitimate" curricular content by addressing the issue head on—by openly talking about her decision not to shave.

A preschool teacher who did not shave was stoutly informed by her small charges that only men didn't shave their legs and underarms. The preschoolers refused to revise their views even when the teacher, whom they adored, pointed out that she was a woman and she didn't shave.

When a university student who did not shave as an undergraduate accepted a faculty position at her alma mater many years later, a former-professor-now-colleague repeatedly introduced the new faculty by stating that he vividly remembered her unshaven underarms, which he proceeded to describe in some detail.

A graduate student in her fifties remarked that when she did observations in the schools she shaved because she was older and figured it was expected of her as a sign of authority. She then added that her older daughter did not shave when on the university's rowing team. I asked what it was about rowing that influenced her daughter not to shave. She replied that women rowers, in general, are a rugged bunch. She added that her younger daughter, a college sophomore, shaves because "she is still trying to catch a man."

A teacher who identified herself as a lesbian described a dilemma she faces: not shaving, because it may be read as a marker of sexuality, may unwittingly out her in a context—the workplace—where she has decided she does not want to be out.

The topic of women's body hair removal has surfaced from time to time in a graduate course I teach on sex/gender issues in education. Anecdotes from students have convinced me that women teachers, like many other women, are under considerable pressure to remove body hair and that choosing not to do so is often read as an exotic or rebellious transgression. Teachers' stories prompted me to take a closer look at hair removal as a cultural practice and to consider possible implications for teachers and teaching of a stringently enforced hair-removal imperative.

I begin this essay with excerpts from pre-twentieth-century sources that hint at a discursive environment ripe for the establishment of the shaven women's body as a "regulatory norm," to borrow a phrase from Judith Butler.[1] Next, I review scholarship that outlines the recent history of this cultural practice and theorizes about why hair removal gained widespread acceptance in the U.S. during the interwar years of the twentieth century (c.1920–1940). Some of this scholarship situates removal practices within then-prevalent discourse about social class, race, and gender. Third, I summarize research on current hair removal practices and on perceptions of women who do not remove body hair. Fourth, because the cooperating teacher in Janine's story pointed to teens as the enforcers of body hair norms, I analyze what two popular magazines for teenage girls are reporting to girls about body hair. Finally, I return the discussion to teaching. I examine hair removal as a governmental practice consistent with other regulatory norms applied to teachers, and I explore one possible reading of the hair-removal imperative, namely that it is a patrolling mechanism, delineating the boundaries of who does or does not constitute an acceptable teacher. I argue that the imperative is a microtechnology of power, providing subtle commentary on which groups of people are not yet welcomed into the profession. The anecdotes that opened this essay highlight strands or themes that repeatedly surfaced in my exploration of this topic.

Historical Overview

A Selection of Pre-Nineteenth-Century Sources

In order to gain a sense of the discursive environment that may have fostered hair-removal norms in the U.S. today, I turn first to some pre-nineteenth-century folkloric and scientific sources, specifically to those that associate body hair with the bestial. When contemporary writer and critic Marina Warner describes hair as a "sign of the animal in the human, and all that means,"[2] she is referring to an understanding of hair that dates back at least to the twelfth century in European myth and folklore. For example, a corpus of stories exists describing a mythic "wild man," a man or woman belonging to one of the so-called "monstrous races."[3] This wild man has long been associated with terrifying, uncivilized, antisocial, violent, and aggressive behavior, as well as with mental illness and godlessness.[4] Timothy Husband, in the introduction to a catalogue for the New York Metropolitan Museum of Art's exhibition *Wild Man: Medieval Myth and Symbolism*, traces the wild man in European medieval visual art and literature. Husband observes that although myths about wild men and women date back to ancient times, the first known reference appearing in a fifth century B.C. text by Herodotus,[5] and although some of these sources, including ancient Babylonian texts, refer to hairiness,[6] it was not until the twelfth century that a hairy body became the distinguishing visual feature of wild men and women: "During the twelfth century, hairiness became an iconographic convention. . . . hairiness was a visual cipher bestowed upon the medieval wild man to indicate, in part, his existence outside man's civilized order."[7] In addition to being an iconographic convention, Husband notes, a hairy body was the mark of distinction: "In physical appearance he [the wild man] differed from man mainly in his thick coat of hair, which left only his face, hands, feet—and with wild women, breasts—bare."[8] Some early descriptions of the wild man were racialized;[9] Husband quotes a passage from a thirteenth-century German epic by Wirnt von Gravensberg, which alludes to the skin color as well as to the hairiness of a particular wild woman: "'Diu was in einer varwe gar swarz ruch als ein beer' ('She was of a black color, hairy as a bear')."[10] During the twelfth century, according to Husband, a hairy body also came to be associated with mental illness, specifically insanity.[11] The wild man, Husband states, figures prominently in European art from the fourteenth through the sixteenth century;[12] the prevalence of artistic representations indicates that wild men simultaneously were a source of revulsion and fascination. By the fifteenth century, Husband observes, in large part due to changing social and political conditions, the wild man began to be viewed in a favorable light and was idealized, especially by the urban bourgeoisie.[13]

This new assessment was a sign, Husband argues, of the increasing popularity of primitivism, a concept that "encouraged a return to a life free of social impositions."[14] The transformation to ideal was never quite complete, however; the "foreboding side persisted well into the sixteenth century. Indeed the wild man as both a mythic and folkloric figure has survived to modern times."[15] Thus, in the more recent sources Husband examined, the wild man was perceived dually, as both "benevolent and malevolent."[16] A link between early sources and the present is provided by Husband, who notes that in parts of Europe the wild man myth persists to the present time and continues to be "celebrated in festivals, masquerades, and dramas," as well as in visual art.[17]

Scientific discussions of hair as they are found in European treatises from the seventeenth and eighteenth centuries continued a tradition that associated hair with the less-than-fully human. Hair—its texture, color, location, quantity, and presence—was a classifying characteristic in taxonomies of the day. In some early scientific sources, quantity of hair was a mark that distinguished humans from animals; significantly, hairlessness was evidence of humanity. For example, in his 1651 anatomy text "Mikrokosmographia," English surgeon Helkiah Crooke observed that "man of all Creatures is covered with the fewest hairs, unlesse [sic] it be on his head."[18] Eighteenth-century anthropologist Johann Blumenbach similarly enumerated differences between humans and other animals; humans, he maintained are distinguishable by an absence of hair, hide, and feathers: "Besides his erect position and his two hands there are some other things to be considered which also seem peculiar to man. Of all animals he alone seems to be placed on the earth *altogether naked.* . . . [emphasis in original]"[19] Blumenbach further implied that hairiness on humans indicates bestiality and savagery. In support of this assertion he mentioned a "man-eating shepherd" who revealed to the public copious back hair when he was executed at "the wheel."[20]

Londa Shiebinger, in recent commentary on Blumenbach, points out gendered and racialized inconsistencies in his assertions, however. For example, she notes that he considered the absence of facial hair on native American males and on women to be a flaw or imperfection while simultaneously establishing hairlessness as a sign of humanity:

> That the absence of chin hair should have been taken as a sign of imperfection in native American males and in women is curious, given that Blumenbach had listed relative hair*less*ness as one of the traits distinguishing humankind from animals [emphasis in original]. Other hairy parts of the body—the armpit and groin, for example—carried no particular prestige.[21]

Distinguishing humans from animals was not the only classificatory role early sources gave to hair. In a 1799 treatise by scientist Charles White, hair—its color, texture, density, and abundance—was one of the characteristics that figured heavily in White's attempt "to establish that of a *gradation* [emphasis in original], as well of the human race, as of the animal and vegetable kingdoms in general."[22] White justified his taxonomic efforts by arguing that "[because] . . . various species of men were originally created and separated, by marks sufficiently discriminative, it becomes an important object, in general physiology, to trace the lines of distinction."[23]

White Europeans stood at the pinnacle of White's hierarchy:

Ascending the line of gradation, we come at last to the white European; who being most removed from the brute creation, may, on that account, be considered as the most beautiful of the human race. No one will doubt his superiority in intellectual powers; and I believe it will be found that his capacity is naturally superior also to that of every other man.[24]

Meanwhile, African "Negroes" were relegated to the bottom of the ladder, one rung away from monkeys. Arguing at one point that "the lowest degree of the human race" lives in Africa, White asserted the following:

2. Taking the European man as a standard of comparison, on the one hand, and the tribe of simiae on the other; and, comparing the classes of mankind with the standards, and with each other, they may be so arranged as to form a pretty regular gradation, in respect to the differences in the bodily structure and economy, the European standing at the head, as being farthest removed from the brute creation.

3. That the African, more especially in those particulars in which he differs from the European, approaches to the ape.

4. That the following characteristics which distinguish the African from the European, are the same, differing only in degree, which distinguish the ape from the European. . . . [25]

White's discussion is a clear example of scientific discourse constructing race. White attempted to distance himself from the slave trade by claiming that he staunchly opposed slavery, but his gradations stemmed from and reinforced some of the same discourses used in support of the trade.[26] His allegiance to a racialized hierarchy was evident even in his disclaimer, which also attempted to assert his scientific neutrality:

. . . the Author had not the Slave Trade at all in view in this Enquiry; his object was simply to investigate a position in natural history. He is fully persuaded the Slave Trade is indefensible on any hypothesis, and he would rejoice at its abolition. The Negroes are, at least, equal to thousands of Europeans in capacity and responsibility; and ought, therefore, to be equally entitled to freedom and protection.[27]

White articulated a long list of defining and distinguishing characteristics, which ranged from manner of walking to penile size.[28] In each case, however, White Europeans displayed the characteristics designated most "human," while Black Africans invariably were relegated to the bottom rung. Significantly, as I mentioned earlier, hair was among those distinguishing characteristics. White dismissed the belief, found in earlier sources,[29] that hair texture, density, and length are consequences of environment, specifically of climate; instead he attributed differences to innate causes:

Of the perennial hair, there are various species; as that upon the head of an European; that upon the chin, and on other parts of the body. The hair of the negro's head seems to be a different species from the European hair, and not a variety occasioned by any difference of climate, or from any peculiar mode of living, dependent on their want of civilization.[30]

His treatise is germane to my analysis because White used hair as a racialized mark of hierarchical distinction and maintained that differences in hair were innate. Unlike other early sources, however, he did not equate hairlessness with his so-called highest forms of humanity. Quite to the contrary, using hair length as a confirmation of his hierarchy, he associated long hair with White Europeans and short hair with Black Africans: "The hair of the head, chin, &c is shorter and more woolly [sic] in the African than in the European, and still more so in monkeys."[31] He later elaborated:

The long ornamental hair of the head, beard, &c. in the human species, exhibits a gradation in the same line as the other marks of distinction. The European has the longest hair; next to him the Asiatic; then the American; and lastly, the African.[32]

These particular observations, however, focused on facial hair on men and on head hair, both of which may be in a category apart from other types of body hair.

The early sources I consulted did not appear to be much concerned with women's body hair, but the breaks in silence are significant. Crooke, for example, in a discussion of the differences between men and women, asserted that hairlessness is a defining characteristic of womanhood: "Women are also smooth and without hair."[33] In addition, in an argument that naturalizes differences and distinctions between the sexes, he suggested that hairlessness, specifically the absence of a beard, is a "natural" sign of woman's subjectivity. After claiming that the hairy portion of a man's face is the wild part, Crooke explains women's lack of an "Ensign of Majesty":

Nature therefore hath made the upper part of the cheek and Nose without Hair, lest the whole Face should be wild and fierce, unbeseeming a mild and sociable Creature, such as a Man is. In Women the smoothnesse [sic] of their Face is their proper Ornament; they needed no Ensign of Majesty [i.e., beard] because they were born to subjection.[34]

Evidence from Nineteenth-Century Discussions

Ideas that emerged in treatises from earlier centuries are evident in the writings of the nineteenth-century German philosopher Georg Hegel. Hegel's lectures on aesthetics, which were published posthumously in 1835, not only describe hair as a mark of distinction between animals and humans, but also state that hair on humans is a sign of aesthetic imperfection. In a section entitled "The Idea of Artistic Beauty" and under the subheading "Deficiency of Natural Beauty," Hegel attempts to articulate differences between the ideal perfect beauty of art and the imperfect beauty of nature. He describes hair, along with feathers, scales, pelts, prickles, and shells, as a bodily covering of animals that masks the soul:

> Such covering does belong to the animal kingdom, but in animals it has forms drawn from the [lower] kingdom of plants. Here at once lies one chief deficiency in the beauty of animal life. What is visible to us in the organism is not the soul; what is turned outwards and appears everywhere is not the inner life, but forms drawn from a lower stage [i.e., from plants] than that of life proper.[35]

In a comparison of animals and humans, Hegel asserts that the human body is "at a higher stage" than that of an animal, partly because the soul is more clearly revealed in the absence of these bodily coverings, but he adds the following caveat, which enumerates human imperfections:

> But however far the human, in distinction from the animal, body makes its life appear outwardly, still nevertheless the poverty of nature equally finds expression on this surface by the non-uniformity of the skin, in indentations, wrinkles, pores, small hairs, little veins, etc.[36]

Similarly, echoes of the seventeenth- and eighteenth-century scientific treatises reverberate in the writings of nineteenth-century biologist Charles Darwin. In *The Descent of Man, and Selection in Relation to Sex,* which is his application of evolutionary theory to humans, Darwin speculated that hairlessness in humans is a product of the evolutionary process, specifically of sexual selection. He pronounced that "in all parts of the world women are less hairy than men. Therefore we may reasonably suspect that this character has been gained through Sexual Selection."[37] He thus suggested that our male progenitors found hairless women sexually attractive and, as a consequence, hairless women and their progeny eventually survived in the evolutionary competition. Significantly, he indicated that women's sweeter voices and greater beauty were also by-products of sexual selection; he further claimed that although bearded males were sexually selected by females over beardless males, males passed along bearding solely to their male offspring, while hairless females passed along hairlessness to both sexes, to varying degrees:

> . . . it appears that our male ape-like progenitors acquired their beards as an ornament to charm or excite the opposite sex, and transmitted them only to their male offspring. The females apparently first had their bodies denuded of hair, also as a sexual ornament; but they transmitted this character almost equally to both sexes. It is not improbable that the females were modified in other respects for the same purpose and by the same means; so that women have acquired sweeter voices and become more beautiful than men.[38]

Darwin associated hairiness with "idiots" and primordial conditions but he did so in a way that protected hairy Europeans from unfavorable assessment. In a comparison of "races," rather than concluding that hairy Europeans were primordial, he claimed that European hairiness was an example of reversion:

> Some races are much more hairy than others, especially the males; but it must not be assumed that the more hairy races, such as the European, have retained their primordial condition more completely than the naked races, such as the Kalmucks or Americans. It is more probable that the hairiness of the former is due to partial reversion; for characters which have been at some former period long inherited, are always apt to return. We have seen that idiots are often very hairy, and they are apt to revert in other characters to a lower animal type.[39]

In a twentieth-century commentary on Darwin's discussion of sexual selection, Bernard Campbell suggested that juvenile characteristics in females were sexually attractive to male progenitors: "The retention of paedomorphic features (e.g., unbroken voice, retention of childlike complexion and more rounded body form), suggests that a greater degree of neoteny has been positively sexually selected in women than in men."[40] Hairlessness is another paedomorphic feature. According to Campbell it is not merely the feature but also the youthfulness associated with the feature—in this case, with hairlessness—that early males supposedly found sexually attractive.

Thus, in Darwin's treatise women's bodies were terrain, sites on which the signs of humanity were or were not marked. His writing is, in this respect, consistent with mid-nineteenth-century middle-class discourse that portrayed women as the refiners, bearers, and conservators of civilization. Darwin's views, which emphasized hairlessness as an indicator of evolutionary ascendency and which asserted that hairlessness in women was sexually attractive to men, may have helped set the tone for the hair-removal imperative of the first half of the twentieth century. Feminist scholar Rebecca Herzig assesses Darwin's role in the creation of fertile ground for this imperative:

> Yet if unwanted hair and techniques for its removal have been around . . . since "hoary antiquity" the years after 1870 saw an increasing fascination with "superfluous" hair in the United States. In the wake of Darwin, body hair became newly invested with evolutionary significance and attendant questions of racial and sexual difference. Changing patterns of immigration stimulated further attention to comparative physiognomy, while shifting economic and political roles for white, middle- and upper-class women provoked particular interest in "woman's" proper physical appearance.[41]

In a chapter entitled "Hair, Dirt, and Beasts," twentieth-century scholar Alison Ferris observes that in addition to associating hair with the less-than-fully human, many members of the Victorian middle class had come to equate hair with filth and filth with specific social classes:

> By the nineteenth century, the Victorian middle class vividly illustrated that the iconographic role of hair had been elided with that of dirt and beasts, especially when referring to the lower classes and "fallen women." The lower classes, like the fictional wildman, were objects of both fascination and disgust to the nineteenth-century middle class. . . . More than ever, these segments of society were described by the middle class as "dirty" and as violating the boundary separating humans from animals. The poor were constantly equated with descriptions of their living conditions until filth symbolically stood for them.[42]

Ferris notes that these classed discourses about filth and hair tended to focus on women:

> These . . . discourses affected nineteenth-century literature and art, which in turn focused more on women than on men. Women of all classes were thought of as being closer to nature and thus more susceptible to transgressing the boundary separating human and animal. Their bodies, behavior, and movements, even the way they wore their hair, were disciplined by social and religious mores and guidelines of etiquette, beauty, and fashion.[43]

Women's body hair was pathologized in Caesar Lombroso and William Ferrero's volume *The Female Offender*, published in 1898. Lombroso and Ferrero argued that criminality could be discerned and predicted by studying a woman's physical features; they posited that substantial body hair and specific hair colors were signs of villainous tendencies. In an introduction to the book, W. Douglas Morrison summarized Lombroso's assumptions:

> . . . he [Lombroso] finds that the criminal population as a whole, but the habitual criminal in particular, is to be distinguished from the average member of the community by a much higher percentage of physical anomalies. These anomalies consist of malformations in the skull and brain and face.[44]

Lombroso and Ferrero did not limit themselves to study of "anomalies" in these body areas, however. Morrison continued:

> The criminal population also exhibits a considerable percentage of anomalies connected with the limbs, such as excessive development of the arms or defective development of the legs. We have also sexual peculiarities, such as femininism [sic] in men, masculism in women, and infantilism in both. Where a considerable number of deep-seated physical anomalies are found in combination in the same individual, we usually see that they are accompanied by nervous and mental anomalies of a more or less morbid character. These mental anomalies are visible among the criminal population in an absence of moral sensibility, in general instability of character, in excessive vanity, excessive irritability, a love of revenge, and, as far as habits are concerned, a descent to customs and pleasures akin in their nature to the orgies of uncivilised tribes. In

short, the habitual criminal is a product, according to Dr. Lombroso, of patho-
logical and atavistic anomalies; he stands midway between the lunatic and the
savage; and he represents a special type of the human race.[45]

Significantly, Lombroso and Ferrero claimed that female criminals and
prostitutes have a "virile quantity" of hair, as well as darker hair than "nor-
mals," and they cited statistics from other criminologists to support their
assertion.[46] The authors pointed out that in one portrait, included in the volume, the woman's hair "is seen to form almost a beard."[47] Morrison, in dis-
cussing a possible flaw in Lombroso and Ferrero's theory, argued that the
characteristics outlined in the book are not unique to criminals but may be
shared by other categories of "degenerates" as well:

> The most weighty objection to the doctrine of a distinctively criminal type is
> to be found in the circumstance that the mental and physical peculiarities
> which are said to be characteristic of the criminal are in reality common to him
> with the lunatic, the epileptic, the alcoholic, the prostitute, the habitual pau-
> per. The criminal is only one branch of a decadent stem; he is only one mem-
> ber of a family group; his abnormalities are not peculiar to himself; they have
> a common origin, and he shares them in common with the degenerate type of
> which he furnishes an example.[48]

In a study of turn-of-the-century medical discourse, Herzig observes
that circa 1878 a new women's disease, hypertrichosis (i.e., "excessive hairiness"), was identified.[49] Significantly, according to Herzig, because there
was no universally accepted, unchanging definition of what constituted a
"normal" female body, there was no consensus among the medical community about the criteria for determining pathology:

> If fluctuations in fashion weren't confusing enough, physicians also grappled
> with differing national, racial, and ethnic standards of hair growth. As
> European and North American medical practitioners readily acknowledged,
> definitions of "excessive" hair not only varied across time, but also across
> physical and cultural distance.[50]

An additional conundrum faced by physicians, according to Herzig, was
that the medical community subscribed to a "radically dimorphic" two-sex
model and used body hair as a marker of sex,[51] but body hair, as some
attempts to definitively establish criteria for pathology revealed, manifests
itself on a continuum that defies the creation of unequivocal dimorphic distinctions.[52] Herzig notes that some physicians, rather than looking to the
sometimes confusing physical body to define "femaleness" (or to hormones
and chromosomes as has been the case in the twentieth-century),[53] turned
to the patient's psyche to determine who were the "real" women behind the
"excessive" body hair:

> These texts thus answer the question of what "woman" really is, her essential difference from the male, through recourse to a particular instinctual quality— namely, her drive to appear "feminine" The individual who exhibited a desire to appear feminine counted as female, no matter how lush and virile "her" hair growth might have been. . . . Sexual identity, the index of femaleness, was removed from the confused and confusing surface of the body and situated in the subcutaneous realm of womanly desire.[54]

Herzig observes that physicians of the day often used a woman's emotional distress as justification for treatment of hypertrichosis and notes that although the disease was diagnosed in women and men, emotional pain or illness was only mentioned in reference to women.[55]

In summary, the early sources discussed here associate hairlessness with humanity and femaleness. They use hair as a defining characteristic in racialized taxonomies of humans that celebrate Whites at the expense of all others. In the latter part of the nineteenth century, "excessive" hairiness, although it eluded definition, became a pathology that predicted criminality in women and was identified as a disease having especially devastating effects on women patients. Hairiness on females, thus, was rendered as an anomaly associated with filth, poverty, criminality, degeneracy, and pathology.

Hair Removal in the Early Twentieth Century

As we have seen, the discursive stage clearly was set at the turn of the twentieth century for hair removal to be fashionable, but according to Christine Hope's history of U.S. women's hair removal practices, prior to World War I, most American women did not remove underarm or leg hair, even though dark body hair on women was considered undesirable.[56] In fact, because vaudeville dancers were among the few women who removed body hair, the practice was deemed as immoral as vaudeville.[57] Thus, early advocates needed to convince a doubting public of the practice's decency. Beauty guides were venues for arguments in defense of the morality of hairlessness; Hope quotes an example from a 1922 beauty book by Virginia Kirkus: "'Because the practice of underarm depilatory or shaving started with chorus girls is no reason for considering it beneath the dignity of the social leader. Lucky the woman who has no superfluous hair; let the rest of her sex get rid of it as best they can.'"[58]

An array of factors may have contributed to a change in hair-removal practices during the 1920s; among these was the Gillette Company's introduction in 1915 of the Milady Decollete, a razor designed specifically for women. Russell B. Adams, Jr., in his history of Gillette, quotes unnamed sources that forwarded a rationale for the product:

In mid-1915 Gillette introduced its Milady Decollete—"brought out after frequent requests from Palm Beach, Virginia Hot Springs and other pleasure resorts," the field force was solemnly assured. It was the first razor designed and marketed specifically for women, and was billed in the extensive national advertising campaign as the "safest and most sanitary method of acquiring a smooth underarm." This was, apparently, a somewhat ticklish subject in those barely post-Victorian times, and Gillette salesmen were sternly ordered: "Do not use the term 'shaving' [emphasis in Adams] as applied to this operation." Men could shave with impunity; women merely smoothed.[59]

According to Adams, Gillette engaged in forceful marketing tactics and sought complete domination of the market, regardless of the product in question.[60] The company's aggressiveness is clear in a bellicose 1912 memo in which King C. Gillette outlines a plan to pulverize his competitors:

> 'All it requires for us to drive them from the field,' he said in the steel-tipped language of a military commander, 'is to train a Gatling gun on them—they could never stand the fire.' Later, becoming even more bloodthirsty, he cautioned, 'We must be the aggressor—we must be continually advancing and drive them back at the point of the bayonet, and our ammunition must be money for advertising.'[61]

Hope asserts that it was advertisers who "'educated'" women into believing that hair removal was necessary.[62] The earliest advertisements only mentioned hair on the face, neck, and underarms; underarm hair, which by the 1920s was called a "'disfigurement,'" was the principal focus.[63] Discussion of "limbs" (i.e., legs) appeared in 1918, but according to Hope, legs were not the focus of these early advertisements.[64] By 1945, according to Basow, the majority of U.S. women removed leg and arm hair; Hope notes, however, that even into the 1940s many women did not regularly or ever remove leg hair.[65]

Changing fashion, specifically clothing that revealed more of a woman's body, is a second factor that contributed to the hair-removal imperative, according to Hope. She specifically mentions sheer sleeves and sleeveless dresses:

> Sears first offers dresses with sheer sleeves in 1922 (sleveless [sic] dresses do not appear on catalog pages until 1925). That same year marks the first time that products designated to remove hair other than that on the face, neck and arms are offered to the general public. The fall 1922 catalog features both a woman's decollete safety razor (identical to a standard safety razor except for its somewhat smaller size and fancier case) and a depilatory ad mentioning underarm hair, complete with picture of a young woman admiring her hair-free underarms in a mirror.[66]

While acknowledging that the hair-removal imperative was a result, at least in part, of changing fashions and aggressive marketing campaigns, Hope also suggests that fads, fashions, and marketing campaigns, in order to be successful, must be consonant with "larger cultural configurations," and she quotes fashion theorist Edward Sapir to support her assertion:

> "An important principle in the history of fashion is that those features of fashion which do not configurate with the unconscious system of meaning characteristic of the given culture are relatively insecure."[67]

In short, successful fashions may tap deep-seated beliefs, hopes, fears, and desires.

Hope is among a body of scholars to have explored the possible desires, needs, and beliefs that created fertile ground during the interwar years for the hair-removal imperative. Specifically, these scholars have situated this change in cultural practice within a context of then-prevailing discourses about social class, race, and gender. Let us examine some of these hopes, fears, and desires more closely.

Hope and Basow suggest that during the interwar period the hair-removal imperative was a by-product of a changing vision of female beauty; this new vision, according to Basow, was more overtly sexy and revealed more skin.[68] She suggests that in an era when women's sexuality is on display, hair removal may signify controlled or contained sexuality:

> Since hair has long had sexual associations for men and for women, its removal also may have conveyed two closely associated sexual messages—that a woman's mature sexuality is controlled at the same time as her "tamed" sensuality is on display. . . . The current taboo against showing pubic hair reflects this process. Women's bathing suits increasingly reveal the pubic area; women now are encouraged to remove or bleach those hairs that show. Visible hair, not the pubic area itself, is too risqué to reveal.[69]

Desire to control women's sexuality may not have been the only regulatory issue at stake, however. Basow indicates, for example, that for White women the interwar period was marked by a dramatic increase in public-sphere opportunities and by changes in social status; she theorizes that hair removal may have been a reactionary containment response, an attempt to reassert distinctions between the sexes and to put women back in their place by portraying them as juvenile, i.e., hairless.[70]

In addition to being sexy, the new image of female beauty was youthful. Basow points out that because hairlessness is generally associated with juvenility, the hairless ideal is part of a discourse that equates female beauty with youthfulness.[71] Cleanliness was also underscored in this new image,[72] and Hope believes that America's overall obsession with hygiene during this period, which equated cleanliness with goodness, contributed substantively to the hair removal imperative.[73] To accept at face value the premise that shaving was instituted for hygienic reasons, however, is to overlook a whole host of deeper questions. For example, if shaving is hygienic, why isn't all body hair removed and why don't men similarly remove body hair? Is cleanliness good, and if so, why? Delving into some of the deeper issues, Basow hypothesizes that America's obsession with cleanliness and cleansing was both racialized and ethnocentric, an assimilationist reaction to massive immigration in the early part of the century.[74] Hair removal, as obliquely intimated in advertisements of the day, is a way to accentuate Whiteness. A 1937 advertisement, quoted in Hope, is rife with overtones of race and class: "'The smooth, fair skin of the female denotes gentility and womanly charm.'"[75] Basow points out that "shaving makes skin smooth and *white* [emphasis in original]."[76]

Rebecca Herzig's discussion of possible reasons why North American women of the first half of the twentieth century patronized X-ray epilation parlors summarizes some of the hopes, fears, and desires that may have been tapped by the hair-removal imperative. According to Herzig, the need to remove hair was so strong that women continued to frequent X-ray parlors into the 1940s, even after the establishments had been outlawed in many parts of North America and this form of epilation had been proven hazardous.[77] She argues that hair removal was related to issues of ethnicity and social-class mobility, observing that the parlors targeted particular audiences, specifically, non-English-speaking urban women.[78] According to Herzig, one source singled out Jewish and Celtic women as having "excessive" hair.[79] She adds, "Medical and legal records indicate that most epilation clients were working women employed in low- or middle-income positions."[80] Clients were promised that the parlors would be clean and luxurious, and that if they undertook the procedure, previously closed doors would be opened to them.[81]

In addition Herzig calls X-ray epilation a technology "used to produce 'race' in this period of U.S. history."[82] The title of her article, "Removing Roots," alludes to the assimilationist tone of the hair-removal discourse. Pointing to the use of hair as a distinguishing characteristic in racial taxonomies of the nineteenth century, Herzig observes, "In the United States, where questions of racial identity have long focused on perceived morphological characteristics, discussions of physical appearance carry particular histories of race and racism."[83] She notes that "removing the 'dark shadow' that barred access to the world of 'social enjoyments' appears to have acquired a certain urgency during the interwar period, an era of increasingly restrictive U.S. immigration laws, widespread interest in eugenics, and increasingly desperate economic depression."[84] Herzig states that in this instance the production of Whiteness is both "a symbolic *and* material process,"[85] and she points to other similar examples of racialized uses of X-ray technology, lightening of African American skin, among them.[86] Misplaced hope in science, Herzig claims, also contributed to the attractiveness of X-ray epilation: "Despite experiencing the dire physiological effects of attempts to reform bodies rather than social structures, some clients continued to seek personal salvation in the advancement of science."[87]

Women's persistence in frequenting these parlors even in the face of evidence that X-rays caused cancer, exemplifies, according to Herzig, one of the multiple ways in which hair and hair removal were tied to morbidity. She reports that some women became severely depressed or suicidal over their body hair.[88] The supposed solution to the body hair problem, however, was also tied to death. Herzig cites a 1970 study that attributed "more than 35 percent of all radiation-induced cancer in women . . . to X-ray hair removal."[89] Thus, she concludes that "however irrelevant or ridiculous the subject of hair removal may appear to readers today, for many women in the interwar period epilation was nothing less than a matter of life and death."[90]

To summarize, when attempting to understand why revealed hair would be considered a disfigurement, why Americans would be obsessed with cleanliness and youthfulness, why standards of female beauty were changing, and why women would risk their lives to remove body hair, we should not overlook the role that hopes, fears, desires, and anxieties—rooted in issues of race, ethnicity, class, and gender—may have played.

Current Practices and Perceptions

Studies of current practice suggest that the vast majority of U.S. women remove body hair, but statistics may be deceiving because sampling has focused primarily on White, middle-class women. Also, some women may not remove body hair because they have little or no non-head hair to remove. That said, however, a 1998 study by Tiggemann and Kenyon concluded that about 92 percent of the female high school and university students surveyed, almost all of whom were White, removed leg or underarm hair.[91] Similarly, in a study of professional women's hair removal practices, Basow reported that

> . . . the majority (85%) of professional women began to remove their leg and/or underarm hair, most by age 14. Approximately 81% continue to do so, at least occasionally. About half of the respondents remove hair at least once a week, although about 25% of those who remove hair do so only seasonally. . . . [92]

These studies also allude to some of the groups of women that are less likely to remove hair. For example, Basow suggests that until fairly recently European women did not, by and large, do so; she also indicates, however, that what had once been primarily U.S. discourses and discursive practices have been exported in recent years.[93] Brownmiller, writing in 1984, confirms this point:

> Influenced by Hollywood's sexpot starlets, only in the last twenty years have European women followed the American lead and begun to denude their underarms and legs. In her autobiography, Shelley Winters recalled her mortification in Rome during the Fifties when she realized that in a roomful of women wearing formal, strapless gowns, she was the only one whose underarms were pink and hairless. Today at a similar event a woman who neglected to shave would probably be mortified by her conspicuous breach of good taste and grooming.[94]

Based on a small number of Black participants, Basow concludes that Black women are less likely than White women to remove leg hair. Twenty-one percent of Black women reported doing so, while 50 percent of White women did.[95] In addition, Basow reports that self-identified lesbians and women who described themselves as strongly feminist were among the least likely to remove underarm and leg hair: "Whereas only 13% of exclusively heterosexual women do not remove leg hair, 39% of lesbian and bisexual women do not."[96] Furthermore, according to Basow, "About one out of three very strongly identified feminists does not remove underarm hair, and nearly that percentage does not remove leg hair, about triple the frequency of low to moderately identified feminists."[97] Basow's study, however, was of professional women; as I will discuss shortly, practices of women in careers defined as professions may be somewhat different from those of women in general. Basow concludes that there is enormous pressure on women to remove leg and underarm hair; as evidence, she reports that although women in the lesbian and strongly feminist categories are among the least likely to remove leg or underarm hair, the majority do so, nevertheless.[98] She speculates that norms of the 1990s were even more restrictive than those of thirty years earlier.[99]

A study of perceptions of White women who do not remove body hair may shed light on why most women opt to do so. In a 1998 study, Basow and Braman showed a videotape to two groups of college students, nearly all of whom were White and from the upper-middle class.[100] The video featured a White model, poolside, drying off her body. One group was shown a video featuring a model who removed body hair, and the other viewed the same video of the same model with underarm and leg hair. Based on responses to the videos, Basow and Braman concluded:

> ...a [White] woman with body hair will be seen [by White observers] as less sexually and interpersonally attractive than the same woman without body hair. Specifically, the woman with body hair was viewed as less sociable, intelligent, happy, and positive, and as more aggressive, active and strong.[101]

In a discussion of their results, Basow and Braman suggest that because body hair on women tends to be associated with lesbians and feminists, negative stereotypes ascribed to these groups may have negatively influenced student perceptions of the model with hair.[102] After viewing the video, each group was administered a survey of feminist attitudes; the researchers note that the group viewing the model with body hair scored significantly lower on this measure than did the group viewing the model with body hair removed. Rather than simply ascribing this difference to chance variation, the authors hypothesize that viewing the model with body hair may have prompted viewers to hold or express more negative attitudes about feminism.[103]

When asked why they remove body hair, respondents in Basow's 1991 study of women professionals indicated they do so either for femininity and attractiveness reasons or to avoid social disapproval; some indicated they felt their credibility in the workplace would be damaged if they did not.[104] The women in Basow's study tended to begin hair removal as adolescents for "social and normative reasons," and Basow suggests that hair removal may serve as a rite of passage for many young women.[105] If they continued to remove hair, they tended to do so for feminine/attractiveness reasons. Basow concludes that today the hairless female body is an aesthetic ideal largely accepted by feminists and nonfeminists alike.[106]

Themes that emerged in literature from and about the first half of the twentieth century also surface in discussions of current practice. Some feminist sources situate hair removal within a larger body of repressive practices that imply the female body must be altered and contained in order to be acceptable.[107] Others point out the political implications of a desire to keep females looking eternally youthful, which is manifest in the removal of signs of adulthood and sexual maturity.[108] Tiggemann and Kenyon cite sources suggesting that infantilization of females tends to surface during periods when women are perceived to be too powerful.[109] Faced with shifting demographics, power relations, and political opportunities, today's women, like many women of the first half of the twentieth century, may be responding to desires and anxieties rooted in issues of ethnicity, race, gender, social class, and sexuality.

Teen Magazines and the Hair-Removal Imperative

Recalling that teenagers were identified in Janine's story as the enforcers of the hair-removal imperative, I decided to gain some insight into the messages teenage girls may be receiving concerning body hair. To do this I turned to two popular magazines for teenage girls, *Seventeen* and *Teen,* along with the websites maintained for each magazine.[110] I chose these publications because of their substantial readership. According to statistics provided by Primedia, the publisher of *Seventeen,* the magazine annually reaches 87 percent of all U. S. teenage girls.[111] The publisher claims a paid circulation of 2.4 million and a readership of over 13.9 million per month.[112] *Teen* magazine has a circulation of more than 2 million and a website that boasts more than 20 million views per month.[113] I located six print and six website references.[114]

The references clearly indicate that body hair is a problem in need of a solution. Discussions often appeared in Q&A advice columns, beleaguered readers reporting that they are "grossed out" by a body hair difficulty.[115] The question, thus, is never whether to remove hair, a topic that was never broached, but how. Usually the references focus on underarm and leg hair, but eyebrows, bikini lines, face, lower arms, and breasts also come under scrutiny. The references, which typically outline possible hair removal techniques along with the pros and cons of each, often are peppered with brand names of recommended products. Techniques range from waxing to laser. The only references to divert slightly from the hair-removal imperative suggest hiding facial and lower arm hair by bleaching it.[116] Taken collectively, the sources suggest that hair removal is labor intensive, sometimes expensive, and often painful. They also suggest that removal is necessary: all American women do or should remove hair. One techniques article is surrounded by shaving statistics, credited to the Gillette Company: "87% of American women begin shaving between the ages of 11 and 13."[117] The mentioning of "American" in this quotation seems to make shaving an almost patriotic thing to do, the passage ringing with assimilationist overtones. Readers are not told what happens to the other 13 percent of American women, whether they shave at ten, fourteen, or never. Furthermore, readers do not find out who these "other" women are and why they don't remove body hair.

The references also tend to link hair removal to contentment, or more precisely, nonremoval to unhappiness and anxiety. One guide to removal techniques begins, "You can't be carefree unless your skin is smoothly hair-free."[118] Another article injects anxiety: "If you've never worried about arm hair, don't start now. But if the thought of donning short sleeves is enough to keep you up at night, read on."[119] That article talks about bleaching cream.

In indirect ways several articles connect hair removal to sexual attractiveness. Only one event is specifically identified as a source of hair-removal anxiety, but it is mentioned in two articles: an upcoming prom.[120] One of these articles, which consists of shaving tips, begins with a word of general advice: "If your promwear includes something sexy, short and strappy, your skin should be your best accessory."[121] Thus, proms are linked to sexuality and the message is clear: hairless bodies are sexy.

By and large, the magazines do not discuss hairiness as a medical problem, but two website Q&As introduce the possibility that hairiness on particular parts of the body may result from a biochemical condition or a hormonal imbalance.[122] One of these also states that hair-growth patterns may be genetic.[123] In both instances hairiness remains a problem in need of a solution; one website uses a bellicose metaphor, suggesting that as a last resort the reader may need to "bring on the major artillery—like electrolysis or laser treatment."[124] The problem lies with the body and its hair, not with the surrounding discourses.

Thus, if 87 percent of American teenage girls are reading these magazines, then the desires and anxieties of nearly all American girls are being shaped and schooled into accepting hair removal not only as normal but necessary. The hair-removal imperative also circulates in magazines for adult women, where I found articles sporting such evocative titles as "Hasta la vista body hair!"[125] Finally, in a recent article describing fashion "transgressions" that even celebrities sometimes commit, *People* magazine called women's hairy armpits one of the "Seven Deadly Sins."[126] A photograph of celebrity Gillian Anderson's unshaven underarms was accompanied by a caption underscoring both the importance and the American-ness of hair removal:

> When in Rome (or in many other places in the world) fine. But in the U.S. women with unshaven underarms, such as Gillian Anderson's at an April pro-choice rally in Hollywood, are "associated with being not well-groomed," says Cindy Barshop, Manhattan-based hair removal guru to celebs and models. "It's a cultural thing."[127]

The fact that Anderson displayed her underarms at a rally for a liberal political cause did not exempt her from criticism, which, significantly, was delivered by a purveyor of hair-removal services. Thus, it appears that in the United States today women of all ages, including celebrities, are being pressured by an almost univocal message.

Some Implications for Teachers and Teaching

Theorizing Hair Removal

In order to frame some implications of the hair-removal imperative for teachers and teaching, let us delve a bit deeper into theory. I begin with the cautionary assumption that reading, whether of texts or bodies, is an interpretive process. I thus recognize that meanings are multiple, discursive-community specific and not transhistoric. Hair on a woman's body, like print texts concerning hair removal, can be read in multiple, imprecise, and ever-changing ways.[128]

That said, the evidence presented here suggests that discourses surrounding hair and hair removal play a role in the materialization of the body as sexed, gendered, raced, and classed. These groupings themselves are dynamic and have distinct historical trajectories, implications, and consequences. In addition, however, they are interrelated in complex ways. For example, applying theory articulated by Judith Butler, which focuses primarily on the construction and performativity of sex, I maintain that in discourses that construct gender as "radically dimorphic" the hair-removal imperative is "a regulatory norm by which sexual difference is materialized."[129] Hair removal is one among myriad technologies that construct sex and gender, assuming as Butler does, that construction is a dynamic, reiterative process, and that sex is a cultural norm rather than a prediscursive given.[130] Butler argues that in order to think of construction in this manner, however, we need to view "matter, not as site or surface, but as *a process of materialization that stabilizes over time to produce the effect of boundary, fixity, and surface we call matter*" [emphasis in original].[131] I argue in addition, however, that several other materialization processes surrounding hair are occurring simultaneously. For example, in discourses that construct race as a series of distinct categories and sexuality (i.e., what is sometimes called sexual orientation) as dichotomous, racial and sexual categories are similarly created, in part, by the materialization and marking of difference. Presence, color, density, and location of body hair play a role in this process. At the same time that articulated differences between people placed in the category "women" and people placed in the category "men" materialize sex, articulated differences among people categorized as "women" help to materialize bodies as raced and sexually oriented. The hair-removal imperative, a regulatory norm, stems from related discourses that attempt to erase discursively materialized variations among people categorized as "women" while simultaneously reinforcing distinction between the categories "women" and "men." Thus, dominant discourses concerning hair and hair removal not only help to create race, sex, gender, and sexuality by constructing difference, but in addition, they support homogenization, by advocating erasure of *some* of these differences.

When attempting to understand how this is accomplished, Butler's concept of a domain of abjection is particularly useful.[132] Butler speaks of "erasures and exclusions" that create and maintain a zone of abjection to which bodies that do not matter are relegated, "a domain of abjected bodies, a field of deformation, which, in failing to qualify as the fully human, fortifies . . . regulatory norms."[133] The hair-removal imperative places women's bodies that are not removed of hair (recognizing that the definition of "excessive" is always shifting) in that domain of abjection, and in the process, fortifies itself.

Butler posits, however, that bodies relegated to the abject realm may present challenges to a "symbolic hegemony," and thus "force a radical rearticulation of what qualifies as bodies that matter, ways of living that count as 'life,' lives worth protecting, lives worth saving, lives worth grieving."[134]

Significantly, the categorized materializations accomplished, in part, by dominant discourses concerning hair and hair removal are integrally related to power, specifically, to the new forms of power described by French philosopher Michel Foucault. Foucault asserted that Europe in the seventeenth and eighteenth centuries saw the emergence of a modern age of power, characterized by different mechanisms of disciplinary power and by the "invention" of a "new political anatomy."[135] One characteristic of modernity has been its attention to the body, more specifically, to the regulation and discipline of the body. According to Foucault, "The classical age discovered the body as object and target of power,"[136] this age being marked by "a meticulous observation of detail, and at the same time a political awareness of these small things, for the control and use of men. . . ."[137] Discourse, he stated, is central to these new power relations.[138]

Hair removal seems to be a classic example of such attention to the body and to its regulation. It is a detailed act performed on the body, regulatory in the sense that it promises much to those who comply to the norm while threatening much to those who do not. Significantly, it exemplifies surveillance and regulation of *women's* bodies.

Second, Foucault argued that power is not merely that which forbids, but also that which allows, constructs, and produces:

> What makes power hold good, what makes it accepted, is simply the fact that it doesn't only weigh on us as a force that says no, but that it traverses and produces things, it induces pleasure, forms knowledge, produces discourse. It needs to be considered as a productive network which runs through the whole social body, much more than as a negative instance whose function is repression.[139]

Its realm, thus, includes pleasure and desire as well as exclusion, fear, and repression. Women remove body hair not only because of a constructed fear of rejection but also because of constructed desires and hopes, including a desire to be acceptable, beautiful, and sexually attractive. Evidence from the teen magazines, for example, suggests that both desire and fear are constructed and then tapped in discourses about hair removal.

Third, Foucault asserted that there is interdependence between major dominations and local mobilizations. Maintaining that "power comes from below," he claimed that major dominations, which have been the subject of much modernist theorizing about power, are "hegemonic effects"[140] of small-scale mobilizations and microtechnologies. In a discussion of a concept he called "double conditioning," Foucault posited that although power exists on continua such that there are no clear lines of distinction between macro and micro power, and although power writ large is not merely an enlargement of power writ small (or vice versa), nevertheless a supportive and productive relationship exists between major dominations and small-scale mobilizations.[141] He might have argued, for example, that major dominations coalescing around gender, sexuality, race, class, and ethnicity are effects of a multiplicity of relations that operate locally. Arguably, hair removal, as a discursive practice, is one such microtechnology, which is in symbiotic relationship with several major dominations. Just as there can be multiple simultaneous readings of the female body removed of hair, hair removal can signify multiple positions in various relations of power. For example, hair removal can signify the power of social-class status while simultaneously signifying subjection in gender relations.

Teachers, Regulation, and Power

Keeping these theoretical perspectives in mind, let us turn to teachers and teaching. First, as Michael W. Apple, Sue Middleton and others have pointed out, historically and currently teachers and teaching have been heavily regulated.[142] Some of this regulation has focused on the body; significantly, the majority of teachers are women. In his book *Teachers and Texts* Apple reproduces a 1923 teaching contract that exemplifies this regulation: the contract forbade women teachers from dying their hair, wearing bright colors, smoking, drinking, loitering in ice cream parlors, staying out after 8:00 P.M., marrying, keeping company with men, wearing dresses more than two inches above the ankles, and from wearing face powder, mascara, or lipstick.[143] Although not written into current teaching contracts, the hair-removal imperative operates as unofficial policy that similarly focuses on women and exemplifies continued heavy regulation of women teachers' bodies. The anecdote about Janine that opened this essay has an interesting twist. Her differences, deemed unacceptable in the classroom, did not bar her from admission to a service-based government job. This suggests that although regulation may be gendered, among women and social spaces differential regulation applies, i.e., not all women's bodies and not all occupations are subject to the same degree or kinds of control.

Second, Foucault's assertion that regulatory norms produce effects not only by prohibiting and repressing, but also by producing, constructing, and capitalizing upon desire, is applicable here. In the case both of the 1923 teaching contract and of the hair-removal imperative one motive for compliance may be the desire to be a "good" employable teacher.

Recalling that Basow's study focused on shaving practices of women professionals and elicited responses suggesting that a high percentage of the participants shave, it is reasonable to surmise that for teachers the hair-removal imperative may be tied to specific dominant visions of professionalism and to a desire to be considered a professional. Hair removal may be a corporeal mark of distinction or status that distinguishes women professionals from other women. The desire to be viewed as a professional may hold special appeal to those in occupations that have never achieved or have lost the status accorded to a "profession." Teaching may fit this description. As appealing as professional status may seem, however, dominant discourses about professionalism, while neither static nor univocal, have their own problematic historical trajectories that are racialized, gendered, sexed, and classed. Ironically, equity initiatives that seek to diversify exclusive occupational fields may be undercut by dominant understandings of professionalism.

Dominant discourse, which plays a central role in the regulation of the body, also assists in the process of the materialization of the "good," the acceptable teacher. Recognizing that there is no consensus about what constitutes good teaching, by examining the implications of the hair-removal imperative we can, nevertheless, catch glimpses of one construction of the "good," of which groups of people, which bodies, tend to be included or excluded. Internal or external enforcement of the hair-removal imperative helps to materialize the "valued and valuable" woman teacher as compliant, conventional, White, heterosexual, sexually attractive, and from the middle class. It also helps to construct a zone of abjection: all others need not apply unless they are willing to fall in line, i.e., to adopt practices and beliefs consistent with the valued norm. The hair-removal imperative, like other regulatory norms, enforces not merely by what it promises and allows but also by what it relegates to a zone of abjection. A traditional vision of the "good" teacher constructs her as a role model for her students. This study raises the question, however, of precisely what "good" women teachers are expected to model via adherence to the hair-removal imperative, given its checkered history.

As we have seen, the hair-removal imperative is a regulatory norm tied to more than one major domination, and it can have different consequences and implications for different groups of women teachers. Let us consider, for example, its links to a cluster of dominations surrounding what Butler calls "heterosexual hegemony."[144] Because the fictive "lesbian body" is constructed as unshaven, bending the rules by not removing body hair is likely to bring a woman teacher's body under suspicion regardless of how the rule breaker identifies herself on a sexuality spectrum. As one of the anecdotes that opened this essay illustrates, however, for some lesbian teachers discourses about hair, together with homophobia, create a "confessional" dilemma, a burden not borne by heterosexual women. The absence of this confessional dilemma is but one example of heterosexual privilege supported by discourses about hair. It also exemplifies differential regulation. Thus, my earlier assertion that an acceptable woman teacher is sexually attractive requires qualification: apparently she is acceptable only if she simultaneously signals contained sexuality and heterosexuality, heterosexuality being accorded privilege.

Obviously, the effects of the major dominations surrounding heterosexual privilege are not felt solely by women or women teachers. Males, male teachers in particular, may face rigid regulatory norms, some of which are deeply rooted in homophobia and heterosexual privilege. While some schools may hire and accept female teachers who do not remove body hair, I submit that the same may not be true about males exhibiting behavior that is stereotypically ascribed to gay men.

The hair-removal imperative speaks at a different decibel level than pronouncements from hate-mongering groups such as Rev. Ralph Ovadal's "Wisconsin Christians United," but the core message is the same: only heterosexuals should be allowed the privilege of becoming a teacher. A dose of Ovadal's distilled hatred may remind us of the grave implications of homophobic discourse and discursive practice, whether subtle or strident. Erroneously linking "homosexuality" to mass murder and pedophilia, a brochure entitled "Homosexuality: The Truth," distributed by Ovadal's group, condemns the granting of full civil rights to gays and denounces the hiring of gay, lesbian and bisexual teachers: "If out-of-the-closet homosexuals are permitted the same civil rights as moral citizens," the brochure argues, "then there is no basis for denying those caught up in this perversion the right to adopt and teach children. . . ."[145] The brochure's creators neither recognize nor acknowledge the potential benefits for all of practicing humane tolerance.

Janine and the Three Strikes Theory

Just before I accepted my first job in academe, a trusted friend and tenured professor, "Jeff," offered me frank advice: "The key to academic success is not having three strikes against you, and through no fault of your own you already have two. It will be your job to prevent the third. Strike one is that you're a woman, and strike two is that you're very bright." Caught off guard by the idea that intellect may not be a treasured attribute in colleges and universities, I asked Jeff to explain. He replied that competence is valued but anything more, especially anything more in women, is likely to engender suspicion and jealously. He advised me to maintain a low profile and to say little about my achievements. He then enumerated many other strikes that may hinder an academic's career, the only one of which I can remember anymore is obesity. His message was clear: academe accepts some variance but the difference tolerance is relatively small, and significant difference is a liability rather than an asset.

Even though Janine was being inducted into public school teaching and not academe, the "Three Strikes Theory" came to mind as I tried to understand why her cooperating teacher considered leg hair to be a serious problem. I suspect that Janine's unshaven legs were the fourth, fifth, or sixth strikes against her and perhaps embodied differences the cooperating teacher was unwilling to openly discuss. The fact that Janine was Jewish marked her, at least in that part of the Midwest, as a different, exotic other, as did her New York home. As the sources I cited earlier indicate, there is historical precedent for identifying Jewish women as exotic others in need of remedy and assimilation. Recall, for example, that they were among the women targeted in advertisements for the X-ray epilation parlors and singled out as having too much hair. To further complicate matters, Janine's curricular specialty was music, a minefield for the brave Jewish teacher outspoken enough to challenge a curricular canon that continues to rely heavily on Christian music, particularly holiday music. Next, in her interactions with students Janine chose not to use a hierarchical power model. Her perspective on power in the classroom, which I find compelling, does not represent the mainstream, especially not in music where teachers routinely face masses of students—class sizes unheard of in most other curricular areas; it may not be valued by teachers or administrators who measure a teacher's competence by his or her ability to "control" students. In addition Janine's politics and even her dietary habits marked her as different. Within this context, and given the prevalent perception—at least prevalent among the White middle class—that unshaven legs signify a whole host of "unsavory" characteristics, including lesbianism and feminism, it is less surprising that Janine's legs elicited criticism. By contrast, the teachers from my graduate class who successfully weathered the storms their unshaven legs created tended not to have long lists of other "strikes" against them. However, I cannot shake off the feeling that students are impoverished by Janine's absence from the teaching profession, as well as by the narrowness of the range of acceptability.

Official policy in schools of education often calls for a more diverse pool of teachers; this study implies, however, that by examining microtechnologies we may see multiple and conflicting discourses and discursive practices in circulation, some of which may undercut diversity initiatives or reveal conflicted views about whether and how much diversity is sought. Microtechnologies may be at odds with avowed "official" policy, may suggest unspoken ambivalence, or may reflect lack of consensus about the merits of welcoming people from historically excluded groups. The hair-removal imperative appears to play a role in a rigorous patrolling of the bounds of acceptability, at least the bounds of who constitutes an acceptable female teacher. However, if we educators seek to make the teaching profession more inclusive, we need to, in Judith Butler's words, "expand the very meaning of what counts as a valued and valuable body in the world,"[146] recognizing the potential benefits for all of such expansion.

Final Thoughts

To the question of whether women's body hair is a trivial and frivolous topic, I respond that it is not. The level of interest this study has generated supports the assertion that for many people, body hair and hair removal involve deeply held desires, beliefs, and values. Second, I argue that we as educators can learn much from an awareness of the seemingly small, nuanced microtechnologies that help to materialize race, class, gender, sexuality, and ethnicity. Foucault posited that microtechnologies are germane to the exercise of power and, thus, he challenged scholars to study power's "capillary form of existence, the point where power reaches into the very grain of individuals, touches their bodies and inserts itself into their actions and attitudes, their discourses, learning processes and everyday lives."[147] In this essay I have examined but one among many such points of power. Finally, I remind readers that while hair removal is a cultural practice having implications and ramifications for women teachers, it is unrelated to a teacher's knowledge of subject matter or competence in helping students learn curricular content. Today, as has been the case in the past, however, what is expected of teachers, women teachers, in particular, apparently far exceeds these narrow qualifications.

NOTES

1. Judith Butler, *Bodies that Matter: On the Discursive Limits of "Sex"* (New York: Routledge, 1993), 10.

2. Marina Warner, "Bush Natural," *Parkett* 27 (March 1991): 7.

3. Timothy Husband, in *The Wild Man: Medieval Myth and Symbolism* (New York: Metropolitan Museum of Art, 1980), 5–8, uses the phrase "monstrous races" to

describe a corpus of mythic figures appearing in ancient texts, including dog-headed men and other "aberrational human forms [that] were reported to live in India, Ethiopia, Libya, and other remote lands."

4. See Husband for descriptions of wild man as terrifying (p. 5), uncivilized (p. 5), antisocial (p. 5), violent (p. 3), aggressive (p. 3), mentally ill (pp. 7–9), and godless (p. 4).

5. Ibid., 5.

6. Ibid., 10.

7. Ibid., 7.

8. Ibid., 1.

9. See Husband's discussion of ancient sources, 5–6.

10. Ibid., 1, cites Friedrich von der Leyen and Adolph Spamer, *Die Altdeutschen Wandteppiche im Regensburger Rathaus* (Das Rathaus zu Regensburg, Regensburg: J. Habel, 1910), 93.

11. Ibid., 9.

12. Ibid., 4.

13. Ibid., 14–16.

14. Ibid., 15.

15. Ibid., 17.

16. Ibid.

17. Ibid., 2, 17.

18. Helkiah Crooke, *Mikrokosmographia: A Description of the Body of Man Together with the Controversies and Figures Thereto Belonging. . . .* (London: Iohn Clarke, 1651), 8.

19. Johann Blumenbach, "On the Natural Variety of Mankind, 1775," in *The Anthropological Treatises of Johann Friedrich Blumenbach . . . and the Inaugural Dissertation of John Hunter, M.D. . . . ,"* trans. and ed. Thomas Bendyshe (London: Longman, Green, Longman, Roberts, & Green, 1865), 88.

20. Ibid.

21. Londa Schiebinger, *Nature's Body: Gender in the Making of Modern Science* (Boston: Beacon Press, 1993), 125.

22. Charles White, *An Account of the Regular Gradation in Man, and in Different Animals and Vegetables; and From the Former to the Latter* (London: C. Dilly, 1799), 125.

23. Ibid.

24. Ibid., 134–135.

25. Ibid., 134, 83.

26. Ibid., 137.

27. Ibid.

28. Ibid., 79–80, 61.

29. See, for example, Crooke, 54; and John Hunter, "Inaugural Disputation on the Varieties of Man, by John Hunter, June, 1775," in *The Anthropological Treatises of Johann Friedrich Blumenbach . . . and the Inaugural Dissertation of John Hunter, M.D. . . . ,"* trans. and ed. Thomas Bendyshe (London: Longman, Green, Longman, Roberts, & Green, 1865), 385.

30. White, 98.

31. Ibid., 58.

32. Ibid., 92.

33. Crooke, 201.

34. Ibid., 55.

35. G.W. F. Hegel, *Aesthetics: Lectures on Fine Art,* trans. T.M. Knox (Oxford: Clarendon Press, 1975), 145.

36. Ibid., 146.

37. Charles Darwin, *The Descent of Man, and Selection in Relation to Sex: Part II,* 3rd ed., (London, 1877; 1st ed., 1871), *The Works of Charles Darwin,* ed. Paul H. Barrett & R. B. Freeman, vol. 22 (London: William Pickering, 1989), 625 or bracketed [600/1].

38. Ibid., 629 or bracketed [604/5].

39. Ibid., 626 or bracketed [601/2].

40. Bernard Campbell, *Sexual Selection and the Descent of Man, 1871–1971* (Chicago: Aldine, 1972), 251.

41. Rebecca Herzig, "Removing Roots: 'North American Hiroshima Maidens' and the X Ray," *Technology and Culture* 40, no. 4 (Oct. 1999): 725–726.

42. Alison Ferris, *Hair* (Sheboygan, WI: John Michael Kohler Arts Center, 1993), 19–20.

43. Ibid., 20–21.

44. Caesar Lombroso and William Ferrero, *The Female Offender,* ed. W. Douglas Morrison (New York: Appleton, 1898), xv.

45. Ibid., xvi.

46. Ibid., 82–83, 70, 71.

47. Ibid., 83.

48. Ibid., xvi–xvii.

49. Rebecca M. Herzig, "The Woman Beneath the Hair: Treating Hypertrichosis, 1870–1930," *NWSA Journal* 12, no. 3 (Fall 2000): 52.

50. Ibid., 53.

51. Ibid., 55, 53.

52. Ibid., 55.

53. Ibid., 56.

54. Ibid., 57.

55. Ibid., 58.

56. Christine Hope, "Caucasian Female Body Hair and American Culture," *Journal of American Culture* 5, no. 1 (1982): 93, 94.

57. Susan A. Basow, "The Hairless Ideal: Women and Their Body Hair," *Psychology of Women Quarterly* 15 (Mar. 1991): 84.

58. Hope, 96, quoting Virginia Kirkus, *Everywoman's Guide to Health and Personal Beauty* (New York: Martin & Murray, 1922), 195.

59. Russell B. Adams, Jr., *King C. Gillette: The Man and His Wonderful Shaving Device* (Boston: Little, Brown and Company, 1978), 92. [Adams does not cite primary sources.]

60. Ibid., 85.

61. Ibid. [Adams does not cite primary sources.]

62. Hope, 95.

63. Ibid., 94; Basow, 84; Susan Brownmiller, in *Femininity* (New York: Linden Press, 1984), 147, quotes an advertisement for Neet in *The Delineator,* October 1924. The ad uses the term "disfigurement."

64. Hope, 94.

65. Basow, 85; Hope, 97. My mother, who came into adulthood in the early 1940s, shaved her underarms and legs as a young adult, as did one of her older sisters. My mother's eldest sister and my grandmother did not, however.

66. Hope, 95.

67. Ibid., 97, quoting Edward Sapir, "Fashion," in *Encyclopedia of the Social Sciences,* vol. 6, ed. R.A. Seligman and Alvin Johnson (New York: Macmillan, 1930), 141.

68. Hope, 96; Basow, 84–85.

69. Basow, 86.

70. Ibid., 85–86.

71. Ibid., 84, 86.

72. Ibid., 85.

73. Hope, 98.

74. Basow, 84.

75. Hope, 98. Hope quotes from Everett G. McDonough, *Truth About Cosmetics* (New York: The Drug and Cosmetic Industry, 1937), 187.

76. Basow, 94.

77. Herzig, "Removing Roots," 724–725.

78. Ibid., 739.

79. Ibid., 728.

80. Ibid., 739.

81. Ibid.

82. Ibid., 744.

83. Ibid., 728, 727.

84. Ibid., 741.

85. Ibid., 744.

86. Ibid.

87. Ibid., 745.

88. Ibid., 726–727.

89. Ibid., 724. Quotes H. Martin et al., "Radiation-Induced Skin Cancer of the Head and Neck," *Cancer* 25 (1970): 61–71.

90. Ibid., 742.

91. Marika Tiggemann and Sarah J. Kenyon, "The Hairlessness Norm: The Removal of Body Hair in Women," *Sex Roles* 39, nos. 11–12 (Dec. 1998): 873.

92. Basow, 87.

93. Ibid., 95.

94. Brownmiller, 148.

95. Basow, 94.

96. Ibid., 83, 92.

97. Ibid., 90.

98. Ibid., 95.

99. Ibid.

100. Susan A. Basow and Amie C. Braman, "Women and Body Hair: Social Perceptions and Attitudes," *Psychology of Women Quarterly* 22, no. 4 (Dec. 1998): 638.

101. Ibid., 637.

102. Ibid., 643.

103. Ibid., 644.

104. Basow, 83, 94.

105. Ibid., 92.

106. Ibid., 94.

107. Ibid., 95; and Basow and Braman, 644; containment is discussed by Brownmiller, 142.

108. Hope, 99; and Brownmiller, 143.

109. Tiggemann and Kenyon, 874.

110. The websites are www.seventeen.com and www.TeenMag.com. I accessed the web-sites on January 17, 2001. The search feature at *Seventeen*'s website searched sources from January 1998 through December 2000. Print articles were examined for the period from January 1995 through September 2000.

111. Statistics from website, "Seventeen." Available: http://www.primediventures.com/html2/media/consumer/seventeen.html. 9 September 2000.

112. Ibid.

113. "Teen Magazine Files Suit Against Link to Porn Site." 6 January 2000. Available: http://mediapeak.com/0100-newsbriefs.htm. 24 April 2001.

114. I culled out all articles referring to hair or shaving for the five-year period from January 1995 through September 2000, eliminating those articles that referred exclusively to top-of-the-head hair. A reference consists of an article or website search hit that mentions the topic one or more times. Jennifer K. McIlhenny, "Bare Necessities," *Seventeen* 58, no. 6 (June 1999): 50. Sabrina Solin, "Bare Essentials," *Seventeen* 56 (June 1997): 58. Sophia Knight, "Faking Perfect Skin: Daring to Bare," *Seventeen* 55 (March 1996): 66. Susan Kaplow, "Beauty Q & A," *Seventeen* 55 (March 1996): 68. Dorothy Nelson, "Go-Bare Guide," *Teen* 43, no. 7 (July 1999): 22. "The Razor's Edge," *Teen* 40, no. 6 (June 1996): 18–19. "Hair Be Gone." Available: seventeen.com. 17 January 2001. "Help, I Have a Mustache!" Available: seventeen.com. 17 January 2001. "I've Got Hair on My Face." Available: seventeen.com. 17 January 2001. "Back to School: 101 Terrific Tips." Available: Teenmag.com-Teen Matters: Back to School. 17 January 2001. "Sex + Body. Help! I Have Hair on My Breasts." Available: Teenmag.com-Teen Matters: Sex + Body. 17 January 2001. "Beauty Q & A. I Can Never Figure Out How to Tweeze. . . ." Available: Teenmag.com-Beauty Q & A. 17 January 2001.

115. Kaplow, 68.

116. "I've Got Hair on My Face;" "Help, I Have a Mustache!" and McIlhenny.

117. "The Razor's Edge," 18.

118. Nelson, 22.

119. McIlhenny.

120. Knight, 66; and Kaplow, 68.

121. Knight, 66.

122. "Sex + Body;" and "I've Got Hair on My Face."

123. "I've Got Hair on My Face."

124. Ibid.

125. Christine Fellingham, "Hasta la vista body hair!" *Glamour* 97, no. 3 (March 1999): 138.

126. "Seven Deadly Sins," *People* 56, no. 12 (17 September 2001): 162.

127. Ibid., 163.

128. As Saul M. Olyan points out in a discussion of biblical shaving rituals, scholars need to "avoid misleading generalizations that do not apply transhistorically, transcultur-

ally, or even in all cases within the same culture at a single time. There is no intrinsic meaning to hair or its manipulation; all meaning is culturally dependent and context-bound." See Saul M. Olyan, "What Do Shaving Rites Accomplish and What Do They Signal in Biblical Ritual Contexts?" *Journal of Biblical Literature* 117, no. 4 (Winter 1998): 622. Africanist art expert and teacher educator Mariama Ross supports this assertion, for example, in her discussion of cross-cultural readings of rasta hair. See her museum catalog entry: Mariama Ross, "Rasta Hair," in *Hair in African Art & Culture,* ed. R. Sieber and F. Herreman (New York: Museum for African Art, 2000).

129. Butler, 4.

130. Ibid., 9, 3.

131. Ibid., 9.

132. Ibid., 3, 8, 16.

133. Ibid., 16.

134. Ibid.

135. Michel Foucault, *Discipline and Punish: The Birth of the Prison,* trans. Alan Sheridan (New York: Vintage, 1979), 138.

136. Ibid., 136.

137. Ibid., 141.

138. Michel Foucault, *Power/Knowledge: Selected Interviews and Other Writings 1972–1977,* ed. Colin Gordon, trans. Colin Gordon, Leo Marshall, et al. (New York: Pantheon Books, 1980), 93.

139. Foucault, *Power/Knowledge,* 119.

140. Michel Foucault, *The History of Sexuality: An Introduction: Volume 1,* trans. Robert Hurley (Pantheon, 1978; rpt. New York: Vintage, 1990), 94.

141. Ibid., 99–100.

142. See, for example, Michael W. Apple, *Teachers and Texts: A Political Economy of Class and Gender Relations in Education* (New York: Routledge, 1986), 72; and Sue Middleton, *Disciplining Sexuality: Foucault, Life Histories, and Education* (New York: Teachers College Press, 1998).

143. Apple, 73.

144. Butler, 16.

145. "Homosexuality: The Truth." Flyer distributed by Wisconsin Christians United to selected homes in my neighborhood, including mine, in the fall of 1998. The organization is based in Monroe, Wisconsin.

146. Butler, 22.

147. Foucault, *Power/Knowledge,* 39.

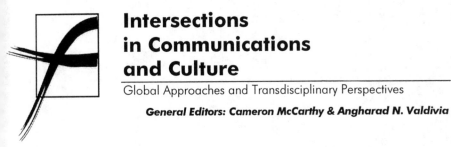

Intersections
in Communications
and Culture
Global Approaches and Transdisciplinary Perspectives

General Editors: Cameron McCarthy & Angharad N. Valdivia

An Institute of Communications Research, University of Illinois Commemorative Series

This series aims to publish a range of new critical scholarship that seeks to engage and transcend the disciplinary isolationism and genre confinement that now characterizes so much of contemporary research in communication studies and related fields. The editors are particularly interested in manuscripts that address the broad intersections, movement, and hybrid trajectories that currently define the encounters between human groups in modern institutions and societies and the way these dynamic intersections are coded and represented in contemporary popular cultural forms and in the organization of knowledge. Works that emphasize methodological nuance, texture and dialogue across traditions and disciplines (communications, feminist studies, area and ethnic studies, arts, humanities, sciences, education, philosophy, etc.) and that engage the dynamics of variation, diversity and discontinuity in the local and international settings are strongly encouraged.

L I S T   O F   T O P I C S

- Multidisciplinary Media Studies
- Cultural Studies
- Gender, Race, & Class
- Postcolonialism
- Globalization
- Diaspora Studies
- Border Studies
- Popular Culture
- Art & Representation
- Body Politics
- Governing Practices
- Histories of the Present
- Health (Policy) Studies
- Space and Identity
- (Im)migration
- Global Ethnographies
- Public Intellectuals
- World Music
- Virtual Identity Studies
- Queer Theory
- Critical Multiculturalism

Manuscripts should be sent to:
Cameron McCarthy OR Angharad N. Valdivia
Institute of Communications Research
University of Illinois at Urbana-Champaign
222B Armory Bldg., 555 E. Armory Avenue
Champaign, IL 61820

To order other books in this series, please contact our Customer Service Department:
(800) 770-LANG (within the U.S.)
(212) 647-7706 (outside the U.S.)
(212) 647-7707 FAX

Or browse online by series:
w w w . p e t e r l a n g u s a . c o m